CONFEDERATE STRATEGY
from Shiloh to Vicksburg

Archer Jones

CONFEDERATE STRATEGY

from Shiloh to Vicksburg

Louisiana State University Press
Baton Rouge

E
470.8
.J6

Preface

As a collateral descendent of General Joseph E. Johnston, I was brought up in the "General Joe" Johnston tradition rather than the more usual tradition for Virginians, that of General Lee. I early read one of the family's many copies of Johnston's memoirs, *Narrative of Military Operations*. This reading made a vivid impression and served not only to impress on me the great injustices visited on General Johnston by the petty and obtuse Jefferson Davis but to fix my attention on Johnston and the West rather than on General Lee and the East.

After I had entered graduate school in history at the University of Virginia, I thought that, in spite of my personal involvement, I would try to write a needed impartial study of the Johnston-Davis feud. Instead of writing a research paper on some phase of this subject while taking Professor Bernard Mayo's seminar, I decided to write a paper on George Wythe Randolph, Confederate Secretary of War from March to November, 1862. This would be pertinent to my thesis, and I had always been interested in the mysterious "General

v

Randolph," whom Johnston mentioned briefly in his *Narrative* as having retired from the War Department in connection with troop transfers from the Trans-Mississippi to Vicksburg, "to the great injury of the Confederacy." I had been reading B. H. Liddell Hart's *Sherman, the Genius of the Civil War,* and was impressed with his analysis of strategy in the West and the importance of the West in the Civil War. Perhaps Randolph had held some of the views later expressed by Liddell Hart, as his desire to secure mobility of forces in the West seemed to indicate.

Randolph turned out to be an interesting figure, and the Alderman Library of the University of Virginia had much unused material on him. So, after writing a paper on "Secretary Randolph and Confederate Strategy," I decided to exploit fully the materials on Randolph. While I never found that Randolph had enunciated the ideas later advanced by Liddell Hart, Johnston's *Narrative* made it clear that the appointment of Johnston to supreme command in the West had originated while Randolph was Secretary of War, though the appointment itself was made under Randolph's successor, James A. Seddon. Rembert W. Patrick, in his scholarly and important *Jefferson Davis and his Cabinet,* praised Seddon for his concern with the West but did not notice that the decision to appoint Johnston, the heart of the Seddon plan, had been made when Randolph was Secretary. Thus, some of the credit given Seddon for trying to remedy the problems of the West should be shared by Randolph.

Beyond this point, Randolph proved to be more significant than Professor Patrick, hampered by his limited manuscript resources, found him. His background made his public acts more intelligible, and his role in shaping the Confederate Conscription Act became clear. While working on Randolph and the origins of Johnston's Department of the West, I discovered several clear hints that Johnston had not been as inactive a western commander as his *Narrative* indicated. John Fiske in his *Mississippi Valley in the Civil War* had spoken of Federal General William S. Rosecrans as unable to move, being practically besieged at Nashville by Confederate cavalry during the winter and spring of 1863. I had noticed that Johnston had sent General Earl Van Dorn's cavalry from Mississippi to Tennessee. This agreed well with Johnston's expressed concern for Tennessee and indicated that he may have had some plan for his department not expressed to the War Department nor in his *Narrative*. Once more postponing the Johnston-Davis feud, I decided to write a history of Johnston's Department of the West. My work on Randolph developed the origins of this department and properly concluded with a study of how the decision to march to Gettysburg had affected operations in the West.

Again I was surprised by what I found. The beleaguerment of Nashville by Confederate cavalry, described by Fiske, ceased when Van Dorn arrived in Tennessee; all of the cavalry was needed to protect the subsistence areas of the Army of Tennessee. Johnston had, however, entertained hopes, when he originally dispatched these forces, that they might do much more. All who have treated Johnston in this period have approached it in the light of his *Narrative,* and his reiterated complaints to the War Department that his command, the Department of the West, was unworkable. A careful reading of Johnston's correspondence as commander reveals that he had comprehensive, if implicit and unrealized, plans for the defense of his department. While Patrick's analysis of Johnston's unsatisfactory relations with Secretary Seddon is borne out, his regular correspondence with President Davis was cordial and informative on his side and conciliatory and helpful on Davis' part. It seemed that I, as had most others, had been reading the later bitter feud between Johnston and Davis back into their earlier relations. While they certainly were not friends, they appeared to be loyally and cordially working together, with Davis needing and relying on Johnston's ability and giving him wide discretion, while the secretive Johnston was expounding his views and plans as well as captiously criticizing the nature of his command.

The task of providing conclusions to this treatise proved a difficult one. Randolph had proven to be significant, and Johnston had been partially reinterpreted. General Lee's peculiar views on the Southern climate and Southern strategy, revealed when his correspondence was read in the context of Confederate strategy, were important. However, no general conclusion based on these facts seemed indicated.

On the other hand, I had earlier come to the conclusion that Davis regarded his departmental organization of the Confederacy's territory as a very important element in his strategy and in his method of strategic direction of the war. I came to realize that Davis really did little more than to provide departments in managing and directing the western war effort. Also my studies of Randolph bore out Patrick's point that Davis was his own Secretary of War and that the Secretaries were significant largely as they influenced the President and could sell him ideas of their own. Conclusions of this type necessitated going back and treating Confederate western strategy from the beginning.

So, at last, a treatment of Confederate strategy from Shiloh to Vicksburg emerged, reinterpreting not only Randolph and Johnston but Davis as well. Davis now appeared, not as arbitrary and interfering, but as one who wisely delegated great authority to the generals in the West, while trying to shape their commands to enable them to have the territory and resources to do the job best. Davis appeared no longer as a narrow and ignorant despot, surrounded by mere clerks and running the war according to the ideas of the battle of Buena Vista and Pierce's War Department. He now seemed to be more a man burdened with great authority and responsibility which he felt that he could not share. His self-imposed burden, that of keeping the limited central direction of Confederate strategy entirely in his own hands, was lightened by the considerable use which he made of the advice and assistance of his Secretaries of War and of consultation with General Lee.

Acknowledgments

I WISH TO EXPRESS MY APPRECIATION TO PRO-
fessor Bernard Mayo of the University of Virginia for
his great assistance. The entire work bears the stamp
of careful correction, expressing his enmity for obscurity, obliquity and slipshod scholarship. While the
conclusions are my own, they were produced in response to his suggestions. Professor Thomas Cary
Johnson of the University of Virginia kindly consented
to read the manuscript also and to give it the benefit
of his knowledge, especially that in the field of military
history. I am grateful to Professor Frank E. Vandiver
for helpful criticisms and to Professor T. Harry Williams for emphasizing to me the importance of Jomini.
Mr. Gilbert E. Govan of the University of Chattanooga
was kind enough to engage in a long correspondence
explaining in detail his reasons for disagreement with
parts of this work. Thus I am much indebted to Messrs.
Vandiver, Williams and Govan for their suggestions
and criticisms, but they are not responsible for the
conclusions.

My colleague, Professor Edward L. Henson, rendered

valuable assistance through reading the manuscript, and my old friend Albert H. Woodruff indirectly contributed much over the years as a tireless listener and sharp critic. I am particularly obligated to Professors Gary Dunbar and Wayne Wallace of the University of Virginia for help with the design of the maps and to Mrs. Charles V. Crittenden for their design and execution.

My wife rendered valuable assistance of all kinds. Of especial value was her help in typing and in carefully reading the entire rough draft. I am also indebted to Mrs. George M. Van Sant for careful reading and suggestions. Mrs. Morrison Benedict was very generous in her typing assistance, and I wish to thank Mrs. Tyree Finch and Miss Georganne Smith for their important assistance in typing the manuscript.

To the Public Documents Division of the Alderman Library of the University of Virginia; to Mr. Paul Grier, librarian of Hampden-Sydney College, and to Mr. John Stonis, librarian of Clinch Valley College of the University of Virginia, I am very grateful for permission to check out volumes of the *Official Records*. Without this courteous service, completion of the book at this time would have been impossible. I am obligated to the manuscript divisions of the following institutions: the Alderman Library, Virginia State Library, Confederate Museum, College of William and Mary, Mary Washington College, Virginia Historical Society and the Library of Congress.

The importance of the papers made available to me by Dr. Robert H. Kean is clear in the text; permission to use them and the loan for typing is very much appreciated. Mrs. R. M. Hughes, Jr. and Mr. R. M. Hughes, III, were very kind in making available, not only their rich collection, but also use of the cool and comfortable library of the late Mr. Hughes.

Table of Contents

	Preface	v
	Acknowledgments	xi
	Introduction	xvii
1	The North's Grand Strategy	3
2	The South's Strategic Policy	16
3	The First Crisis	33
4	The Western Kaleidoscope	51
5	Western Reorganization	70
6	A New Adviser and New Commander	89
7	Johnston and Davis Survey the Situation	111
8	The Inception of Departmental Strategy	131
9	Complications with Personnel	151
10	The Realization of Departmental Planning	174
11	The Gettysburg Decision	198
12	Shiloh to Vicksburg—An Evaluation	219
	Bibliography	241
	Index	251

Maps

THREE MAPS ARE AT THE END OF THE VOLUME, to be consulted in conjunction with the text.

MAP 1: The Theater of the War—showing the Department of the West

MAP 2: Kentucky and Tennessee

MAP 3: Mississippi and Alabama—showing railway connections with Tennessee

xvi

Introduction

STUDY OF THE STRATEGY OF THE AMERICAN
Civil War has been neglected, particularly by American
writers. Emphasis on biography and battlefield strategy
has tended to obscure the larger picture. One aspect
of Civil War strategy which has received attention is
the creation of a super command in the West in 1862
under Joseph E. Johnston. The plan for such a command has been praised and attributed to Secretary of
War James A. Seddon, and its failure laid to Johnston.[1]
The Secretary of War when this plan was actually originated, George Wythe Randolph, was once so obscure
a figure that one historian of the Civil War referred
to him in one work as Thomas Jefferson Randolph
and in another as George Washington Randolph.[2]
While this obscurity surrounding his career was ably
remedied by Rembert W. Patrick in his 1944 book,
Jefferson Davis and His Cabinet, little significance has

[1] Rembert W. Patrick, *Jefferson Davis and His Cabinet* (Baton
Rouge, 1944).

[2] H. J. Eckenrode, *Jefferson Davis, President of the South* (New
York, 1923), 31; H. J. Eckenrode and Bryan Conrad, *Longstreet,
Lee's War Horse* (Chapel Hill, 1936), 174.

been attached to Randolph's work as Secretary of War. In 1956, however, Frank E. Vandiver pointed out his important role in shaping the plan for Johnston to command in the West. Nevertheless, the lack of both narrative and documentation in Vandiver's book makes a complete account and evaluation of Randolph's work necessary.

More important than the origins of the "western plan" is its execution. There has been discussion of the merits of the plan, but little of its execution. Proponents of Johnston hold that he was given an unworkable assignment, while his critics say that he wasted opportunities, was inert, or at best failed to use his power, brooding "for months over the proper exercise of his command, bemoaning the fact that he had so much authority that in reality he had none." [3] Both sides are agreed, however, that he did nothing while in purely departmental command. His biographers consequently concern themselves with his relations with the government and his problems in Braxton Bragg's army.

The curious failure to scrutinize Johnston's operations during this critical period stems in large measure from Johnston himself. His memoirs, offered as his "contribution of materials for the use of the future historian of the War between the States," contributed very little beyond a brief for his increasingly bitter feud with Jefferson Davis.[4] Concerned with proving his case and showing that he was right in the various con-

---

[3] Frank E. Vandiver, *Rebel Brass, the Confederate Command System* (Baton Rouge, 1956), 30, 49–54, 59–60.

[4] Joseph E. Johnston, *Narrative of Military Operations* (New York, 1874), dedication.

troversies of the time, he neglected his own activities during this Western period. Historians can hardly be blamed for assigning no higher value to him than he did to himself and for thus neglecting significant activity on his part.

Though trying specifically to fill these gaps in Civil War scholarship, I have found it desirable to fit them into a general narrative of Confederate western strategy from Shiloh to Vicksburg. First, Union and Confederate strategy is surveyed in order to acquaint the general reader and remind the expert, thus setting the stage for concentration on the restricted period and geographical area under consideration. Before embarking on western strategy itself, I have discussed the Confederate manpower crisis of the spring of 1862, both because of the general significance of the remedy applied and to show the important contribution of Randolph, the author of the remedy—conscription.

A brief general narrative of western strategy in 1862 follows, with emphasis on illustrating the methods of the President and the Secretary of War. When command and coordination faltered in the West, Davis and Randolph intervened and constructed a new department, which was not actually activated until Seddon had replaced Randolph. A detailed account of Joe Johnston as commander in the West has been provided because western strategy was specifically entrusted to him by the government. The period naturally ends with an account of the crisis in strategic planning during the spring of 1863. At this time the relative merits of action in the East and West were debated, strongly influenced by Johnston's trusteeship in the West.

While an effort has been made to have the record

as presented speak for itself, the obligation to provide conclusions has not been evaded. Two Civil War figures are, I think, vitally affected and significantly remolded. Randolph, the sociable and affluent Richmond lawyer who had entered the public service in time of crisis, fruitfully brought to the problems of the Confederacy a penetrating and thoughtful intellect and a fresh approach based on his military studies and field experience.

If Randolph emerges more a statesman than an amiable cipher, Johnston the soldier gains new stature while Johnston the man suffers. His strategic insight was almost flawless, his plans were comprehensive and effective, but his secrecy about his plans and the brevity and paucity of "his jejune and ice tempered character of correspondence" [5] with the War Department (though not with the President) destroyed the confidence Secretary of War Seddon had in him. His touchiness with superiors and excessive generosity to subordinates tended to nullify much of his effectiveness in an era when military relationships were far more personal and informal than they are today. The plan of a western department, conceived during Randolph's tenure in the War Department and, in a modified form, executed under Seddon and Johnston, emerges as significant and realistic. Although important, it was not a new concept nor an innovation that would in itself have changed the course of the war.

Viewing Confederate command and strategy on the

[5] R. G. H. Kean, *Inside the Confederate Government, The Diary of Robert Garlick Hill Kean, Head of the Bureau of War,* ed. Edward Younger (New York, 1957), 50, entry of April 12, 1863.

basis of a year's performance in the West, one is convinced that President Davis met the problems with an open mind and considerable flexibility; his system of decentralized command not only seems well-suited to the circumstances but, in both concept and execution, displayed considerable growth during the period. If the President slighted the West at first, events there and the attention of his Secretaries of War soon brought his sympathetic consideration.

CONFEDERATE STRATEGY
from Shiloh to Vicksburg

"Come out West; take to yourself the whole Mississippi Valley; let us make it dead sure, and I tell you the Atlantic slope and the Pacific shores will follow its destiny as sure as the limbs of a tree live or die with the main trunk! . . . Here lies the seat of the coming empire; and from the west, when our task is done, we will make short work of Charleston and Richmond, and the impoverished slope of the Atlantic."

Sherman to Grant,
February, 1864.

Chapter One

The North's Grand Strategy

1

ESSENTIAL TO ANY CONSIDERATION OF PARTIC-
ular strategic planning in the Civil War are the fundamental conceptions and overall plans of both the North
and the South. In some respects Union strategy is more
important since, by the fact that it was offensive, it
imposed its character on much of the Southern planning. By the political nature of the war the North was
on the offensive. Also, from the point of view of the
Union, the Civil War was a total war. The United
States was fighting for unconditional surrender rather
than for a favorable settlement. Whereas Solferino or
Sadowa were decisive in ending a war by the concession
of a province, the capture of Vicksburg and its army
could not be decisive in this way; complete victory
against a resolute national resistance was necessary in
order to secure unconditional surrender. Thus, as in
the Second World War, total military victory was essential in order to attain total political victory.

The grand strategic plan for the war was only gradually evolved. The North "drifted into the Civil War
. . . without so far as is known, any general plan for its

3

prosecution having been considered or adopted, or any move made to bring together our most capable military men for such purpose." While there "were more or less conferences in regard to separate campaigns," the war, "as a whole, was allowed to drift from year to year without intelligent guidance under nominal commanders-in-chief until 1864, when, at length, it was turned over to a mastermind to direct and control it." [1]

Thus there was little strategic direction in the early years of war beyond the guidance given by Lincoln, who, though he "became a fine strategist," had much to learn.[2] Little direction or long range planning was provided by the first commander-in-chief, the feeble septuagenarian, Lieutenant General Winfield Scott, nor much practical and effective guidance by his youthful successor, Major General George B. McClellan. If McClellan's absorption with operations in Virginia deprived the Northern war effort of much strategic direction, the man who succeeded him in July, 1862, Major General Henry W. Halleck, was little more effective. "Old Brains" Halleck, a successful California lawyer and businessman with a West Point background, expanded most of his efforts in administration and devoted "his time to minutiae" which "seemingly obscured in his own mind the sound strategy of the main army." [3]

[1] George A. Bruce, "The Strategy of the Civil War," *Papers of the Military Historical Society of Massachusetts*, XIII (1913), 393.

[2] T. Harry Williams, *Lincoln and His Generals* (New York, 1952), 7.

[3] William A. Ganoe, "Henry Wager Halleck," *Dictionary of American Biography*, eds. Dumas Malone and Allen Johnson (20 vols., New York, 1928–36), VIII, 150–52 (cited hereafter as *D. A. B.*).

Finally, however, comprehensive central direction according to "a plan of action . . . that covered the concerted movements of all the Union forces" was provided after March, 1864, when Lieutenant General U. S. Grant "kept in touch" with the Union armies, "directing and coordinating their operations." [4]

Nevertheless, Union operations were not without some grand strategic planning before Grant. In spite of confusion and false starts, logic, politics and personalities compelled the evolution of a plan. Most important was the fact that the nature of the country made its impression on early campaigns until "at length, trial and error, those gropings in the dark, were by geography forced into line, and compelled to march forward according to a fixed strategical plan." while it was probably not clear as such to many of its lesser executors, Lincoln and the more important generals gradually perceived their strategy in all its phases. While there was conscious planning according to the accepted plan, there were certainly disagreements as to emphasis and diversions from the principal objectives.

The strategy was a three-pronged drive into the South, aimed at three different objectives, the selection of which was governed by somewhat different considerations. One prong, or rather in this case a giant pincer, was on the Mississippi River. One arm of the pincer was a drive from the south, beginning with the taking of New Orleans on May 1, 1862, and culminating in the capture of Port Hudson, Louisiana, on July 9, 1863. The other arm was a drive downstream, which began with the battle of Mill Springs, Kentucky, in January, 1862,

[4] Christian A. Bach, "Ulysses Simpson Grant," *ibid.*, VII, 492–97.

and the fall of Forts Henry and Donelson in February of that year. It was pressed on in the battles of Shiloh (April, 1862), Corinth (October, 1862), and in Grant's setback at Holly Springs (December, 1862), and was ultimately successful in the final brilliant campaign which ended with the fall of Vicksburg on July 4, 1863. This prong had the triple purpose of cutting the Confederacy into two parts, economically as well as militarily, re-establishing for the Union navigation of the Mississippi and protecting "the right flank of any army operating from Nashville round the southern extremity of the Alleghany mountains." It prevented the Trans-Mississippi area, with not only its considerable agricultural resources but its valuable connection with Europe through Mexico, from being of assistance to the eastern part of the Confederacy. It also enabled the Union to concentrate its military resources against that part of the South which could stand alone, the stronger eastern section, and destroy it. The weaker section then naturally fell and the Confederacy was thus, in effect, destroyed piecemeal.

The second prong was to advance from Kentucky into Tennessee, through middle and east Tennessee and break the Alleghany barrier. This began, or rather diverged, from the northern Mississippi River pincer, with Buell's ill-fated advance along the railroad from Corinth, Mississippi, to Chattanooga, Tennessee, in June of 1862. After it was checked by Bragg's invasion of Kentucky, the advance was begun again in earnest by Rosecrans at the battle of Murfreesborough, Tennessee (December, 1862). The offensive was continued when Rosecrans maneuvered Bragg out of Chattanooga. Though checked at Chickamauga, the penetration of the Alleghany barrier was finally brought to a successful conclusion by Grant, William T. Sherman, and George H. Thomas in the battle of Missionary Ridge in November, 1863.

The incidental fruits of this drive were the completion of the conquest of Tennessee and, to Lincoln, the important political goal of liberating the Unionists in east Tennessee. The major results were the cutting of the best east-west communications of the Confederacy, breaking into the heart of the South with the ability to occupy and paralyze that large and vital agricultural area, and its center, the important city of Atlanta with its shops and railways. The great advantage conferred by the advance into Georgia, which outflanked the Appalachian Mountains, was not only that it enabled the heart of the South to be penetrated and the sea reached, which then cut the Confederacy into thirds, but the way was opened to the Carolinas thus taking Lee from behind. As a "right flank wheel of more than a 1,000 miles extending in time over three years" it ranks as "one of the most amazing maneuvers in military history." [5]

The third prong was an advance from Washington down the eastern seaboard between the mountains and the sea. This began with the battle of First Manassas in July, 1861, and the well-conceived but ill-fated Peninsula campaign (April–July, 1862), continued through the long bloody struggles of 1862, 1863, and 1864 in Virginia, and finally ended at Appomattox. Advantages and results of this drive were assurance of the safety of Washington and the capture of the Confederate Capital,

[5] J. F. C. Fuller, *The Generalship of Ulysses S. Grant* (London, 1929), 49–52.

with its munition plants and railroad connections as well as its political significance. The capture of Richmond would have effectively eliminated from the war Virginia, the state many regarded as the South's strongest prop. Presumably, the final result, though never realized, was to have been an advance south into the heart of the Confederacy on a route the reverse of that actually followed by Sherman.

These three land attacks had important naval assistance. In fact, together, the land and naval attacks made up what is rather grandiosely called the "Anaconda" plan of constant and unremitting pressure on all sides of the South. The Navy's mission was that of blockade, capturing and closing ports, and diversionary expeditions along the coast. This well-unified strategy was, as has been pointed out, put into operation early and pressed with considerable energy and fair continuity of effort throughout the course of the war. Proportionate effort and attention were not always allotted to the various fronts, and there were some egregious diversions, such as Banks's Red River expedition.

2

THIS MILITARY PLAN WAS ESSENTIALLY A VERY fine one and it won the war, but one serious objection can be advanced. This concerns the amount of military force lavished on the eastern seaboard offensive when even the advisability of anything more than demonstration and defense in that theater was questionable. The contention is that this drive was essentially a frontal assault in a very restricted area.

In placing such great emphasis on the enemy's capital, the Union leaders "were obsessed by conventional strategical considerations," when they "struck at strength and political powers." Even if the Confederacy's capital had been captured, the results would have been disappointing, and a continued advance would have been an equally great task "because topographical conditions in the East would have proved as difficult to overcome as they did to the English in 1775–83." The best policy, striking at weakness, would have been "to have launched a strong, well-organized offensive in the West." [6]

While the difficulties of invading North Carolina from the North were considerable, especially the problem of communications, those of reaching even Richmond were considerable. The terrain in Virginia was admirably suited to defense, in that it was traversed by rivers running east and west (Rappahannock, James, etc.) which lay athwart the route of advance and usually provided an excellent barrier for the defenders. Obstructed by the rivers, hedged in between the mountains and the Chesapeake Bay, and restricted as to objective, Union generals had little opportunity for more than battlefield maneuver. They were constantly facing an enemy deployed, and later entrenched, before them.

Thus a frontal assault was necessary at a time when the power of the defense was beginning to assert that mastery of the battlefield which, with the introduction

[6] J. F. C. Fuller, *Grant & Lee, A Study in Personality and Generalship* (New York, 1933), 39–42.

of the Maxim gun, was to reach its zenith in the 1914–1918 period. Technological advances which had been made since the Napoleonic wars had a profound effect on tactics. The invention of expanding rifle bullets, which could be easily inserted through the muzzle and which, on being fired, expanded to make a tight fit with the barrel, so improved the rifle that it was adopted for military purposes in the 1850's. The efficiency of small arms was also improved by the introduction of the waterproof percussion cap which made weapons reliable in wet weather.

Not only was the rifle much more accurate than the musket, its range was greater. The rifle would reach to 1,000 or 1,200 yards and was effective at 400 yards, as compared with the 100 yards effective range of the British army's old "Brown Bess" musket. This at least tripled the danger space before a defending line, providing more time in which to shoot at the enemy. In addition, the increased accuracy of the rifle made it possible to hit a target, thus virtually eliminating fusillades of relatively unaimed fire. The firepower of infantry was, in a sense, increased by a multiplying effect, especially that of veteran infantry who had developed their marksmanship. During the Civil War the rifle dominated the battlefield almost to the same degree that the machine gun did in World War I.

While developments in artillery had been equally striking, they were later in reaching the field. Military inertia and opposition to change, retarding the introduction of new weapons, had been almost overcome in the case of the percussion cap rifle. However, the opposition to the first improvements in artillery, rifling and the use of steel, overlapped the Civil War. Many authorities preferred bronze guns as their salvage value made them cheaper. So steel or breech-loading guns were rare, and rifled guns did not prevail.

The development of weapons at differing rates had an important effect on tactics. The range of artillery was not increased in proportion to that of the rifle. The smoothbore, twelve pounder "Napoleon" cannon, used extensively by both armies, had no greater range than that of a good rifle. Thus the highly effective Napoleonic method of using artillery to annihilate a section of the line of the defending troops prior to commencing the attack could no longer be employed with the same decisive results. In this way the potency of infantry firepower in the defense was further augmented.

One other development of the war, resulting in large part from the improvement in small arms, was the practice of entrenching when on the defense. This practice was limited to fortifications and permanent works at the outbreak of the war, but it gradually spread until it was universal in the last year of the war, with troops entrenching to some degree almost whenever they paused. This tremendously enhanced the power of the defense because of the much smaller target offered by the man behind entrenchments and because of his ability to fire more rapidly with the ease of reloading. One man in entrenchments was worth three or perhaps as many as five men in the attack.

Thus, technological advances at an uneven rate, together with the increasing practice of field fortifications and entrenchments, introduced the era when the defense was definitely in the ascendency. This is best illustrated by the failure of seven out of every eight assaults in the Civil War.

This augmented power of defense, which made the Civil War the precursor of the Great War of 1914–1918, increasingly gave, as the war wore on, the advantage on any battlefield to the defender. After 1863 there were hardly any offensive victories, and the advances which took place were largely the result of outflanking operations. When Grant had exhausted his capacity to outflank Lee, his progress stopped. So when Grant was within sight of his goal, Richmond, he was faced with the stalemate of trench warfare. This plight never beset operations in the West for long, though it was apparently General Joseph E. Johnston's intention to produce a similar situation before Atlanta.

The opportunities for maneuver and the avoidance of a stalemate found in the larger theater of the West, as well as the strategic importance of the objectives in that area, have led many authorities to conclude that the "West was the really decisive theater" where "the decisive blows were struck." [7] On the other hand, the fact that the war was won in the West while the eastern theater was locked in what might be said to be a four-year deadlock may lead too easily to the conclusion that the efforts in Virginia were, therefore, ill-advised and wasted. The Confederate forces held in the East by the Union offensives, as well as the tremendous and constant casualties suffered by Lee's army, had an important influence both on the course of the war in the West and on the final outcome.

It may be contended that the victory in one area and

[7] W. Birkbeck Wood, "American Civil War," *Encyclopedia Britannica* (14th ed., Chicago, London, Toronto, 1951), I, 767; B. H. Liddell Hart, *Strategy, the Indirect Approach* (New York, 1954), 154.

deadlock in another were entirely fortuitous. The talented commanders of the North—Grant, Sherman, Rosecrans, Don C. Buell, Thomas, John M. Schofield, and others—were to be found in the western theater. On the other hand, the East had to get along with such men as John Pope, Joseph Hooker and Ambrose E. Burnside. While eastern generals had to face Lee and such capable subordinates as James Longstreet and "Stonewall" Jackson, those in the west faced mediocrity, if not incompetence, in such men as John C. Pemberton, John B. Hood, Bragg, and Theophilus H. Holmes. If the commanders had been reversed, so might have been the course of the war.

Whatever evaluation may be made of Union strategy or the causes of the outcome of the war, the influence of geography must be emphasized. Union strategy was guided, and in a sense made, by geography. While in Virginia the rivers for the most part obstructed offensives, in the West they were vital routes of advance. Federal seapower in the form of gunboats and transports enabled the armies to advance into the heart of the Confederacy along the Mississippi, Tennessee, Cumberland and other rivers. River transport not only helped to make up the deficiency in transportation by rail and road but, by its greater security, helped to remedy the problem of long and very vulnerable lines of supply, the curse of operations in the big spaces of the West.

While the direction and application of Northern strategy was influenced by geography and the progress of technological changes, so also was its overall concept. Since the defensive had again asserted its preponderance and there was rough equality in the character of the armies, smashing victories against any but demoralized or incompetently led armies could only be obtained by tactically or numerically superior forces. The difficulties in producing quick or decisive action were compounded by the immense size of the theater of operations. Napoleonic concepts had the same limitations on their applicability in the American Civil War as they had had in Russia and eastern Europe.[8]

Northern strategy was responsive to these conditions. The South was attacked on the political and economic, as well as military, fronts in application of what may be called a strategy of exhaustion. Appropriately, though for a variety of motives and often against Lincoln's urging, Union generals applied this strategy, one which was based on the realization that, as in the Second World War, "to deny to the enemy what may be called his 'vital area of operations'—that part of his country essential to the maintenance of his forces—became even more important than winning victories in the field, because it knocked the bottom out of the enemy's fighting power." [9] When this objective had been sufficiently attained by Grant's conquest of the Mississippi and Sherman's march to the sea, a strategy of annihilation was at last possible.

Related to the adoption of this strategy by Union generals was the pervasive influence of the ideas of the eminent theorist and interpreter of Napoleon, Jomini. West Point and the professional thinking of American soldiers were dominated by his theories. Though an

[8] Frederic N. Maude, "Strategy," *Encyclopedia Britannica* (13th ed., New York, London, 1926), XXV, 989, 993.
[9] Gordon A. Craig, "Delbruck: The Military Historian," *Makers of Modern Strategy*, ed. Edward Mead Earle (Princeton, 1952), 273–82; J. F. C. Fuller, *The Second World War, 1939–1945* (New York, 1949), 35.

expounder of Napoleon and an advocate of the offensive, Jomini had been profoundly influenced by eighteenth century ideas and strategy, especially those of Frederick the Great, not only in his geometrical conceptions and his stress upon lines of operation and supply, but in his emphasis on victory through maneuver. This caused his doctrine to value the conquest of territory rather than the destruction of the enemy's army. For implementing a strategy of exhaustion and avoiding an unrealistic pursuit of a strategy of annihilation, these ideas had a real application. Parenthetically, it should be noted that the Jominian influence was not all good. It often had an inhibiting effect, especially upon the more pedantic generals, and Jomini was pre-eminently the advocate of "sound" strategy and of "safety first." [10]

This analysis of Northern strategy is perhaps more descriptive of what happened than of the guiding principles of its directors. But for a variety of reasons—the fortuitous applicability of Jominian concepts and, in the case of Sherman and perhaps Grant, the explicit application of the principles of the strategy of exhaustion—this was the Northern grand strategy. On the other hand, President Davis consciously oriented his strategic policy towards a defense against the strategy of exhaustion.

[10] B. H. Liddell Hart, *The Ghost of Napoleon* (New Haven, 1935), 105–16.

Chapter Two

The South's Strategic Policy

1

"THE CONFEDERACY WAS UNFORTUNATE IN ITS
failure to work out a general strategy of the whole
war." [1] There was no grand strategic plan of the same
type as developed by the Union; there was no large
overall plan of defense and/or offense which was followed throughout the war. The responsibility for this
lack of grand strategic plan rests on President Jefferson
Davis.

The President's West Point education and his sub-
sequent seven years service as a lieutenant in the regular
army provided useful training and experience for his
role as military leader. His military background had
been expanded during the Mexican War when, serving
as a colonel, he compiled a splendid combat record,
gaining special distinction at the battle of Buena Vista.
He gained experience in military administration when
he served brilliantly as Secretary of War in President
Franklin Pierce's cabinet and on the Military Affairs
Committee of the United States Senate. This experience

[1] The following discussion is based on E. Merton Coulter,
The Confederate States of America (Baton Rouge, 1950), 342–48.

served him well in selecting officers and in creating and organizing a Confederate army and war department where none had existed before.

As President and constitutional Commander-in-chief, Davis was the commander-in-chief in actuality. Though he had five secretaries of war and two nominal commanders-in-chief, all decisions and policies were those of the President. Consequently, his views and theories are essential to an understanding of Confederate strategy.

In late 1864 President Davis "advocated a bold, correct strategy . . . when he argued that even if Richmond should fall, enemy victory would be as far away as ever, for the government could function in some other place just as well. There are no vital points on the preservation of which the continued existence of the Confederacy depends." Then, stressing guerilla warfare possibilities, he pointed out that there "is no military success of the enemy" which can destroy the Confederacy. "Not the fall of Richmond, nor Wilmington, nor Charleston, nor Savannah, nor Mobile, nor all combined, can save the enemy from the constant and exhaustive drain of blood and treasure which must continue until he shall discover that no peace is attainable unless based on the recognition of our indefeasible rights."

Here Davis was not really enunciating any special system of elastic defense but rather an extension of his "policy of considering the war solely defensive," and applying it to the then deteriorating military situation. This advocacy of the tenacious and unremitting defense was "part of the mass thinking promoted by Davis to show the world that the Confederacy did not want war

and that it would do nothing more than defend itself—
a 'simple demand that the people of the United States
should cease to war upon us, and permit us to pursue
our own path to happiness, while they in peace pursue
theirs.' "

This theory of the war held that the Confederate
States of America were the victims of aggression by the
United States of America, whose people did not lend
wholehearted support to this war of conquest. Therefore, a tenacious defensive resistance would be the best
means calcuated to wear down the will of the Northern
people to win and, thus, lead them to abandon the war;
or, that failing, hold out until foreign powers intervened, a development on which considerable hope was
long placed. However, this purely defensive theory of
war may have had an adverse effect on Southern offensive operations in that this "school of strategists thought
that to invade the North would belie this position," and
so "stir up a hornet's nest."

With this principle there is not too much quarrel,
except that it may have hampered offensive strategy.
However, the manner in which this defense was to be
carried out and the points to be defended were the
subject of much debate and many pressures. Arguments
of the advocates of the defensive were intermingled
with those of the offensive. "From the beginning
counsels were divided between an offensive concentration of forces and a dispersal to suit the whims of every
local-minded governor and states-rights enthusiast. The
philosophy which adventitiously controlled was a sort
of combination of dispersal with a definite concentration around Richmond."

Davis was under many pressures to adopt the defensive toward which he was inclined. These pressures tended to convert Confederate strategy into a very rigid and inflexible doctrine which insisted that every threatened point and every inch of territory be defended. He was under constant pressure from local authorities, especially governors, for forces for local defense. Pleas, threats, harrassment and obstructionism were used to extort from the Richmond government men and resources for the defense of locally important points. This situation was aggravated by the fact that "Northern strategy was planned to force a dispersal of Confederate forces by attacks at widely scattered points and McClellan especially advised attacking Southern seaports as part of this plan." However, adherence to a policy of defending localities was especially important because "localism was so strongly embedded in the Southerners that little enthusiasm could have been developed for the war, had important forces not been maintained in the states."

The President was, however, especially responsive to these appeals for detachments for the defense of exposed or threatened points. He interpreted his doctrine of defense in the light of certain economic, social, military and political considerations. These brought him to the independent adoption of a policy stressing the defense of the complete territorial integrity of the Confederacy, which harmonized very well with local demands. This view that the protection of territory should be the paramount objective of Southern military strategy was urged by important considerations.

In the early stages of the war there was uncertainty as to the effect of the war upon the Negro, especially when large numbers of white men went to the armies. It was felt that Federal incursions might be the signal for slave insurrections and, of course, there were many demands for the protection of menaced points, particularly on the seacoasts, against this supposed menace. Later in the war, although this bugaboo had been dispelled, Davis' general policy still included the holding of territory at all costs.

This strategy was continued because the President felt that once United States troops had occupied a portion of Southern territory, however briefly, that area would be virtually worthless to the Confederacy when and if it were reoccupied. He thought that this would be so because, during the occupation, the Union authorities would free the slaves, seize cotton and cause so much other havoc with the peculiar and delicate social and economic fabric of the Southern States that any military policy not based on a territorial defense would result in the crippling of the country in spite of victories and success in the field.

An important political consideration also prompted President Davis to adopt and maintain his policy of territorial defense. It was essential to do nothing which would discourage or hamper recognition of the South. This was a keystone of the early war policy of the President and the country. It was necessary to prove that the South was really a viable nation and could defend itself. Loss of territory naturally prejudiced the prospects of European recognition.

Moreover, the President had also an important military reason for his policy of territorial defense. Problems of supply, subsistence and recruitment of the Confederate military forces imperatively urged the protection of the Southern territory from which were drawn these sinews of war. Considering the alternative, the President remarked that the "general truth that power is increased by the concentration of an army is, under our peculiar circumstances, subject to modification," as the "evacuation of any portion of territory involves not only the loss of supplies, but in every instance has been attended by a greater or less loss of troops." [2] Not only under these circumstances would the Southern soldier's propensity for desertion and desire to defend his own home weaken the retreating army, but the area would be lost as a source of conscripts for the armies.

Thus Southern strategy was based on territorial defense, not only for political and social motives, but for sound logistical reasons. Confederate strategy was responsive to the Northern strategy of exhaustion, defending the same objectives at which the Union forces were aiming. Hence, President Davis explicitly saw the war in the same terms as the North was fighting it and sought to protect areas vital to the supply and recruitment of the Confederate armies.

Jomini's influence and his emphasis on territory were congenial with this strategy. Further, Confederate defense was not passive, but offensive-defensive. Though the natural propensities of the field commanders would account for this, it was both a policy actively encouraged by Davis and was in accord with the prevailing Jominian climate of military theory. Davis encouraged offensives to regain territory for the same reasons he concentrated

[2] Jefferson Davis to Edmund Kirby Smith, November 19, 1863, *The War of the Rebellion: A Compilation of the Official Records of the Union and Confederate Armies* (Washington, 1880–1901), Ser. I, XXII, Part 2, 1071–72. This work will be cited hereafter as *Official Records* and abbreviated *O. R.*

on its defense, and his generals found the policy consonant with Jomini's insistence that no defense be inactive, but should be offensive-defensive.[3]

In implementing this strategy, the President had to choose between two schools of thought. Generals P. G. T. Beauregard and J. E. Johnston advocated concentration on a nationwide scale to strike at the enemy's weak point, while General Lee, taking into consideration the weakness of the Southern transportation system, advocated that each theater commander exploit opportunities for the offensive with locally available forces, both for the purpose of regaining territory and taking the pressure off other and hard-pressed areas.

Thus the personal inclination of the commander-in-chief reinforced his theory of the politically defensive nature of the war. This concept was strengthened by important socio-economic considerations as well as by the Confederacy's diplomatic goals. All of these, together with important military reasons and the clamor of influential local authorities, committed the South to a policy of territorial defense. In practice, this meant an attempt to post adequate forces at all threatened points along an enormously long land and sea frontier—not an equal distribution of forces along the front, of course, but enough of a distribution to amount to a very considerable dispersion.

There was certainly strong merit in the strategy of territorial defense and, while the consequences of a

[3] Frank E. Vandiver, "Jefferson Davis and Confederate Strategy," *The American Tragedy* (Hampden-Sydney College, Virginia, 1959), 20; the very phrase is Jomini's and was also used by Davis. See: Davis to Mrs. Davis, May 28, 1862, Dunbar Rowland (ed.), *Jefferson Davis, Constitutionalist, His Letters, Papers and Speeches* (10 vols., Jackson, Mississippi, 1923), V, 254.

different policy might have been more serious, the policy itself had definite drawbacks. This policy weakened the main armies in the field and precluded the adoption of an elastic defense. An elastic defense—the trading of space for time, retreating in order to embarrass the enemy's communications and giving up of territory in order to concentrate large forces at a critical point— would have yielded more military victories and defeated more invasions than the Davis plan. Though its adoption would have led to many of the consequences which Davis sought to prevent by his policy, the failure to defeat major offensives which took vital points and areas could only mean certain defeat. Thus, the plan followed resulted in being too weak everywhere, in clinging to areas unimportant strategically and in permitting the enemy to employ the principle of concentration with greater safety and effect. The advantage of interior lines, which the Confederacy enjoyed to some extent, with the consequent capability for rapid concentration, was nullified by this policy. Real opportunities for more effective defense were thrown away when a system of elastic defense was rejected.

The implementation of Federal strategy made a strong imprint on that of the Confederates. This is true because, as the Federal armies were advancing along three great and clearly distinguishable routes, the South naturally had to concentrate larger forces in the paths of these advances. Since the importance of thwarting the three great prongs of the Union attack was clearly realized and special efforts were made to meet them, the Southern organization for war had necessarily to include three major fronts. These were on the Mississippi River, the middle and east Tennessee or Appalachian barrier front, and the Virginia or eastern seaboard theater.

However, the policy of defending everywhere made it impossible to develop on these critical fronts a concentration of force which was proportionately equal to that of the Union. In January, 1863, for example, the Confederacy had 259,000 men in the field opposing 529,000 for the United States. Concentrated in the three major theaters, the Confederacy had 85,000 in Virginia (except southwestern Virginia), 33,000 men at Vicksburg and in northern Mississippi, and 57,000 men in central and eastern Tennessee. In these same major theaters the United States had 224,300 in Virginia (except southwestern Virginia), Washington and Maryland, 91,000 in western Tennessee and northern Mississippi, and 96,000 in central and eastern Tennessee. Thus, sixty-eight percent of the Confederate armies were concentrated on the three major fronts as opposed to eighty-one percent of the Union armies on these same fronts.

While these percentages overstate the case somewhat, since some of the Union troops included were committed to defensive purposes, the amount and nature of Confederate dispersion is graphically illustrated in the following respective dispositions: In South Carolina, Georgia and Florida, 18,100 Confederates opposed 10,800 Union troops, while in western Florida, Alabama, and southeastern Louisiana, 23,600 Confederates faced 31,000 Federals whose mission included an advance north to help open the Mississippi. In North Carolina 27,000 Confederate troops opposed 16,240 Federals; in southwestern Virginia 6,000 Confederates faced a Union force of 7,000; and in Texas there were 7,000 unopposed Confederates. In the Trans-Mississippi area, which does not properly fall into either the major or minor classification, 15,000 Confederates in Arkansas opposed 38,000 Federals, of which 13,000 were temporarily detached from the down-river advance on Vicksburg.[4]

Thus it can be seen that, though the South was outnumbered by about two to one in the total number of troops in the field, she was outnumbered by about two and one-half to one in forces on the major fronts. On the other hand, in the minor theaters, the South enjoyed a numerical superiority of about one and a quarter to one. Although this distribution was in some measure due to the Union's effective exercise of its seapower, the pressure of local authorities and the deliberate policy of President Davis were quite as much responsible.

2

CONFEDERATE STRATEGY WAS THEN A DEFENSIVE policy which viewed *all* territory as important, with some concentration against the major Union efforts. The application of this policy was systematized by President Davis in such a way that the method was in a sense elevated to a strategy itself.

The country was organized into departments and districts, all commanded by officers of appropriate rank and all fitting into a logical, though frequently changing, system. However, this departmental organization which was largely founded on state lines and on geo-

[4] William Roscoe Livermore, *The Story of the Civil War* (2 vols., New York, London, 1913), I, 70–94.

graphical features, while excellent for peace-time administration, was not always adapted to war purposes, especially as the organization was sometimes slow to reflect changes in the military situations.

Captain R. G. H. Kean, the chief of the Confederate Bureau of War, alleged that the President seemed "to have no plan—to be drifting along on the current of events," also that he "is not a comprehensive man—he has no broad policy—either of finance, strategy or supply." There were complaints of "hair splitting, and the absence of all *policy*—no line of action tending to foreseen results." Secretary Seddon, when asked if the President had a plan "for meeting the emergency," responded "that he has none . . . and that he never *had had* any."

The chief of the Bureau of War spoke of the "absorption of the President's time in trifles (comparative)," and said that "certainly the style of business with which his time is now consumed is in our present circumstances almost a *scandal*—little trash which ought to be dispatched by clerks in the Adjutant General's office." Thus Kean's observations confirm the view that the President consumed his time, attention, and energy in details and in the army administration. However, this had a greater importance to Davis as it was, in a sense, his military policy. This organization, meticulously managed, became an end in itself, as it was his war policy and his strategy. This preoccupation with administration and his reliance on it as a strategy or in lieu of one had important effects on military operations. The foundation of Mr. Davis' system was the department or geographical administrative area which controlled the forces within it.

The numerous instances when departmental autonomy and integrity seemed to have been preserved at the expense of inter-departmental cooperation led Captain Kean to complain that the stress laid on "the inviolability of a departmental line" caused the "separate departmental organization" to become the "radical vice of Mr. Davis' whole military system." The effect of this system in which the departments reported only to the President was that it made "each department depend only on its *own* strength," depriving "them of the mutual support and combination which might else be obtained."

Kean's criticism that it was a "fatal notion" which made "each military department a separate nation for military purposes without subordination, cooperation or concert" [5] is valid only if the system of territorial defense is rejected. Each department had its area to protect and might suffer invasion if it lent assistance to another. One of the most striking examples of the evil of this policy was exhibited during Sherman's advance to Atlanta when General J. E. Johnston sought the aid of the troops in Mississippi under the great cavalryman, Forrest. But Sherman had obtained the assistance of a "threatening movement from Memphis on Columbus, Miss., to prevent Forrest" from breaking his communications. In the face of this menace to northern Mississippi, Davis refused the service of Forrest against Sherman, pointing out that Confederate forces in Mississippi were in "proportion to the enemy confronting them much weaker than General Johnston."

[5] Kean, *Inside the Confederate Government,* 72, 80, 100 (parentheses and italics Kean's), 101 (italics Kean's), 167, 187 (italics Kean's or Seddon's).

Thus perhaps Forrest's men were used not to "insure
the defeat of a great invasion" but rather "to repel a
mere raid." [6]

Criticisms have been leveled against Southern strategy
similar to those against the North. The Confederates
concentrated men in the East in the same way as the
Union Army. This was done by the South naturally
to counter those of the Union, but it was also based on
"the dominant position of Virginia and Richmond in
the minds of the people" which "was such that the loss
of Richmond would have seemed the loss of the war.
If there could have been an equivalent concentration on
the Mississippi . . . and west of it, the back door of
the Confederacy could not have been easily battered
down and disintegration from the rear might not have
set in." [7]

While concern for Richmond was an important
motive, the Federal capital exercised just as strong a
fascination on the Confederates as Richmond did on
the North. The value of this objective, however, was
thus questioned by two Confederate soldiers:

> "I say, Mac, what do you suppose we are going
> to do with the city of Washington when we take
> it?"
> "That question reminds me," replied Mac,
> "of old Simon's answer to Tony Towns when he
> asked Simon if he were not afraid he would lose
> his dog that was running after every train that came
> by. The old darkey replied that he was not thinking

[6] *O. R.*, Ser. I, XXXVIII, Part 4, 294–95, 805; Robert Selph
Henry, *First with the Most Forrest* (New York, 1944), 307–12.
[7] Coulter, *Confederate States of America,* 342.

about losing his dog, but was jus wonderin' what
dat dorg was gwine to do wid dem kyars when he
kotched 'em." [8]

The concentration of men to protect Richmond and
the fortuitous collection there of many of their best
generals made Richmond secure. But these large forces,
plus the skill of General Lee and his subordinates, led
them and President Davis to attempt offensives in the
East which were beyond their strength. The newly
developed power of the defense stopped them just as
it stopped the Union advance. In attacking the Union's
largest concentration, the chances for success were
further reduced, while the other areas of the Confederacy, weaker in both men and geographical advantages
for defense, were being overrun. The analogy with the
criticisms of Northern strategy is complete.

Against this, the argument may be made that the only
chance for a successful offense was to use the largest
army which had the best leaders. More convincing perhaps is the contention that if the Virginia armies were
strong enough for an offensive they were too strong for
the good of the Confederacy. They would have done
better to spare some of their strength to bolster the
sagging West where the war was being lost. The larger
theater of the West, with its greater opportunities for
maneuver, convinced many at the time that this was the
true place for a Confederate offensive. Cogent arguments were advanced for "liberating" Kentucky, capi-
talizing on Southern sympathizers farther north and
of the important strategic significance of the old Northwest.

[8] John B. Gordon, *Reminiscences of the Civil War* (New York,
1903), 315.

3

THESE DISPUTES IN THE SOUTH, TOGETHER
with similar ones in the North, have suggested an interesting and signifiicant analogy. Something may be
learned by comparison with an instance where "Easterners and Westerners fought in council and on paper,"
just as they did during the Civil War.

The similarity in their broad lines of the problems of the American Civil War and of the Great
War has struck more than one critic. In both, one
side held relatively to the other a central position,
and as it happened in each war that side which was
centrally placed was exposed to the rigors of a
blockade. In both the co-ordination of effort was
difficult, yet urgently needed. Unity of command,
is a phrase which appears at an early stage of both
struggles in the correspondence of soldiers and
statesmen. In both wars there were two main fronts,
and in both there was controversy as to which front
should be regarded as decisive.[9]

The only difference between Easterners and Westerners in the Civil and the First World wars was that the
terms were reversed. The Easterners of 1914–1918 corresponded to the Westerners of 1861–1865, and West-

[9] Frederick Maurice, *Statesmen and Soldiers of the Civil War*
(Boston, 1926), 6.

erners of the World War to Easterners of the Civil War. But, the problems, conditions and motivations were the same. In fact, the analogy may be extended to the Second World War, with Mr. Churchill and his Mediterranean schemes as the Westerner of 1861–1865. This is the same role he played with his Dardanelles campaign in 1914–1918. The Easterner of the First World War, like his counterparts of the Civil War and the Second World War, wanted to follow the path of least resistance for offensive action. Erich Ludendorff in 1915 wanted to avoid the stalemate of the western front, with its dense concentrations of troops, relatively narrow front and strong entrenchments, in favor of the relatively open, fluid and less densely held lines of the East. Also, in the vast amount of space in that theater, a breakthrough would have yielded greater opportunities for maneuver, envelopment and for more decisive strategic results.

In the fall of 1914 and in 1915 Winston Churchill was promoting his Dardanelles scheme for a different but related reason, and for one similar to his motives in 1942 and 1943. Since the Allies had become stymied on the western front, he advocated that they seek a weaker opponent or area to overwhelm (Turkey in 1914–1915 and Italy and the Balkans in 1942–1943).

The parallel between the Virginia front of 1862–1864 and the western front of 1915–1918, and that of the western theater in the Civil War and the Russian front in the World War, makes the analogy with Ludendorff's plans startlingly concise. The analogy with the problem of the Allies and the United Nations, while lacking the geographical similarity of the Russian front, has its point in the seeking out of the weaker force, for there were instances of relatively weak Union forces in the

West during the course of the war. Also, the analogy
applies to the interior lines of Germany and the South,
and in the case of the Dardanelles campaign, to the
superiority of Allied sea over German rail communications to that area (in the sense of faster communications
being the equivalent of interior lines). If analogies are
forceful in history, then the case for a western-oriented
strategy of the Civil War should be strengthened by the
fact that both German and Allied Easterners in the
First World War have been pretty well vindicated.

The analogy may be carried still further in that the
1915 problem of Ludendorff in gaining a hearing was
similar to that of Confederate generals during their war.
Their superiors, Chief-of-Staff General Erich von Falkenhayn and Commander-in-Chief President Davis, were
both men in supreme and relatively unfettered command, both with strong wills and definite views. In
Great Britain and France questions of strategy were
decided in cabinets, by discussion, and the opinions of
the generals carried great weight, as did also the views of
politicians influenced by generals. As will be seen, both
analogies are applicable to the Confederacy.

Chapter Three

The First Crisis

1

AFTER THE BATTLE OF FIRST MANASSAS OR
Bull Run in July, 1861, at the beginning of the Civil
War, preparations were made for future campaigns,
and there was much activity in the border states of
Kentucky and Missouri. With the end of Kentucky's
neutrality in the autumn, a continuous military frontier
existed between the North and the South, stretching
from Northern Virginia through Southern Kentucky
into Missouri. But the armies remained quiet while
each side raised and trained troops.

Confederate morale, raised high by the victory at
Manassas, remained so throughout this period. Volunteers rushed to the colors in such numbers that 200,000
had to be turned down due to the critical shortage of
arms with which to equip them. The ominous portent
of Union inactivity in the field was revealed in early
1862 when the newly raised Union volunteer army, now
adequately trained and equipped, at last went into
action.

Confederate complacency was shattered first in January, 1862, by a relatively minor defeat at Mill Springs

in east central Kentucky. Then, despite renowned generals such as Beauregard and Albert Sidney Johnston, the entire front in the West collapsed before the advance of the numerically superior Federal armies. The forts on the Tennessee and Cumberland Rivers, Henry and Donelson, fell with the loss of 15,000 men in February. This involved losing all of Kentucky and western Tennessee, including the capital of Nashville. By early March the Confederate forces were regrouping in northern Mississippi. In northern Arkansas the Confederate defeat at Pea Ridge early that month not only signalized the complete loss of Missouri to the Confederacy but opened Arkansas to invasion.

The disasters in the East, while perhaps less critical, had a no less alarming appearance and an equally depressing effect on public and official moral. In February the Confederate army near Washington was withdrawn in order to be nearer to and provide security for Richmond, while from North Carolina came the news of the fall of Roanoke Island and the capture of most of its garrison. In March the Federals continued their advance in North Carolina by seizing New Bern.

In addition to these military disasters, an even more dangerous situation appeared imminent. It seemed clear that a large portion of the Confederate army was about to be disbanded with little prospect of new volunteers to take their place. In spite of various inducements to enlist, the impulse to volunteer began to fade in early 1862. More alarming was the fact that the "zeal with which men sprang to arms at the outbreak of hostilities had begun to wane. Absence from home, the privations of camp life, and the arduous duties and dangers of the service were no longer dreams; they had become painful

realities to many persons." Not only had the romance
gone out of army life, but the quick and glorious victory
which had been expected had not materialized. This dis-
illusionment contributed strongly to the feeling held by
many in the army "that it was only just that they should
retire and let those who had not yet served have their
turn."

What made this decline of enthusiasm both inside and
outside the ranks so serious was the fact that from one-
third to two-thirds of the men in service had enlisted
for one year only. Their terms of service were already
beginning to expire, and in spite of inducements
offered, they were not re-enlisting in significant numbers, nor were others coming forward to take their
places. It was estimated that by the middle of May the
terms of enlistment of 148 regiments of twelve-month
men would have expired. Since few of them showed an
inclination to remain, it seemed as if, before the end
of May, perhaps one-third of the Southern army would
be disbanded. Furthermore, this was the best third, as
they had had the longest service and the experience of
what few engagements there had been. They would,
presumably, be followed out of the army in the spring
and early summer by the remaining one-year men.

With the Union offensive in full swing in the West
and McClellan beginning to move in Virginia, the Confederate Congress in January and February vainly
sought to stimulate enlistment through five different
legislative enactments.[1] At this critical juncture President Davis reshuffled his cabinet and brought in a new
Secretary of War. The military disasters of the year had

[1] Albert B. Moore, *Conscription and Conflict in the Confederacy*
(New York, 1924), 7, 9–10.

destroyed the reputation of incumbent Secretary Judah P. Benjamin of Louisiana. When an investigation by the Confederate Congress fixed the blame for the Roanoke Island disaster on him, it was politically necessary for Benjamin to leave the War Department.

The feeling that the Secretary of War should be a military man, together with the necessity of recognizing Virginia in the cabinet, led the President at this critical time to select, for Secretary of War, Brigadier General George Wythe Randolph of Virginia, a man who had come to the President's attention through a highly regarded report on coast defense.[2] This proved to be a wise selection for, though probably unknown to Davis, General Randolph was well-equipped by background and interest for his new task. More than any other Secretary of War, with the possible exception of General John C. Breckinridge, Randolph was qualified by knowledge and experience to make a substantial contribution to Southern military policy and strategy. A knowledge of his unusual background is essential to an understanding of his policy and his contributions to Confederate strategy.

2

GEORGE WYTHE RANDOLPH [3] WAS BORN ON March 10, 1818, at Monticello, the home of his grand-

[2] Patrick, *Jefferson Davis and His Cabinet*, 122, 172–75, 180.
[3] Materials used in this sketch of Randolph are: George Wythe

father, Thomas Jefferson. He was the son of Governor Thomas Mann Randolph and Martha Jefferson Randolph and the brother of Colonel Thomas Jefferson Randolph. Educated in Cambridge, Massachusetts, and

---

Randolph Papers, Confederate Museum, Richmond, Va.; some papers of Captain R. G. H. Kean bearing on Randolph's career, courteously made available to me by Dr. Robert H. Kean of Richmond, Va., and cited hereafter as Kean Collection; Edgehill-Randolph Papers and other letters, Alderman Library, University of Virginia, Charlottesville, Va.; Daniel Harvey Hill Papers, Virginia State Library, Richmond, Va.; James L. Kemper Papers, Alderman Library; *O. R.*, Ser. I, II, Part 2, 91–97; H. W. Flourney (ed.), *Calendar of Virginia State Papers and Other Manuscripts* (10 vols., Richmond, 1861), 186, 195, 196; *Journal of the Convention of 1861* (Richmond, 1861), 145, 399; *Ordinances Adopted by the Convention of Virginia at the Adjourned Session in November and December, 1861* (Richmond, 1861), Ordinance No. 93; Richmond *Enquirer*, February 11, 1863; J. H. Chamberlayne (ed.), *Ham Chamberlayne—Virginian* (Richmond, 1932), 66–67; Mary Boykin Chesnut, *A Diary from Dixie*, ed. Ben Ames Williams (New York, 1950), 110; Frederick S. Daniel, *Richmond Howitzers in the War* (Richmond, 1891), 10–11; T. C. DeLeon, *Belles, Beaux and Brains of the '60s* (New York, 1909), 90–91; DeLeon, *Four Years in Rebel Capitals* (Mobile, 1890), 164; Mrs. Burton Harrison, *Recollections Grave and Gay* (New York, 1912), 172; T. J. Macon, *Reminiscences of the First Company of Richmond Howitzers* (Richmond, 1909), 10; Robert Stiles, *Four Years under Marse Robert* (New York, 1903), 48; John S. Wise, *The End of an Era* (New York, 1909), 70; W. Asbury Christian, *Richmond, Her Past and Present* (Richmond, 1912), 194, 213–14; *Drill Book of the Howitzer Company of the First Regiment of Virginia Volunteers* (Richmond, 1860); Henry T. Shanks, *The Secession Movement in Virginia, 1847–1861* (Richmond, 1934), 167–68, 194; Jennings Cropper Wise, *The Long Arm of Lee* (2 vols., Lynchburg, Virginia, 1914), I, 114–19; "Extracts from an old 'Order Book' of First Company, Richmond Howitzers," *Contributions to a History of the Richmond Howitzers* (Richmond, 1878), pamphlet No. 1, 14–84; Captain Henry Hudnall, "The Origin of the First Company," *ibid.*, pamphlet No. 1, 3–10; W. S. White, "A Diary of the War," *ibid.*, pamphlet No. 2, 97.

Charlottesville, Virginia, he was appointed a midshipman in the United States Navy when he was thirteen years old. After six years of service, most of it at sea and including duty on "Old Ironsides," he entered the University of Virginia to pursue "such studies as would be of advantage to him in his profession."

Two years later, deciding to abandon the navy, he took up law, graduating in 1840 from the University of Virginia with a B.L. degree after one year only. Ten years of practice in Albermarle County, Virginia, having availed him little either in his profession or in Democratic politics, he moved to Richmond, Virginia. His purpose in this move being "to make money," he declared himself "ready to tramp over sea and land in search of fortune."

Fortune smiled on bachelor Randolph soon after he reached Richmond, when he married the beautiful, charming and very wealthy widow, Mrs. Mary Elizabeth Adams Pope. Considering her "amiable"—and wealth a *"decided recommendation"* in a match—he pursued her energetically, traveling a good deal and neglecting his practice even though his borrowed capital was "going with fearful rapidity." Success crowned his efforts, however, in April, 1852, and a considerable and immediate change took place in his circumstances. Instead of two rooms, he now occupied a two-story house in the "best neighborhood" provided with illuminating gas, plumbing and four servants.

Though marred by his wife's and his own bad health, the next few years were pleasant for Randolph. His childless married life was a happy one, and his wife's affluence enabled them to enjoy sociability, comfort and travel, while Randolph indulged his tastes as a dandy with such items as cashmere pantaloons and shirts at sixty dollars per dozen. His industry and talent, however, gave him such an important and lucrative trial practice that he was regarded as one of the "rising men of the bar," and this expansion of his own revenues enabled him to be generous with the less fortunate in his own family.

A respected and well-liked member of the social and professional community in Richmond, he was prominent in civic affairs and continued his penchant for politics, serving on the Richmond City Council. He had a reputation as a speaker, but his availability was diminished by his very moderate stand on the issue of Southern rights and slavery extension. His ambitions were not political and politics remained very much a sideline with Randolph, law, leisure and books continuing as his principle interests.

Randolph, who was "said to have read a Latin or Greek author in the original every morning before breakfast," was widely read in history and could quote La Rochefoucauld and Bacon, as well as Shakespeare and the Bible. But most significant for his and the Confederacy's future was his continuing absorption in naval affairs. Moreover, he had extended this interest to include land warfare. He was especially concerned with current European military developments. Continued warfare abroad gave him an opportunity to be an armchair strategist, for during the Italian war of 1859 he studied "the geography of the scene of the War," and planned "campaigns for the belligerents."

It was only natural, then, that when Virginia should seem to be menaced by John Brown's raid, this latent interest should manifest itself in the military sphere.

He ingeniously combined his military and naval inclinations when he "conceived the idea of converting the ordinary naval boat howitzer into an efficient arm of the land service." He promptly organized a howitzer company in the Virginia militia which was on active service during the crisis. His military erudition enabled him to discuss the role and importance of artillery as well as to describe its drill and give "a detailed and interesting history of the howitzer and its efficiency."

After serving at Harpers Ferry until the hanging of John Brown, Captain Randolph devoted himself to turning his howitzer company into a "crack corps" of the Virginia militia. Energy, indicated by weekly meetings, and efficiency, to which a twenty-eight page drill manual testifies, must indeed have produced a superior unit. The company commander gave the character to the unit, for though the military and technical were stressed, neither the social nor the intellectual aspect was ignored. Attention to all of these aspects was combined when "the burial of a tame crow" was dignified "not only by salvos of Artillery but also by an English speech, a Latin oration and a Greek ode."

The scope of Randolph's military career was broadened in January, 1860, to include service on a special military board created to provide arms for the state of Virginia. But soon his primary interest was diverted from military affairs to politics in Virginia. John Brown's raid turned him into a defender of Southern rights and the election of Lincoln, into a secessionist. Though immediately after the election of Lincoln he predicted the organization of a Southern Confederacy, he felt that Virginia would not join until compelled to do so by the policies Lincoln would follow when he actually took office. Strongly favoring Virginia's early secession, he argued also that it was to the state's economic advantage, for a southern tariff would make Virginia the Massachusetts of a Southern Confederacy. To promote these views he became, in December, 1860, a candidate for a convention called to consider whether Virginia should secede.

After "a very exciting contest," Randolph was the only advocate of secession of the three members elected to the convention from Richmond. There he played an important and creditable role, advocating secession on economic grounds. He was selected to represent the secessionist point of view on a three-man commission sent on an abortive mission to President Lincoln in April, 1861, in an effort to learn his views and intentions toward the seceded states. His interest in the militia had already been extended to legislation, and while in the convention he served on its military affairs committee, where he was influential and rendered "valuable service."

Randolph's politico-military career, which had already taken much time from his law practice, was radically altered when Virginia seceded and he and his howitzers were called to active service in April, 1861. His rise in his new career of full-time soldiering was meteoric. Recruiting efforts had been so successful that the company was immediately transformed into a battalion, of which he was elected the major commanding. Service on the York-James peninsula gave him an opportunity to distinguish himself on June 10, 1861, in the battle of Big Bethel, the first Confederate victory on Virginia soil. Acting as the Confederate chief of artillery, he not only displayed "conspicuous gallantry" but his professional skill made such an impression that Colonel D. H. Hill thought he had "no superior as an artillerist in any country." His labors with his unit had not been in vain, for the "firing of the howitzers was as perfect as the bearing of the men."

Public notice of the battle and the unstinting praise and strong endorsements of the two professional officers commanding, Hill and John Bankhead Magruder, earned Randolph promotion to colonel. His promotion in September, with its increased responsibilities, made his absence from his post at Yorktown necessary in order to attend to ordnance and quartermaster affairs in Richmond. This provided him with an opportunity to return from the sphere of military operations to that of policy by participating in the continuing deliberations of the Virginia secession convention.

The problem of manpower for the Confederate armies was already worrying Randolph before he attended the November, 1861, sessions of the Virginia convention. He anticipated that, by the spring of 1862, enlistments of most men would have expired and "every man of them will go home." While he thought that many would return, better opportunities of promotion would attract them into new units, thus entailing the necessity "to organize anew in the face of the organized forces of the enemy." His remedy was a draft, with the militia "classified" into groups according to training and service obligation "as in France, Prussia and in all military nations," thereby not only raising men but allowing the "burden of war" to be more "equally distributed." With these measures and the abundance of experienced officers and men, the army in the spring of 1862 would no longer be the "mere mob" of the preceding year.

These ideas were the basis of his influential efforts in the Virginia convention to remedy the manpower problem at least as far as the Virginia forces were concerned. With the assistance of his brother, Colonel Thomas Jefferson Randolph, his bill for conscription in Virginia passed on November 19, 1861, after a legislative struggle. Modeled apparently after the system prevailing in Prussia, it provided for an active militia embracing male citizens from twenty-one to thirty-one years of age and a reserve containing those too old for the actives. Compulsory service of three years was required for those under twenty-six and of two years for those over that age, before they became eligible for entry into the reserves. The actives and the reserves were organized into separate companies, regiments and brigades so that they would be mobilized independently of each other. There was a penalty of three additional days of service for each day missed through failure to enroll promptly or for absence without leave.

While this law was subsequently amended by the legislature, it would have been of little effect, in any case, as the Confederate Government soon largely pre-empted state action in the field of recruiting the army. This law gives a good indication of Randolph's views and of his knowledge of European conscription legislation and methods, which he took into the Confederate Cabinet.

Randolph's continued eminence as a soldier caused him to be promoted to brigadier general in February and sent to Suffolk, in southeastern Virginia, where he was charged with the defense of the coastline as far south as northern North Carolina. Despite his promotion and his undoubted patriotism, he desired to leave the army. His health, already bad, suffered from service in the field, and the army had already taken him from his books and home "to swelter in the pestilent marshes of the Peninsula." It was probable that a taste for legislative service had been developed by Randolph while in the Virginia convention. These, together with a feeling that he could do more for the Confederate cause on the policy level, induced him to enter at a late date the race for Confederate Congressman from Richmond. He was badly defeated, running third in a field of three. His late entry caused him to lose the votes of his supporters because the other "two horses" were "halfway to the goal when he put his foot on the tract."

Not only did General Randolph have a manpower policy which he desired to put into operation on the national level, but he was a discerning observer of the whole military scene. When President Davis selected a secessionist grandson of Thomas Jefferson, who would represent both the army and Virginia in the Cabinet, he probably did not anticipate getting also a man with a ready-made manpower program for the Confederacy. Nor had Randolph's service in the field obscured the interest in strategy manifested when he planned campaigns for Louis Napoleon and *Feldzeugmeister* von Benedek less than three years before.

3

Appointed Secretary of War on March 17, 1862, General Randolph reached Richmond on Saturday, March 22, and immediately began his new duties, though Secretary Benjamin remained a few days until he became familiar with the work in progress. The manpower crisis was uppermost in Randolph's mind, and in "his first interview with President Davis he pressed upon him the absolute necessity of Conscription." [4] While a resort to conscription had been urged in the press, President Davis had taken no public stand on the question at the time Randolph entered upon his duties.[5] Even today his attitude is unknown, no record of his views at that time being available. In all proba-

[4] Sketch of Randolph, 5, 7, Kean Collection. Not having access to the Kean Collection nor utilizing the Edgehill-Randolph Papers, Rembert W. Patrick, in his able and scholarly *Jefferson Davis and His Cabinet,* 123–24, states that Benjamin "aided in drafting the conscription bill, and helped to push it to enactment by Congress," while Randolph's influence was "negligible." As Patrick cites no source for this statement, presumably he reasonably concluded that the capable and experienced Benjamin, rather than the novice Randolph, had done this important work. Patrick concluded (*ibid.,* 130) that Randolph was the least influential of the Secretaries of War. This conclusion, well-warranted by the information at his disposal, must be modified by this new evidence.

[5] Edward A. Pollard, *Life of Jefferson Davis with a Secret History of the Southern Confederacy* (Philadelphia, Chicago, St. Louis, Atlanta, 1869), 202.

bility, however, he was inclining toward the measure as the only solution. If he were still undecided or had any lingering doubts, Randolph's thorough grasp of the problem and the remedy must have convinced Davis of the necessity and efficacy of the measure.

On March 28 the President asked the Confederate Congress for conscription legislation. Legislation was made necessary by the excessive complication of the numerous existing laws, he said, and by conflicts with state laws. Though "these reasons would suffice" for enacting a comprehensive law, the preparations for an enemy offensive had created a "spirit of resistance so general, so resolute, and so self-sacrificing that it requires rather to be regulated than stimulated." Therefore, action was necessary to keep those under eighteen years of age and those over thirty-five at home as a reserve and "for maintaining order and good government." For these reasons, and to keep the burden of service from falling "exclusively upon the most ardent and patriotic," it was necessary to declare everyone from age eighteen to thirty-five "in the military service of the Confederate States, and that some plain and simple method be adopted for their prompt enrollment."

Whatever his role in bringing the President to the advocacy of the measure, Randolph was vigorous in urging the adoption of a bill which would not only retain the existing one-year men in the ranks but the existing organizations as well. In addition, he wished a general conscription of all within the age group specified in order to increase the armies. To secure the adoption of the kind of law he desired, Randolph "sought interviews with the chairman of the Military Committee of both houses" [*sic*] of the Confederate Congress. Ignoring the President's specious arguments about regulating enthusiasm, he insisted that "a bold and strong measure was absolutely, demonstrably necessary to save the South from instant subjugation." He supported his argument before the military committees with a statement prepared at his direction by the Adjutant and Inspector General's office. This statement carried the alarming intelligence "that in ninety days from the first of April, 130 regiments would go out of service, being twelve-month men enlisted in April, May and June, 1861, and constituting quite half of the whole force in the field." [6]

Randolph awaited with impatience passage of the law which he thought "will at once relieve all our difficulties by continuing the army as it stands." A bill substantially embodying Randolph's views reached the Senate floor in April, where, after considerable debate, it was amended, allowing men who were to be continued in service privilege of reorganizing and electing new officers. Randolph, having seen this type of reorganization with the demoralizing effect of officers and men running for office, strongly opposed this feature. But the Senate felt this, together with a bounty and furlough, was necessary to conciliate the one-year men. Even two members of the Military Affairs Committee voted for the amendment. However, with the support of the committee, especially that of two important Administration supporters, Louis T. Wigfall of Texas and the chairman, Edward Sparrow of Louisiana, the bill went through without further change, passing 19

[6] James D. Richardson (ed.), *Messages and Papers of the Confederacy* (2 vols., Nashville, 1906), I, 206–207; Sketch of Randolph, 7, Kean Collection.

to 5 on April 11. After fighting off a number of amendments, such as one requiring the consent of the individual and of the governor of his state before he could be drafted, the Senate bill passed the House, 53 to 26, on April 14.

Apparently Randolph's efforts had secured a bill which did not suit the President. The objectionable feature, which Randolph regarded as essential, was that of keeping the one-year volunteers in service. The President "was distrustful of the system," because "he regarded it as a breach of faith on the part of the Government with the soldiers to legislate them into an enlistment for three years or the war, when they had volunteered for one year." These doubts of the President about this feature, for which he had not asked in his message, were aired in a cabinet meeting convened to consider the bill. The President, however, decided in favor of the measure as it stood, and it became law on April 16, 1862.[7]

The Conscription Act "retained in service the 148 regiments of one-year volunteers and by encouraging voluntary enlistment enabled Lee to save Richmond." In addition to saving "the Confederacy in the summer of 1862," it systematized manpower. The Conscription Act was of lasting significance, not only by impelling conscripts and volunteers into the service "just at the moment when they were absolutely necessary to check the onrush of the enemy," but because "powerful armies built up in the summer and fall of 1862 were the backbone of the Confederate military system that distin-

[7] George Wythe Randolph to Joseph E. Brown, April 2, 12, 15, 1863, Allen D. Chandler (ed.), *The Confederate Records of the State of Georgia* (8 vols., Atlanta, 1909–11), III, 175–77, 183–85; Sketch of Randolph, 7–8, Kean Collection.

guished itself on the bloody battlefields of 1863 and 1864." [8]

The role of Randolph in giving the Administration a policy for recruiting, infusing "some vigor and consistency into the chaos which reigned in the War Office on March 24, 1862," was largely overlooked at the time. It is not clear whether he persuaded Davis to adopt conscription, crystallized his decision, or merely advocated something on which the President had already resolved. His conspicuous and important service in framing the bill is clear. The plan to keep one-year men from leaving the service, even for a short while, was decisive. Had they done so, their regiments would have been broken up, and the men would have entered organizations "which could never be assembled, or, if assembled, could not be prepared for the field in time to meet the invasion actually commenced." This vital feature he had embodied in the bill through his representations to the Congressional committees.

The strong supposition is, then, that his influence produced a bill holding the volunteers in service, a feature not requested by, and unsatisfactory to, President Davis. The same forceful and expert presentation used with the congressmen was apparently applied to Davis and convinced him of the necessity of the legislation. The new Secretary was in an admirable position to enforce his views. His military erudition and familiarity with European manpower legislation, added to the practical experience gained in the field, gave a convincing appearance of complete expertness. The persuasiveness and authority of this talented trial lawyer had imposed his views in the Virginia convention of

[8] Wood, "American Civil War," *Encyclopedia Britannica*, 767; Moore, *Conscription and Conflict in the Confederacy*, 355–56.

1861, in which he had risen with little political experience or background. Backed by the statistical resources of the War Department, and speaking with conviction and authority, he carried congressmen and the President along with his views.[9]

While a law of Congress could go a long way toward ending the manpower crisis of the Confederacy, no such simple solution was available for the problem of directing military operations on a battle front a thousand miles long and protecting an extensive and vulnerable seacoast. Without a commander-in-chief or modern staff, the President with the collaboration of the Secretary of War grappled with problems of command and strategy on an almost unprecedented scale.

[9] Kean, *Inside the Confederate Government*, 72, entry of June 14, 1863; Randolph to Davis, August 12, 1862, *O. R.*, Ser. IV, II, 42; these conclusions are based on the Sketch of Randolph in the Kean collection. Kean, who was responsible for this sketch, admired Randolph, with whom he became associated in February, 1862, thus being in a position to know Randolph's ideas and actions. The only added support for his role is the Charleston *Mercury*, April 3, 23, 1862, and statements that Davis used pressure to secure passage of his bill found in Richard Malcom Johnston and William Hand Browne, *Life of A. H. Stephens* (Philadelphia, 1884), 409, and Alfred Roman, *Military Operations of General Beauregard* (2 vols., New York, 1883), II, 433.

The negative evidence is impressive, however. Albert Burton Moore in his *Conscription and Conflict in the Confederacy* says nothing to indicate anyone's role in framing and passing the conscription bill. That Davis' message to Congress did not ask for retention of one-year volunteers, something clearly anticipated by Randolph in his letter to Governor Brown, gives strong support to the contention in the Sketch of Randolph and the statement in Kean, *Inside the Confederate Government*, 72, entry of June 14, 1863. Unfortunately the sketch stops in the middle of a sentence, immediately after stating Davis' opposition to retaining the volunteers, and Randolph's role in persuading Davis has only been inferred. For Kean's relation to Randolph, see Kean, *ibid.*, xxii.

Chapter Four

The Western Kaleidoscope

1

THE VAST AREA OF THE CONFEDERACY WEST
of the Appalachian Mountains presented the most difficult problem in command to the Richmond authorities, by reason of its great extent and its remoteness
from the capital. On July 4, 1861, the western frontier
of the Confederacy, stretching from the Appalachian
Mountains to New Mexico, had been constituted as
Department No. 2. When on September 10, 1861, General Albert Sidney Johnston, the ranking field officer
of the Confederacy, had been placed in command, this
department had been redefined to include Tennessee,
Arkansas, Kentucky, Missouri, Kansas, the Indian territory and the western part of Mississippi. The Gulf
coast was protected by Department No. 1, under Major
General Mansfield Lovell, who was principally concerned with the defense of New Orleans, while another
force under Major General Braxton Bragg watched
over Pensacola, Florida, and Mobile, Alabama.

During the period of inactive operations in the fall
of 1861 General Johnston devoted himself to building
an army and a military organization from the raw mate-

rial supplied by the western states and the Confederate War Department. Though absorbed with problems of recruitment, organization and equipment, General Johnston kept the Secretary of War informed as to his own dispositions and strength and those of the enemy. As the Federal armies were much stronger, Johnston's plans were purely defensive. The Richmond authorities, while giving advice and directions on the problems of building up his force, left dispositions and strategy largely in his hands.[1]

By January, 1862, General Johnston had his command organized and his men disposed along the frontier. Defending his center in Tennessee, he had about 5,500 men at Forts Henry and Donelson on the Tennessee and Cumberland Rivers. The left wing of his central army was advanced to Columbus, Kentucky, on the Mississippi River, where that capable and versatile ecclesiastic, the Right Reverend Major General Bishop Leonidas Polk, commanded 17,000 men. His right wing was also advanced into Kentucky, and General Johnston personally commanded it with 25,000 men holding Bowling Green. The extreme right based on Knoxville, Tennessee, was an army of three to four thousand men under an energetic but inexperienced Tennessee journalist, Brigadier General Felix K. Zollicoffer. In Arkansas, Major General Earl Van Dorn, a veteran West Point cavalryman, commanded 20,000 men. Against these widely dispersed forces numbering about 70,000

[1] *O. R.,* Ser. I, IV: Special Orders No. 88, Adjutant and Inspector-General's Office, July 4, 1861, 362; Special Orders No. 149, Adjutant and Inspector-General's Office, September 10, 1861, 405; Albert S. Johnston to Secretary of War Judah P. Benjamin, October 22, 1861—February 8, 1862, 468–554 *passim;* VII, 707–864 *passim.*

men, Union forces of 30,000 men were available under the slow and pedantic command of Major General Henry W. Halleck in Missouri. Also subject to Halleck's orders was the army of Major General U. S. Grant, 20,000 strong, in western Kentucky. North of Bowling Green was another Union force, 70,000 men under the competent direction of Major General Don Carlos Buell.

Johnston received a significant reinforcement at the beginning of February when he was assigned a new officer, General P. G. T. Beauregard, the hero of Fort Sumter and Manassas and the fourth-ranking field officer of the Confederacy. This talented soldier with a flair for publicity and controversy, was sent from Virginia to remove him to an area with less opportunity for military and political disputes. If President Davis doubted Beauregard's capacity, Johnston did not, and he immediately began to rely heavily on him. Beauregard's energy, insight and ability were to be important assets in the West, when the imposing and majestic-looking Johnston proved to be much less impressive in action.

Already at the Battle of Mill Springs on January 18, 1862, Zollicoffer's army had been defeated, Zollicoffer killed, and his army precipitously driven from Kentucky. Reporting this defeat, General Johnston wrote General Cooper on January 22 that he was about to be overwhelmed, that all of "the resources of the Confederacy are now needed for the defense of Tennessee."

On February 8, two days after Grant's advance had taken Fort Henry on the Tennessee River, the War Department took strong action to strengthen Johnston. Reinforcements were rushed from every point. General Bragg was ordered to send all of the troops he could spare to Knoxville, "at least four regiments," while General Lovell in New Orleans was directed to send 5,000 of his best-equipped men to Columbus, Kentucky.[2]

The reinforcements were too late to save Fort Donelson. General Johnston had strengthened it with part of his Bowling Green troops, so twelve to fifteen thousand men were lost to the heavily reinforced Grant in the surrender of the fort on February 16. With the Tennessee and Cumberland Rivers open to the Federal fleet, the whole Confederate position in western and central Tennessee was untenable, and General Johnston began an evacuation. General Beauregard was given charge of the troops along the Mississippi River, and Johnston undertook to lead the Bowling Green force southeastward through Tennessee and then westward through northern Alabama to rejoin Beauregard at Corinth, in northern Mississippi. Johnston did not complete this long march until March 22. Meanwhile, Beauregard had ordered a concentration in northern Mississippi, abandoning Columbus in order to economize on men. General Van Dorn was ordered across the Mississippi to join the concentration at Corinth. Time was allowed for these movements because the Union armies were under the slow and timid direction of General Halleck, supreme commander in the West since March 11, 1862. The armies of Buell and Grant, totaling 80,000 men, were assembling near Pittsburg Landing on the Tennessee across the Mississippi border from Corinth.

[2] Stanley F. Horn, *The Army of Tennessee* (New York, 1941), 80; *O. R.*, Ser. I, VI: Benjamin to Braxton Bragg, February 8, 1863, 823–24; Benjamin to Mansfield Lovell, February 8, 1862, 824.

The reaction of the President and the Secretary of War to these disasters was swift and decisive. General Bragg had advocated concentration of all available forces in a letter to Benjamin on February 15, 1862, and, in a telegram on February 18, had asked: "Should we not give up the seaboard now and concentrate all our means on the vital point?" The same day Benjamin wrote in a similar vein, pointing out that the "heavy blow which has been inflicted on us by the recent operations in Kentucky and Tennessee renders necessary a change in our whole plan of campaign." He and the President had "had in contemplation the necessity of abandoning the seaboard in order to defend the Tennessee line which is vital to our safety." Though lacking sufficient information from General Johnston, the Secretary informed General Bragg that the "decision is made and the President desires that you proceed as promptly as possible to withdraw your forces from Pensacola and Mobile and hasten to the defense of the Tennessee line." Retaining Mobile, however, Bragg sent 10,000 men and, at Beauregard's earnest request, went in person with his troops, though he retained the command of his department.

Efforts were also made to strengthen east Tennessee and to defend Knoxville and the vital railroad which linked Virginia with Chattanooga and Atlanta. Reinforcements for the army in east Tennessee were sought, and a talented and experienced officer, Major General Edmund Kirby Smith, was sent out from Virginia to take charge and defend the area and, if possible, make a diversion to help the defeated armies in the center. Though General Cooper felt that the District of East Tennessee "need not be separated" from Johnston's department, the new commander was instructed to communicate directly with the War Department—in fact, east Tennessee became an independent department.[3]

President Davis retained his confidence in General Johnston and sustained his friend, writing an "unofficial letter" to obtain his side of the recent defeats in order better to defend him from his critics. Davis also took into his own hands communication with General Johnston, directing him to send information frequently on his "condition and purposes." But the conduct of operations remained in the hands of Johnston, though he himself had delegated most of his authority to Beauregard during a good part of February and March. The President offered no more than speculations as to what military operations might be possible.[4] Thus the policy of the President remained one of delegating all strategic decisions in the West to the commander there. The vigorous, if tardy, intervention from Richmond to provide needed reinforcements had only been necessary in order to reach across departmental lines. In response to the changing situation, the District of East Tennessee had, in effect, been reorganized into an independent department, and General Bragg's presence with the armies of Johnston and Beauregard had effectually united his department with Department No. 2.

Concentrating at Corinth their forces from Tennessee

[3] *Ibid.:* Bragg to Benjamin, February 15, 18, 1863, 826–27, 894; Benjamin to Bragg, February 18, 1863, 828; VII—Benjamin to Albert S. Johnston, February 8, 1862, 863; Davis to Johnston, March 12, 1862, 257–58; X, Part 2—Samuel Cooper to Johnston, March 8, 1862, 303.

[4] *Ibid.,* VII: Davis to Johnston, March 6, 12, 26, April 5, 1862, 257, 299, 365, 395.

and their reinforcements from the south, Johnston and Beauregard advanced to attack the army of General Grant at Pittsburg Landing while it was still separated by a few miles from that of General Buell. On April 6, 1862, at Shiloh Church, in one of the bloodiest battles of the war, the Confederates failed to crush Grant. General Johnston lost his life and General Beauregard, assuming command, had to fall back the following day before the united forces of Grant and Buell. Soon General Halleck himself took personal command and began a very deliberate and cautious advance against Corinth. Outnumbered two to one, General Beauregard retreated and on May 30 evacuated Corinth, falling back to Tupelo, Mississippi. The loss of New Orleans at the end of April and of Island Number Ten, Fort Pillow, and Memphis, all of the posts on the Mississippi north of Vicksburg, by the end of June made the western outlook even more depressing. Fortunately Halleck, naturally cautious and fearful of the effect of the summer climate in Mississippi,[5] remained inert after his occupation of Corinth. Keeping the forces of Grant and William S. Rosecrans on the defensive in northern Mississippi, he directed Buell with 35,000 men to advance along the Memphis and Charleston Railroad and strengthen the forces already operating against Chattanooga. But to the Richmond Government, the collapse of the Confederate defense in the Mississippi Valley did not look a bit more menacing than the threat to Richmond presented by the imposing and powerful Federal army assembled at Washington.

[5] John Rodman Ropes, *The Story of the Civil War* (2 vols., New York, 1898), II, 385.

2

PRESIDENT DAVIS, SECRETARY OF WAR RANdolph, and General Lee, who had been in charge of the conduct of military operations since March 13, 1862, were absorbed with the immense Union Army at Washington, commanded by General George B. McClellan. At the beginning of March this youthful West Pointer and railroad executive was about to employ his army against that of his old friend, Joseph E. Johnston. Having thoroughly trained his troops and brought his army to a high pitch of efficiency, General McClellan determined to reach Richmond by utilizing the flexibility given him by Federal sea power. If he should land his men at the end of the York–James Peninsula, he would avoid the long overland route to Richmond from Washington, and his advance up the peninsula would be facilitated by his ability to outflank the defenders by using the rivers to transport his men around the flanks of the Confederate troops on the peninsula. This movement he commenced in March, and General J. E. Johnston made a corresponding movement of a large part of his forces to the neighborhood of Richmond.

The proximity of Virginia operations to Richmond and the availability of the commanders for conference had enabled the President and the War Department to play a role in the strategy of the operations there that was unknown in the West. The overall strategy of First

Manassas was presidential, and in July and October, 1861, the President had consulted with the Virginia commander and his subordinates as to prospective operations. Now a question of strategy arose over which there was disagreement. General Johnston felt that the lower part of the peninsula should be abandoned as McClellan was very strong, especially in artillery, and any position on the peninsula was vulnerable to a flanking movement by water. He recommended a concentration of all available troops from Georgia and North and South Carolina for a counterblow when McClellan drew near Richmond. A meeting was held in Richmond on April 4 in order to discuss his recommendations. Present were General Johnston and his two principal subordinates, Major Generals Gustavus W. Smith and James Longstreet, President Davis, General Lee and Secretary Randolph. General Lee opposed Johnston's plan to evacuate, arguing that it was necessary to hold the lower peninsula in order to gain time. Randolph supported Lee, contending that the abandonment of the peninsula would mean the evacuation of Norfolk and with it the navy yard and one of the major means of creating a navy. General Johnston's subordinates backed him up.

"The conference was protracted and sometimes very heated. During the first four or five hours the President took no active part in the discussion," but "the persistent opinions of the Secretary of War and of General Lee" won him over, and he announced that he favored holding the peninsula, "undoubtedly a sound decision." [6] General Johnston's defense of the peninsula was

---

[6] Gustavus W. Smith, *Confederate War Papers* (New York, 1884), 42. See also: Johnston, *Narrative*, 112; Douglas Southall Freeman, *R. E. Lee* (4 vols., New York, 1935), II, 22.

little more than a delaying action, and he began his evacuation just as McClellan's elaborate preparations for an attack on Yorktown were complete. General Randolph, sent to try to delay Johnston's evacuation, personally ordered a delay at Norfolk long enough to save considerable stores and munitions.

Harmony between General Johnston and his superiors returned when his evacuation to the neighborhood of Richmond was carried out and the troops from southeastern Virginia were concentrated around the capital. On May 31, 1862, Johnston's effort to smash McClellan at Seven Pines failed, and Johnston was severely wounded. The command of the Confederate armies was entrusted to General Lee, and preparations for driving back McClellan were pressed with vigor. Over 20,000 men were brought from North and South Carolina and Georgia. There seems to have been harmony of view and unity of action among Davis, Lee, and Randolph with respect to the concentration and proposed operations. Randolph's absorption with the Virginia front is indicated by the fact that he installed a telegraph line linking the War Department directly to General Lee's headquarters in the field. It was not a success. The key was captured, and some Yankee soldiers telegraphed impertinences to the Secretary of War.[7]

At the end of June Lee attacked McClellan in the Seven Days' Battles, drove him back and destroyed the last of President Lincoln's already waning confidence in McClellan and his plan. Lincoln then brought in the

[7] Robert E. Lee to Davis, June 5, 1862, Douglas Southall Freeman (ed.), *Lee's Dispatches* (New York, 1915), 5–6; Lee to Randolph, June 5, 1862, *ibid.*, 6, n. 1; J. B. Jones, *A Rebel War Clerk's Diary*, ed. Howard Swiggett (2 vols., New York, 1935), I, 169.

swaggering Major General John Pope, fresh from victories on the Mississippi. McClellan's army was reconcentrated in northern Virginia under Pope's command, and Richmond was relieved of any immediate danger.

But while the crisis had been surmounted in the East with the active participation of the Secretary and the President, the *laissez faire* policy toward the West had been carried to an unprecedented degree. The death of the President's good friend, A. S. Johnston, had placed in command Beauregard, a man whose ability Davis distrusted. Yet, after six weeks in command, Beauregard could write General Cooper that since "the battle of Shiloh, when I assumed command of the Western Department [Department No. 2] . . . no instructions from the War Department relative to the policy of the Government and the movements of the armies of the Confederacy have been received by me."

This inquiry elicited a reply from General Lee, then still in charge of military operations. Stating the western command philosophy of the government on May 26, General Lee agreed that "although no instructions have been given as to the military operations within your department since the command devolved on you, yet your condition and movements have been the subject of anxious consideration. Full reliance," he said, "was felt in your judgment and skill and in the bravery of your army to maintain the great interests of the country and to advance the general policy of Government." General Lee expressed optimism that, since "the victory of Shiloh," Beauregard would be able to advance into the country to the north of him.[8]

[8] *O. R.*, Ser. I, X, Part 2: P. G. T. Beauregard to Cooper, May 19, 1862, 52; Lee to Beauregard, May 26, 1862, 546.

But the withdrawal from Corinth and the loss of Fort Pillow on the Mississippi on June 1 confirmed President Davis in his initial judgment of General Beauregard. He wrote Mrs. Davis that the Mississippi would be safe if it were defended by the Mississippi troops lying in camp or retreating with Beauregard. He sent west an aide who subjected Beauregard to a "merciless inquisition" about recent operations. The President's opportunity to remove his western general came when Beauregard placed himself on sick leave in the middle of June, entrusting the command temporarily to General Bragg, the next-ranking officer. President Davis took this opportunity to place General Bragg permanently in command, and Beauregard, when his Alabama furlough was completed, was sent to command at Charleston, South Carolina.[9]

Though he had arrived in Mississippi two weeks too late for the battle of Shiloh, Major General Earl Van Dorn and his men from Arkansas did not recross the Mississippi. While this strengthened the forces in Mississippi, the now anachronistic departmental organization handicapped the Confederates in this area. Department No. 2, sometimes called the Western Department, once an extensive domain, had been diminished by the loss of much of its territory to the enemy, and east Tennessee had effectively made good its independence. The Pensacola and Mobile areas had been added, not by the action of the War Department, but through an informal personal union. General Bragg was, in modern officialese, "wearing two hats," one as commander of Department No. 2 and the other as commander of his

[9] T. Harry Williams, *P. G. T. Beauregard, Napoleon in Gray* (Baton Rouge, 1954), 155–59.

old department. The separate Department No. 1 em-
braced most of Mississippi and Louisiana east of the
Mississippi. General Lovell, commanding when New
Orleans was captured, had finally been superseded by
Van Dorn in June.

When Beauregard was actually retreating out of his
department and into Department No. 1 with almost all
of the troops in the Western Department, he asked
whether to "prevent confusion cannot the Western
Department extend over all the States of Mississippi and
Alabama?" He was given a small extension of territory
only, down to the thirty-third parallel, leaving Department No. 1 still independent, that it might oppose the
advance of the Federal forces from their new base at
New Orleans.

Bragg, too, felt the anomaly of two departments, back-
to-back, in Mississippi. Writing on June 24 he pointed
out that: "The present dividing line between Departments 1 and 2 is exceedingly inconvenient. The only
communication for me east or west passes through Van
Dorn's command." That Bragg's implied request was
promptly granted and Departments 1 and 2 united must
be attributed also to the serious threat posed by Buell's
advance on Chattanooga and the hope that Bragg could
help in its defense.

Department No. 2 now included all of Mississippi
and Alabama and a part of Georgia, extending east to
the railway from Chattanooga, to Atlanta and West
Point, down the Chattahoochee and Apalachicola Rivers
to the Gulf of Mexico. General Bragg organized his
new department, making all of Mississippi west of
Pearl River and the Mississippi Central Railroad the
District of Mississippi under Van Dorn. All of the

remainder of the department south of the thirty-second parallel became the District of the Gulf under the command of Brigadier General John H. Forney. While Van Dorn was piqued, writing President Davis that his command, Department No. 1, was now "reduced to a district subordinate," and complaining: "I have been ever thus trammeled and cannot help but feel it," the arrangement undoubtedly was a great improvement, enlarging General Bragg's resources for the defense of the whole area. This the President made clear to Van Dorn, pointing out that "the junction of the departments arose from no want of confidence, but to render the whole force most available to the paramount objective—the defense of our country."

Apparently the War Department was not explicit nor informative about its departmental reorganizations. Bragg, for example, felt unclear about the Department of East Tennessee, writing to its commander, Kirby Smith, of his doubt as to whether his department was "a separate command or still as formerly, a part of General Johnston's old department and hence embraced within my command." Kirby Smith, in explaining that his department was independent of the "Army of the West" and reported directly to the War Department, displayed his ignorance of the name of Bragg's department, which was Department No. 2 or the Western Department. The Army of the West was Van Dorn's old force from the Trans-Mississippi.[10] Even though

[10] *O. R.*, Ser. I: X, Part 2—Beauregard to Cooper, May 25, 1862, 544; XV—General Orders No. 39, Adjutant and Inspector-General's Office, May 26, 1862, 726; Special Orders No. 146, Adjutant and Inspector-General's Office, June 25, 1862, 766; Davis to Earl Van Dorn, July 15, 1862, 778; LII, Part 2—Bragg to Randolph, June 24, 1862, 325; Van Dorn to Davis, July 12, 1862,

the principal form of strategic control exercised by the War Department was in the arrangement and subordination of the departments, needed changes had been made tardily, and the commanders in the field were apparently not kept abreast of these changes. Constant replacement of commanders undoubtedly aggravated the situation.

While the failure of the Federals to follow up after capturing Corinth left Bragg an opportunity to recruit his strength and reorganize his department, Federal activity pointed to an area of serious weakness in the Confederate front.

3

CONFEDERATE FORCES IN EAST TENNESSEE, AN area of strong Union sympathies and an object of President Lincoln's special solicitude, had long been seriously threatened. The commander of the Department of East Tennessee was harrassed by a disloyal population, confused by misleading reports, and menaced at Cumberland Gap and Chattanooga, the opposite ends of his department. Its commander, Major General Edmund Kirby Smith, commented in June, 1862, that since he had assumed command in February his army had "been

---

328; XVII, Part 2—Randolph to Bragg, June 29, 1862, 627; Bragg to Kirby Smith, July 20, 1862, 562; XVI, Part 2—Randolph to Bragg, June 23, 1862, 701–702; Kirby Smith to Bragg, July 24, 1862, 734–35.

almost broken down by constantly moving from one end to the other of the line" to meet recurring threats.[11] At first considered to be purely on the defensive, he had sent reinforcements to Beauregard after Shiloh and had even decided to go to Mississippi himself. But the breaking of the Memphis and Charleston Railroad intervened to prevent further easy troop transfers to Beauregard, and Kirby Smith proposed that he might threaten Nashville as a diversion in favor of Beauregard, which plan was approved by Richmond.

The picture soon changed, and by the end of May Kirby Smith was hard pressed at Cumberland Gap and Chattanooga. He called for reinforcements and concentrated all forces to save Chattanooga, leaving a small force to hold Cumberland Gap. When he arrived in Chattanooga on June 7, he found the city under bombardment by Federal artillery. While this threat turned out to be transitory, Kirby Smith telegraphed General Cooper on June 12, asking: "In the event of abandoning East Tennessee, with the Georgia and Virginia lines open to me, which shall I take?" General Cooper replied that the President preferred the Georgia line of retreat and suggested that he telegraph Beauregard for reinforcements.

Not only did Kirby Smith ask Beauregard if he could spare any men, but General Cooper inquired of Beauregard whether, under the "present circumstances," he could return the men that had been sent him from east Tennessee. Beauregard replied, however, that it would be "fatal" for him to weaken his army at Tupelo.[12]

[11] *Ibid.*, Kirby Smith to Cooper, June 15, 1862, 685.

[12] *Ibid.*: Kirby Smith to Cooper, June 12, 1862, 679; Cooper to Kirby Smith, June 12, 1862, 679; Cooper to Beauregard, June 12, 1862, 680; Kirby Smith to Beauregard, June 12, 13, 1862, 680, 681; Beauregard to Cooper, June 13, 1862, 681.

When the threat to Chattanooga was renewed, Kirby
Smith decided on June 14 to abandon Cumberland Gap
and on the following day reported to Cooper his intention together with his accurate belief that General
Buell's Union army from northern Mississippi was
advancing on Chattanooga. He was sacrificing the Gap
and concentrating all of his forces. Feeling that the
enemy had made "the most dangerous move of their
campaign," he sent all supplies out of the department,
though he still hoped for aid from Beauregard.

The attitude of President Davis was expressed to two
Tennesseans when he noted that all available men had
been sent to east Tennessee and that, if Beauregard's
successor, General Bragg, had the "power to aid General
[Kirby] Smith he will not fail to do so; but I fear that
there is little hope of that." General Randolph echoed
the same view to General Bragg. The latter had reported
that Buell was moving east with 25,000 men and, since
he was hopeful of taking the offensive soon, could not
east Tennessee be most efficiently aided from Georgia?
The Secretary of War replied, authorizing Bragg "to
attempt the movement you indicate or any other which
in your judgement promises success." The War Department, he said, had sent as many men to Kirby Smith as
could be armed, but "six of his regiments were sent to Corinth and never returned to him. Aid him if you can." [13]

The seriousness of the situation must, however, have
impressed itself on the President and the Secretary of
War. If they were unwilling to order Bragg to reinforce,
they soon had many of the troops in camps in Georgia

[13] *Ibid.*: Kirby Smith to Cooper, June 14, 15, 1862, 683, 684–85;
Davis to W. G. Swan and J. G. M. Ramsey, June 21, 1862, 696;
Bragg to Cooper, June 22, 1862, 701; Randolph to Bragg, June 23,
1862, 701–702.

and Alabama in motion toward Chattanooga. The President wrote to Kirby Smith on June 25 that "re-enforcements to a larger extent than the number named by you have been ordered to Chattanooga, and I will endeavor still further to increase your command." Meanwhile the Secretary of War was combing the training camps for men with an order "to send all organized corps ready for the field to Chattanooga." Directions such as these were dispatched by the Secretary:

> Order all the new infantry regiments and battalions in a condition to march immediately to Chattanooga. Order also Lawton's cavalry regiment and Capers' artillery battalion, the latter to serve for the present as infantry if their battery is not ready. Give this order in my name.
>
> Does the telegraph report you correctly in saying you can move your infantry by the 22d of July? . . . I had hoped that you could move 1,000 men at least in forty-eight hours. . . . I can send arms to Chattanooga. Can you carry the men?

Thus unarmed troops were sent forward, meeting their weapons at Atlanta or Chattanooga. Henry W. Hilliard's legion and one regiment were sent from Alabama, and three regiments and two battalions, from Georgia.[14] General Bragg too had acted, sending over 3,000 men to Chattanooga. The slowness of Buell's advance enabled Kirby Smith to hold Chattanooga and, with his enlarged force, to defend Knoxville and the

[14] *Ibid.*: Davis to Kirby Smith, June 25, 1862, 707; Randolph to J. S. Smith, July 4, 1862, 720; Randolph to John Dunwody, June 29, 1862, 711; Randolph to H. W. Hilliard, June 27, 1862, 709; Randolph to Kirby Smith, July 2, 1862, 717.

railroad as well. His army had been increased from 8,600 in April to 18,000 by late July.

However, Halleck's feeble strategy and the slow progress of Buell presented the initiative to the Confederates, if they would only grasp it. In July the President and the Secretary of War were relieved from pressing worries about the safety of Richmond and the situation in Virginia. Lee moved his army north to meet Pope, and his mastery of the situation was established. The tactful and correct Lee stood in little need of advice from his superiors and so in eastern operations, as the Rebel War Clerk put it, General Lee had "razeed" the War Department "down to a second-class bureau, of which the President himself is the chief." Aside from rationalizing General Bragg's department and meeting the east Tennessee crisis with reinforcements of raw men, Randolph and Davis did nothing. The department commanders in the West were liberally supplied by the War Department with authority, discretion and confidence, but no directives or even suggestions beyond those relating to reinforcement.[15] The confidence of the President and the Secretary had been amply rewarded by Kirby Smith's energy, efficiency, and decisiveness in an emergency. They were about to witness a spectacular performance by General Bragg and his army.

[15] For Randolph's preoccupation with the Seven Days' Battles and his suggestion for Bragg to "strike the moment an opportunity offers," see: Randolph to Bragg, June 29, 1862, *Ibid.*, XVII, Part 2, 627.

Chapter Five

Western Reorganization

1

GENERAL KIRBY SMITH KEPT BRAGG WELL informed of events in east Tennessee. The possibility of doing more than merely sending a small reinforcement to Chattanooga had obviously occurred to Bragg. He wrote Cooper on July 12 that his shortage of transportation had been remedied, but an "almost unprecedented" drought prevented any movement against the enemy, well-entrenched and superior in numbers. He added: "Could I have foreseen the barrier to operations which is now between us a considerable portion of this force would have been thrown into East Tennessee, where successful operations might have been carried on directly into and behind the enemy's lines." As late as July 19 Kirby Smith obviously hoped that his reports would have an effect on Bragg and cause him to move in force to east Tennessee. The next day he telegraphed Bragg: "It is your time to strike at Middle Tennessee."

But Bragg had already made up his mind and announced his intention of moving to Chattanooga immediately with a large force. Explaining his movements to his old commander and friend, Beauregard, he pointed out that he was immobilized by the drought, while feeling "uneasiness for the safety" of the important east Tennessee line. As Kirby Smith had been refused aid "from the east or south," the "whole responsibility" for the safety of east Tennessee rested on himself. Bragg saw positive aspects in the move, however, for he envisaged the possibility of cutting Buell's communications and getting him in a "tight place."

He set 35,000 men in motion on July 21 on the circuitous railway route from Tupelo, Mississippi, to Mobile, north to Montgomery and Atlanta. In order to secure the reinforcement of Chattanooga "at the earliest moment," the garrison of Mobile started first. He explained to Cooper that "as long as we are passing, Mobile is safe, and at the close a sufficient force will be left there." In effect, this expedient placed the head of the movement half way to Chattanooga before it had even begun, while the tail of the moving army would replace the garrison of Mobile.[1]

Simultaneous with this decision on Bragg's part, the "Confederate Government also recognized the importance of Chattanooga and reorganized its Western Commands accordingly," by relieving Bragg of responsibility for the Trans-Mississippi area. But in extending Bragg's department to the Gulf and cutting off the Trans-Mississippi District, the government was doing more than merely completing a reorganization so that Bragg

[1] *O. R.*, Ser. I: XVI, Part 2—Kirby Smith to Bragg, July 4, 6, 10, 20, 1862, 719–30 *passim*; Special Orders No. 4, Headquarters of the Forces, July 21, 1862, 731; XVII, Part 2—Bragg to Cooper, July 12, 1862, 645; July 23, 1862, 656; LII, Part 2—Bragg to Davis, July 17, 1862, 330; Bragg to Beauregard, July 22, 1862, 330–31.

could direct his undivided attention toward Tennessee
and have at his disposal all resources within reach. This
change marked also the beginning of an energetic application of a system of separate departments with specialized missions. These departments were to be assigned
their tasks, and these were frequently changed to meet
the varying military situation. Not only was Bragg given
a free hand to march north, but the Trans-Mississippi
was erected into a separate department under a new
commander, Theophilus H. Holmes. Further, Richard
Taylor, an able officer enjoying the fullest confidence of
the President, was sent from Virginia and "assigned to
duty in the District of Western Louisiana in the Trans-
Mississippi Department" and "especially charged with
the command of the troops serving in the southern part
of the district." He was directed to "establish such lines
of communication as the state of the country may
require for the regular receipt and transmission of
intelligence" and to "communicate directly . . . information of all important events." [2]

After Van Dorn, who had been directed to "confer"
with Taylor, had to turn his attention northward, two
regiments were, on September 1, ordered from Mobile
"to Louisiana for a purpose not admitting of delay,"
and Henry Sibley's Brigade at Marshall, Texas, was at
the same time placed under Taylor's orders.

When, on September 11, General Daniel Ruggles,
commanding at Vicksburg, telegraphed his recommen-

---

[2] Thomas L. Snead, "With Price East of the Mississippi,"
Battles and Leaders of the Civil War, eds. C. C. Buell and Robert
U. Johnston (4 vols., New York, 1887–88), II, 725; *O. R.,* Ser. I,
XV: General Orders No. 5, War Department, Adjutant and
Inspector-General's Office, July 18, 1862, 770; Cooper to Richard
Taylor, July 30, 1862, 791.

dation of "an immediate movement against New Orleans," he received word that Taylor had been assigned
the "very responsible" duty to which he referred, and
that the "Secretary is at a loss to understand why
Brigadier-General Ruggles . . . should propose to interfere with the authority vested in Major-General Taylor, or why he should give publicity through the medium
of the telegraph to suggestions which should have been
regarded by him as private and are so regarded in the
instructions to General Taylor." Needless to say, Ruggles was bewildered and offended by this testy reprimand
from the Secretary, and pointed out that not only was
New Orleans within his district, not Taylor's, but his
telegram "amounted at most to a suggestion, and if the
[telegraph] agents are disloyal, the plans of the Government are at their mercy." Thus Randolph endeavored
to keep "strictly confidential" his rather unrealistic
project for the recapture of New Orleans.[3]

Complications soon overshadowed this plan, however,
for General Bragg was leading a large part of his force
entirely out of his department for a campaign in Kirby
Smith's neighboring department. What was to happen in
his own command during his absence? During June and
July the Federal naval flotillas from New Orleans and

---

[3] *Ibid.*: Davis to Van Dorn, August 4, 1862, 795; Randolph to
John H. Forney, September 1, 1862, 804; H. H. Sibley to Randolph, October 1, 1862, 819; Daniel Ruggles to Cooper, September
11, 30, 1862, 806, 817; Jasper S. Whiting to Ruggles, September
23, 1862, 810; Cooper to Ruggles, October 21, 1862, 840; Richard
Taylor, *Destruction and Reconstruction* (New York, 1879), 102–
103, 110–15. General Taylor makes no mention of this plan, but
from the destitute nature of his district, denuded of troops, it
is easy to understand why he was not able to give it serious
thought. For the final echo of this project, see: Davis to Johnston,
February 19, 1863, *O. R.,* Ser. I, XXIII, Part 2, 641.

the upper Mississippi had been engaging the Confederate batteries at Vicksburg, the last Confederate strongpoint on the Mississippi and the last link to the Trans-Mississippi. Federal troops had advanced from Baton Rouge and appeared before Vicksburg on the west bank of the river. While the Union efforts had not been successful, they were naturally the subject of great concern to General Bragg and to Vicksburg's immediate defender, General Earl Van Dorn. Van Dorn was fearful of a more powerful Federal land attack and wished to make Vicksburg more secure by fortifying Port Hudson, Louisiana, down the Mississippi from Vicksburg, and also by securing the mouth of the Red River. He too had hopes of recapturing New Orleans, if the enemy were not too strong.

General Bragg's other major concern was the protection of northern Mississippi from invasion by the Federal troops holding Memphis, Corinth, and the line of the Memphis and Charleston Railroad. To provide for these two distinct areas of operation, he left Van Dorn in command of his district, with 16,000 men for the defense of Vicksburg and the prosecution of his projects in Louisiana, and committed the defense of northern Mississippi to Major General Sterling Price. For his task, Price, an intelligent and popular Missouri politician, was given command of the Army of the West, the troops which had originally been brought from Arkansas by Van Dorn and which numbered about 20,000 men. Bragg apparently did not expect to be able to direct movements from beyond the boundaries of his department and so instructed Van Dorn to "consult freely and co-operate" with Price. Van Dorn was expected to "do all things deemed needful without awaiting instructions" from Bragg. Price was given similar instructions.[4]

Bragg's ambitious campaign went very well. Kirby Smith's command, reinforced by two divisions of Bragg's army, crossed the mountains south of Cumberland Gap and advanced into Kentucky. At Richmond, Kentucky, on August 30 he annihilated a small Federal army largely composed of raw recruits and then occupied Lexington, threatening Louisville. Outflanked, the Union forces at Cumberland Gap retreated northward through the mountains of eastern Kentucky. At the end of August Bragg himself began an advance due north from Chattanooga and, by-passing Nashville, entered Kentucky in early September. This move placed Bragg closer to Louisville and Cincinnati than Buell, who was also on the march north and who was passing through Nashville. In the East, as well, the Confederates took the offensive after Lee had severely defeated Mc-Clellan's successor, Pope, at the Second Battle of Manassas near Washington on August 29 and 30. By the middle of September Harpers Ferry had capitulated, and Lee's army was in Maryland.

General Bragg undoubtedly wished Price to pin down the Federal forces in northern Mississippi and western Tennessee and not to let anything Van Dorn might propose interfere with this objective. He soon saw the value of a combined offensive by Price and himself and, shortly after he reached Chattanooga, he intimated his ideas when he reminded Price that "the road is open . . . into Western Tennessee." Price took

[4] *Ibid.*: LII, Part 2—Van Dorn to Davis, July 22, August 2, 11, 1862, 331, 334, 340; Bragg to Davis, July 17, 22, 1862, 330; XVII, Part 2—Thomas Jordan to Van Dorn, July 23, 1862, 656.

up the idea with alacrity, being "extremely anxious for a forward movement." Bragg approved Price's plan to advance, and Price proposed his campaign to Van Dorn, urging him to join him. However, Van Dorn was absorbed with an attack on Baton Rouge and wished Price to aid him before they advanced into Tennessee.

On August 11 Bragg pointed out to Van Dorn the importance of taking the offensive to keep Buell from being reinforced and suggested alternative ways of uniting with Price. But he pointed out that these were "suggestions only," for he could not give "specific instructions" as "circumstances and military conditions . . . vary materially from day to day." He offered the inducement that, if Van Dorn joined Price, his seniority would give him "command of the whole force." But Bragg relied almost entirely on Price, warning him not to "depend much on Van Dorn; he has his hands full." [5]

On leaving Chattanooga Bragg told Van Dorn and Price of his plans and left to their discretion the best way of dealing with the Union troops in Mississippi and west Tennessee, writing that he was "satisfied that you can dispose of them, and we shall confidently expect to meet you on the Ohio and there open the way to Missouri." Except for two messages to Price in early September and one to Van Dorn in late September directing an advance on Nashville, the department commander left his two subordinates to their own devices in working out their campaign. The two generals, com-

[5] Buell and Johnston (eds.), *Battles and Leaders of the Civil War,* II, 726–27; *O. R.,* Ser. I, XVII, Part 2: Bragg to Sterling Price, August 2, 19, 1862, 662, 682; Price to Van Dorn, July 31, August 4, 1862, 665, 663; Van Dorn to Price, August 11, 1862, 675; Bragg to Van Dorn, August 11, 1862, 675–76.

manding adjacent departments, despite long association, were unable to work out a joint plan. Van Dorn could not move as soon as Price desired and preferred to advance due north rather than toward Nashville. In spite of Van Dorn's being the senior major general by seven months, they discussed, persuaded, and traded plans only. Their lack of co-ordination, as well as their cordiality, is indicated by the closing of one of Van Dorn's letters: "However all this may turn out, I shall always be happy to be associated with you in this noble struggle, and I pray to God you may be victorious wherever you may go."

Van Dorn had long been in direct communication with President Davis. On September 9 he applied to Secretary of War Randolph for the service of some recently exchanged prisoners which, he said, were necessary to his proposed campaign in west Tennessee. He continued: "I ought to have command of the movements of Price, that there may be concert of action. . . . Bragg is out of reach; I refer to you." Randolph endorsed the letter to the President: "I suppose the matters would be regulated by General Bragg, and feel some hesitation in giving directions which might conflict with his plans. Something, however, should be done."

The President discussed the disposition of the prisoners and commented that Van Dorn's rank gave him the "command of all the troops with whom he will be operating." [6] This, of course, had been specified by

[6] *Ibid.*: Bragg to Price and Van Dorn, August 27, 1862, 688; Bragg to Price, September 12, 1862, 706; Samuel Jones to Price, September 6, 1862, 694; Bragg to Van Dorn, September 25, 1862, 713; Price to Van Dorn, August 27–September 19, 1862, 697–707 *passim*; Van Dorn to Price, September 3–19, 1862, 691–708 *passim*; Van Dorn to Randolph, September 9, 1862, 697–98.

General Bragg, but Price and Van Dorn were not yet operating together, and it seemed as if they would never agree on a joint plan and unite their armies. However, the War Department was alerted to the fact that General Bragg's departure had given rise to confusion and lack of co-ordination in Mississippi.

2

THE REALIZATION IN RICHMOND OF THE DIVERgent purposes and lack of co-ordination between the forces of Price and Van Dorn produced a prompt response. On September 11 the President telegraphed Van Dorn that the "troops must co-operate, and can only do so by having one head. Your rank makes you the commander." The President added that he had supposed that these were General Bragg's instructions also. In response to these orders, Van Dorn informed the Secretary of War that he proposed "to clean out West Tennessee . . . and then go across the Tennessee and Cumberland into Kentucky," while Price "proposes to follow Rosecrans toward Nashville. Therefore there can be no co-operation." Secretary Randolph replied that it was "impossible for the Department to instruct you as to your line of operations but co-operation between Price and yourself is indispensable to success, and was contemplated by General Bragg." The remedy was to place Van Dorn in command and, referring to the President's earlier instructions making this point, Randolph reminded Van Dorn that he was the senior officer and directed him to use his own discretion, "subject to General Bragg's instructions."

The alarm in Richmond caused by this lack of co-ordination and absence of control was aggravated by ignorance of General Bragg's plans and instructions for operations in that area. The President feared "disaster to all must be the probable result" of this lack of co-operation and "was at a loss to know how to remedy evils" without knowledge of General Bragg's plans. The Secretary, fearing a "serious misunderstanding" between the generals, reiterated his instructions for co-operation and for Van Dorn to "direct the movements" of the united armies.[7]

News of continued separate action by the two commanders, resulting in a minor defeat and narrow escape for Price, undoubtedly put an end to exhortations for co-operation and united action under Van Dorn. On September 29 Secretary Randolph dispatched peremptory orders to Van Dorn to "assume forthwith the command of all the troops left in Mississippi including General Price's column. Concentrate them without loss of time . . . make proper disposition for the defense of the Mississippi River and also for an advance into Tennessee." These instructions actually cut the Gordian knot of dual control of these distant forces by informally separating the Mississippi armies from General Bragg's command, unifying them under Van Dorn and controlling them directly from Richmond.

[7] *Ibid.*: Davis to Van Dorn, September 11, 1862, 700; Van Dorn to Randolph, September 9, 12, 15, 1862, 697, 701, 703; Randolph to Van Dorn, September 16, 19, 1862, 704, 707; Davis to Bragg, September 19, 1862, 707.

This reorganization was to have another and peculiar feature, however, in that an additional distinct command was to be created in Mississippi. This organization was to have as its "chief object" the defense of Mississippi and eastern Louisiana, but its commander was "to act in concert with Major General Richard Taylor" and "communicate with him as speedily as possible and concert with him a joint plan of operations for the defense of the river and the capture of New Orleans." This southward facing command, in a sense a re-creation of Department No. 1 and analogous to Taylor's in western Louisiana, embraced all of Mississippi and eastern Louisiana. Van Dorn would thus be relieved of his responsibilities in Louisiana and Mississippi, "permitting him to command the forces ordered to advance into West Tennessee" and thus presumably give his full attention to co-operating with Bragg, who was now approaching the crisis of his Kentucky invasion.

This novel arrangement presupposed the success of Van Dorn's invasion of west Tennessee. He had, in effect, to conquer for himself a department, as in his present location near Corinth he was poaching on another man's territory. This was a particularly complicated situation as both he and one of his subordinates, Major General Mansfield Lovell, outranked the commander of the new department, Major General John C. Pemberton, who was on his way from Charleston to take up his new duties. Pemberton had probably been selected, not because of his rank, but because he was not only no longer needed in Charleston but was unpopular there.[8] To Davis and Randolph this new

[8] *Ibid.*: Randolph to Van Dorn, September 29, 1862, 715; Randolph to John C. Pemberton, September 30, 1862, 716–17;

divided organization must have seemed an admirable one in the confident days when Bragg was inaugurating a Confederate governor of Kentucky and the New Orleans project was not yet dead.

When Van Dorn attacked and was heavily repulsed before Corinth on October 3 and 4, 1862, the situation of two commanders operating on the same area seemed destined to continue. Van Dorn was now "an isolated body in the field in Mississippi, relieved of command" of his department, while Pemberton found, under "circumstances . . . so much changed by movements of the enemy in the State of Mississippi" that it was "now impossible to carry out instructions," as both Van Dorn and Lovell were his seniors. The situation was regarded as especially critical because it was thought that the enemy was pursuing Van Dorn from Corinth. The remedy, unity of command, was obtained by nominating Major General Pemberton for promotion to lieutenant general, a rank which had only recently been authorized by the Confederate Congress and to which nominations had just been made. That Pemberton should have been selected rather than his more experienced senior, Van Dorn, was probably due to the unfavorable reports of Van Dorn's private life. Van Dorn's failure at Corinth may have contributed as well.

Pemberton was informed on October 14 of his promotion and was also directed to assume command of "the forces intended to operate in Southwestern Tennessee in addition to the command heretofore assigned"

Thomas Robson Hay, "Confederate Leadership at Vicksburg," *Mississippi Valley Historical Review*, XI (March, 1925), 544. See also: *O. R.*, Ser. I, XIV: William Porcher Miles to Lee, June 11, 1862, 560; Lee to Davis, June 25, 1862, 560.

to him. Van Dorn complained that this left him out in the cold. When he had taken chief command he had turned over his own troops to General Lovell, and so now that his army had been placed under Pemberton's department, he was left with no forces to command. This was remedied, however, by Van Dorn's replacing Lovell, and Pemberton assumed active charge of the Department of Mississippi and Eastern Louisiana, beginning measures to resist the advance of Grant. Some confusion continued to exist as to whether Bragg's authority still extended over Mississippi, but apparently the new unified organization under Pemberton had eliminated his authority from that area.[9]

Though a dangerous and anomalous situation had been remedied in Mississippi, unity of command was still sadly lacking in the West. In lieu of the single department confronting the enemy from the Appalachian Mountains to the Indian Territory, such as had existed barely eight months before, there were now four independent commanders responsible only to Richmond. The difficulty, if not impossibility, of these widely separated armies being controlled and co-ordinated from such a distance must have become rapidly apparent. Though Bragg was in full retreat from Kentucky by the middle of October and both Lee in Maryland and Van Dorn in Mississippi had already been checked, the

[9] *Ibid.,* XVII, Part 2: Pemberton to Cooper, October 9, 1862, 724; Van Dorn to Randolph, October 12, 1862, 727; Davis to James Phelan, October 11, 1862, 726–27; General Orders No. 17, Headquarters Department of Mississippi and East Louisiana, December 7, 1862, 787; Randolph to Pemberton, October 14, 1862, 727; Davis to Van Dorn, October 21, 1862, 733; Cooper to Bragg, November 19, 1862, 752; Bragg to Cooper, November 21, 1862, 755; Taylor, *Destruction and Reconstruction,* 116–17.

offensive spirit persisted a little longer in Richmond. Ignorance of Bragg's intentions and capabilities led to the supposition that he was "not seriously weakened" and withdrawing from Kentucky "for the purpose of completing the conquest of Tennessee." This expectation, together with the unity of command just achieved in Mississippi, led to the idea of a combined advance by the armies of Bragg in Tennessee, Pemberton in Mississippi, and Holmes in the Trans-Mississippi—"of converging three armies . . . upon some central point, and of regaining Tennessee and the Mississippi Valley."

The problem of directing from Richmond these three armies, situated as they were in a four-hundred-mile arc segmented by two major rivers, must have presented itself with startling clarity. The task of co-ordination was largely delegated to the three commanders. "To effect this great object co-intelligence among the commanders is absolutely necessary," wrote Randolph to Holmes. Though it was intended that Richmond would arrange a plan of campaign with General Bragg and communicate it to Holmes and Pemberton, co-ordination was left, Randolph continued, to "entire co-intelligence among the separate commanders." The President, too, wrote Holmes, saying on October 21 that the "concentration of two or when practical of all the columns in the attack upon one of the enemy's armies is so obviously desirable," but how and when such concentration should be made can only be determined after "the freest communication between the Generals so that each shall possess exact information in regard to the condition of the others."

The inherent difficulty of this plan, particularly in view of the very slow communication with the Trans-

Mississippi, must have been readily apparent to Randolph and Davis. At Randolph's instance General Bragg was called to Richmond for a conference on October 23 to give the history of his Kentucky campaign and to make plans for his army. At the same time Randolph, in view of the news that Pemberton's forces in north Mississippi were seriously menaced by Grant, ordered a practical implementation of the plans. Perhaps recalling General Bragg's recent Kentucky campaign which had begun as an effort to aid the adjacent department of Kirby Smith, Randolph authorized Holmes to cross the Mississippi with part of his force and, by virtue of being the senior lieutenant general, take charge of operations. At the same time another remedy for these evils had been proposed when General Bragg suggested to the War Department, during his October visit, that General Joseph E. Johnston "be assigned to the whole command in the Southwest with plenary powers."

The creation of a larger command in the West must have already occurred to Davis and Randolph. The expedient of having to issue orders from Richmond for General Holmes to leave his department with a portion of his command in order to secure concentration and unity of action was certainly a makeshift to be avoided. Though sending Holmes to Mississippi was a logical tactic in view of the fact that he was not presumed to be "seriously menaced," this very thing, when done by Bragg, had created disorganization in Mississippi. The necessity for further co-ordination was made clear by dispatches from the field. Pemberton, urging that "more troops are greatly needed," asked, "cannot some of Holmes' be spared?" while Van Dorn warned that "if we are not strengthened here we shall lose this state . . . Can any part of Bragg's force be thrown here?" [10]

The flexibility displayed in the summer and fall and the effort made to reshape departments to the strategic needs of the moment and to give each a specialized mission had been a marked improvement over the conduct of operations during the spring. Departmental organization had been based on a new principle—uniting forces capable of acting together, rather than merely directing a command toward a particular front or objective. Further, this alteration of departments to fit the changing situation obviated much of the need for movement of troops across departmental lines, as departments had been redefined or even created to give their commanders new resources for new tasks. Though this system took better advantage of the field commander's knowledge of the local situation, still this improved direction and these new methods had required far more active direction from the War Department, undoubtedly giving rise to the idea that increased effectiveness would result were someone on the spot in the West to co-ordinate the efforts of all of the departments. There would be a further increase in flexibility were there, in the West, a commander with both the local knowledge and the authority to transfer troops from one department to the other. The creation of a theater command for the West would be somewhat different from the situation a year

[10] *O. R.*, Ser. I: XIII—Randolph to Theophilus H. Holmes, October 20, 27, 1862, 889–90, 906–907; XVII, Part 2—Van Dorn to Randolph, October 22, 1862, 735; Pemberton to Randolph, October 25, 1862, 735; XX, Part 2—Bragg to Johnston, January 11, 1863, 493; Davis to Holmes, October 21, 1862, Rowland, *Jefferson Davis, Constitutionalist*, V, 356–57; Kean, *Inside the Confederate Government*, 30, entry of November 25, 1862.

before. Albert Sidney Johnston had practically started
with nothing and had built his command from the
ground up, while in 1862 the new structure would have
to be imposed upon an already existing organization.

The problem of who would command such a new
overall department was a very acute one. If Bragg himself was considered, there is no evidence of it. He was
fully occupied with his army in Tennessee and to have
employed him would have been to create another problem, that of finding a successor to take charge of his
army. The selection of a commander was thus limited
to the three line officers who outranked Bragg—Lee,
P. G. T. Beauregard, and Joseph E. Johnston. Lee was
fully occupied commanding the Virginia theater, and
Beauregard had only recently been removed from the
western command and relegated to defending the coasts
of South Carolina, Florida and Georgia. He had apparently lost the confidence of the President. General
J. E. Johnston, severely wounded the preceding May,
had, to the regret of the President and the public, not
yet recovered. It may well have been for this reason that
his services were refused General Bragg. Davis still had
respect for Johnston's professional ability, feeling him
to be a "good soldier," one capable of rendering "valuable service." For these reasons he would have been an
excellent choice, had he been well enough to serve.

The problem was soon solved, however. In early
November General Johnston was known to be well
enough to be taking exercise on horseback in Richmond
and, about November 12, reported himself fit for duty.
On reporting himself to the War Department he was
told that it was intended to place all of the area east
of the Mississippi River and west of the Appalachian

Mountains under his command. Though Johnston was not at that moment assigned to this command, he felt that the intention to give him this post justified him in making some suggestions about the area in which he was to serve. He thought that, "as the Federal troops invading the Valley of the Mississippi were united under one commander," the Confederate armies defending it should likewise be united, but east of the river. If Holmes's and Pemberton's forces were thus concentrated, Johnston thought, 75,000 men would be opposed to Grant's supposed 45,000, assuring a victory over Grant and enabling Pemberton's and Bragg's armies to concentrate against and defeat Rosecrans' Federal forces in middle Tennessee and so "transfer the war to the Ohio."

On November 13 General Johnston called on Secretary Randolph to present these views and suggestions for a concentration east of the Mississippi River. But before he had finished his exposition, Randolph, "with a smile," asked him "to listen to a few lines on the subject; and opening a large book," he read Johnston his letter authorizing Holmes to cross the Mississippi and also a "note from the President, directing him to countermand his instruction" to Holmes.[11] Thus Johnston found that the Secretary of War, to a large extent, agreed with him and had authorized his plan, only to have the President disapprove it. Johnston was not appointed to the command for which he had been selected until November 24, 1862. This delay in his

[11] Davis to Mrs. Davis, June 23, 1862, Varina Howell Davis, *Jefferson Davis, ex-President of the Confederate States of America, a Memoir by his Wife* (2 vols., New York, 1890), I, 314; Johnston, *Narrative,* 147–49.

appointment was presumably a result of the week's hiatus in the War Department brought about by the sudden resignation of Secretary Randolph over a dispute with the President about the countermand of the order to Holmes which had embodied Johnston's views.

Chapter Six

A New Adviser
and New Commander

1

SECRETARY RANDOLPH'S RESIGNATION WAS PRE-
cipitated by his October 27 order authorizing General
Holmes to cross to the east side of the Mississippi. The
President sent for the communication some time later
and, though the instructions could easily be deduced
from the President's expressed desire for the armies
to unite, he took strong exception to it on November
12. Davis said that he had in mind only "co-intelligent
action" and that any temporary departure of Holmes
from his department "would have a disastrous effect
and was not contemplated."

The next day Randolph endorsed the communication
to Holmes to be added to his instructions, while Davis
on the fourteenth called Randolph's attention to the
necessity of always going through the "established channel" and referring to him "in these matters and in all
cases of selection of persons to be appointed commis-
sioned officers." In response to a request for clarification,
the President listed items which must be referred to

him, including the "removal of an Army," the "assignment of general officers," and a number of other less
important matters. Randolph promptly sent in his resignation and immediately left the War Department.[1]

The cause of Randolph's resignation was certainly
deeper than the dispute which was the occasion for it.
The position of President Davis' Secretaries of War was
a special one and was widely misunderstood at the time.
On April 13, 1862, General Henry A. Wise, on declaring
"there is no Secretary of War!" was asked, "What is
Randolph?" " 'He is no Secretary of War!' said he; 'he
is merely a *clerk,* an underling, and cannot hold up his
head in his humiliating position.' " General Wise was
undoubtedly correct in believing that the President was
his own Secretary of War and that he kept in his own
hands all decisions.

However, the President wished his Secretary of War
to be more than a mere clerk. The Secretary was an
adviser and collaborator. Together they arrived at decisions in the numerous conferences which were a feature
of the Davis method. Secretary Seddon, Randolph's
successor, later complained of "tedious conferences,"
and perhaps they did not suit Randolph either. Randolph's former aide and nephew by marriage, Captain
R. G. H. Kean, the chief of the Bureau of War, thought
that he was tired of "responsibility without discretion"
and that he felt it impossible to "administer the War
Office, or the Government, on the terms laid down by
the President." Randolph himself said that the Presi-

[1] *O. R.,* Ser. I: XIII—Davis to Randolph, November 12, 14,
1862, 914–15; XXIII—Randolph to Cooper, November 13, 1862,
915; V—Randolph to Davis, November 15, 1862, 372; Rowland,
Jefferson Davis, Constitutionalist, V, 371–72.

dent, who was unable to "discriminate between important and unimportant matters," wished "to impose restrictions which in my judgment were derogatory to the office and hurtful to the public service and to which I could not submit without sacrificing my self-respect and the public interest." [2]

Thus it seems quite probable that Randolph wished to act on his own, to have authority and responsibility delegated to him. The role of assistant, adviser, and collaborator, without any power of free decision, was not one that appealed to him. Any system which required such close collaboration and personal contact between two men had to depend on harmonious relations. There is reason to believe that the two men "did not make a team." Randolph's health was bad, and the President felt he was indecisive and inefficient, an indifferent if not poor administrator. Captain Kean felt that Randolph had "not been treated by the President with proper confidence for some time," and even that the President had become "jealous of the independent character of the Secretary." Davis may have welcomed an opportunity to replace his Secretary of War, or Randolph may consciously or unconsciously have taken the bit in his teeth, and the President had then reined him up rather sharply.

Randolph himself was not a career politician nor public servant, having entered public service under the impulse of John Brown's raid and the secession controversy. He "grunted and sweated" under the tedious

[2] Jones, *Rebel War Clerk's Diary*, I, 120; Kean, *Inside the Confederate Government*, 30—entry of November 25, 1862, 101— entry of August 23, 1863; Randolph to T. J. Randolph, January 20, 1863, Edgehill-Randolph Papers.

routine of the War office [3] and undoubtedly did not find the same fascination in the minutiae of administration as did Davis, for he referred most of the correspondence to the bureau heads for action. Randolph was no doubt happy to leave public life when he felt that he was no longer contributing anything.

The circumstances of his departure strongly support the view that he was unhappy in the advisory role in which the President cast him, desiring some independent authority and discretion. The resignation issue is also indicative that he played a large role in working out the western reorganization leading to the appointment of Joe Johnston to supreme command in the West.

2

IN VIEW OF THE FACT THAT THE PRESIDENT'S method was that of frequent conference and decisions by discussion, changes in the West and the decision to appoint a supreme commander had undoubtedly been arrived at during these numerous conferences. Thus, when Davis made all decisions and arrived at them through consultation with his Secretary of War, the role of the two men is difficult to disentangle, and the part played by Randolph can only be inferred.

[3] Patrick, *Jefferson Davis and His Cabinet,* 127; Kean, *Inside the Confederate Government,* 29–30, entries of November 30, 1862; Randolph to J. Thompson Brown, January 14, 1863, George Wythe Randolph Papers, Confederate Museum, Richmond, Va.

That Randolph's ideas and advice had an important part in making the decisions is indicated by the fact that most of the correspondence was carried out by him. That some of the instructions were sent by the President also strongly supports the view that they were in close collaboration on the problems of the West. The correspondence of the President with Van Dorn was superseded by communications of Randolph *and* Davis with the general—correspondence in which Randolph predominated. The only available endorsement is that of September 9, 1862, in which mutual concern is displayed, Randolph's being expressed first. While the active direction from Richmond was in itself out of the ordinary, Randolph's role was larger than had been usual with western commanders, the President's friend Cooper, the elderly Adjutant and Inspector-General, fading into the background.

That the President almost entirely delegated the interpretation of their views and the writing of instructions for the field commanders to Randolph, rather than keeping it in his own hands or delegating it to Cooper, is significant. It is indicative that Randolph was strongly interested and that his views either coincided with those of the President or that his own were very influential in shaping the decisions. This is supported by Randolph's background. His views could be decisive with the President, as is borne out in the case of the adoption of concription. When an obvious need for War Department direction arose, it is inconceivable that an educated military man, who had planned "campaigns for the belligerents" in the Italian War of 1859, would not also have plans which he wished to apply when his own country was involved and he was its Secretary of War.

The appointment of Joseph E. Johnston to command in the West, a move suggested by two of the most influential commanders there, Bragg and Polk,[4] must have appeared obvious to both the President and Randolph. Here was a general soon to be available for active duty but with no army to command. Here also was a proposed command which could only be filled by an officer of his rank. He was a general who was proven in service, popular with the people, and who enjoyed the confidence of the President. There is no reason to suppose that Randolph disagreed with an appointment so clearly indicated.

That Randolph favored and presumably urged the formation of a western department which would include the Trans-Mississippi is strongly indicated by his instructions to General Holmes. When he authorized Holmes to "cross the Mississippi" with a part of his force when he thought it "necessary" and "direct the combined operations on the eastern bank," Randolph was certainly displaying enthusiasm for combined operations and unity of command. This letter is especially significant when it is realized that this was Randolph's idea entirely, that President Davis had not approved these instructions and, in fact, disapproved them when he later found out about them. The close agreement between Randolph's earlier instructions and the views expressed in writing by the President at the time indicates that this was the first divergence between Randolph's orders and the President's views. Davis also

[4] William M. Polk, *Leonidas Polk, Bishop and General* (2 vols., New York, 1893, II, 158.

clearly indicated that this was the first of the messages sent to the West which he had not seen and the first such instruction not agreed upon in conference.[5]

3

GENERAL RANDOLPH'S ABRUPT DEPARTURE from the War office made it necessary for President Davis to resort to an interim appointment until he was able to find a new man. He resolved to try to secure the services of the prominent Virginia political leader, James A. Seddon, and if he declined, to offer the post to General Joseph E. Johnston, who had not yet been appointed to the western command.[6] Seddon accepted the appointment, however, and took office on November 22, 1862, thus continuing Virginia's representation in

[5] Frank E. Vandiver in his *Rebel Brass,* 51–53, gives Randolph full credit for realizing "the crippling effect of bigness as a factor in strategy" and proposing "a radical scheme of decentralization" which nevertheless applied the "principle of military concentration." Randolph made a lasting contribution in getting the "serious attention of Davis focused on the western theater." Professor Vandiver's work is undocumented, and I have not, on the basis of my sources, been able to be so positive in giving Randolph full credit, though I have every reason to agree with the conclusions in *Rebel Brass* regarding Randolph's importance. I believe, however, that the system that President Davis applied from the beginning of the war recognized the difficulties of war in such a vast theater and took advantage of decentralization as a solution.

[6] John H. Reagan, *Memoirs* (New York, Washington, 1906), 161.

the Cabinet but marking a return to purely civilian control.

James Alexander Seddon, the new Secretary, was forty-eight years old and had enjoyed a distinguished career as a lawyer, planter, and politician. Graduating from the University of Virginia in 1835, he had practiced law in Richmond. After two terms in Congress as a Calhoun Democrat he had in 1851 retired to his estate near Richmond where he remained influential in state politics. He had been a secessionist in 1861 but, after serving in the Confederate Provisional Congress, had not been returned to the regular House. Coming out of retirement to take up his appointment, he soon exercised an important influence on the President. He "became convinced that the weak spot in Confederate defense was in the West." Since "able generalship in combination with departmental planning had resulted in the victories of Lee in Virginia," Seddon, like Randolph, thought "a plan, therefore, should be worked out along similar lines for the West. Because of the distance from Richmond, Seddon thought that the commander of the forces in the West should of necessity have freedom of action in order to co-ordinate all agencies of defense." Believing that great ability was necessary for this post, he thought that General J. E. Johnston "would measure up to these requirements" and so "recommended his appointment." Seddon's concern for the West, his great ability, and his important influence on President Davis were significant for Confederate strategy in the ensuing months.

The man and the policy of his predecessor having been endorsed by Seddon, Johnston was on November 24, 1862, appointed to the western command, which he had been told that he was to have. While E. A. Pollard of the anti-Administration Richmond *Examiner* suggested that he was appointed to quiet the objections of Mississippians to the assignment of Pemberton or, as historian T. Harry Williams has thought possible, that he was given an unworkable advisory post "to lay on the shelf a general who was out of favor," it seems most likely that the President and certainly the two Secretaries of War had great expectations from the unity of command to be achieved under Johnston.[7]

The new "geographical command" embraced the following area:

> Commencing with the Blue Ridge Mountains running through the western portions of North Carolina, and following the line of said mountains through the northern part of Georgia to the railroad south from Chattanooga; thence by that road to West Point, and down the west bank of the Chatahoochee River to the boundry of Alabama and Florida; following that boundry to the Choctawhatchee River, and down that river to Choctawhatchee Bay (including the waters of that Bay) to the Gulf of Mexico.
>
> All that portion west of said line to the Mississippi River is included in the above command.

General Johnston was to establish his headquarters at Chattanooga but could select any other place if it might provide better facilities for communicating with

[7] Patrick, *Jefferson Davis and His Cabinet,* 134–35; Pollard, *Life of Jefferson Davis,* 298–99; Williams, *Beauregard,* 242. On Seddon see also: Roy Watson Curry, "James A. Seddon, A Southern Prototype," *Virginia Magazine of History and Biography,* LXIII (April, 1955), 123–50.

the various forces within his command. He was also directed "to repair in person to any part of said command whenever his presence may for the time be necessary or desirable."

It was intended that he should give the departments within this area "something of the same guiding direction and control as was exercised nearer the capitol" by the War Department, that combined movements by the armies there could be "mutually supporting, and that in certain contingencies even transfers of troops" might be made. Johnston's control was, however, to be purely operational, for the subordinate departments were to continue to report directly to Richmond.[8]

The man whose personality, ability, methods, and opinions were vitally to affect the working out of this new arrangement did not leave Richmond until November 29, 1862, and after five days on the train reached Chattanooga on the morning of December 4.

4

GENERAL JOSEPH EGGLESTON JOHNSTON WAS born in Prince Edward County, Virginia, on February 3, 1807. Upon graduation from the United States Military Academy at West Point, thirteenth in a class of forty-six, he served for eight years in the artillery. He

[8] *O. R.*, Ser. I, XVII, Part 2: Special Orders No. 275, November 24, 1862, 757–58; James A. Seddon to Johnston, February 5, 1863, 626–27.

then resigned to take up a career as a civil engineer. While with an expedition in Florida in 1837, he led the rear guard after an Indian attack, being twice wounded. As a result of this exploit he was recommissioned as a first lieutenant in the Topographical Engineers without loss of seniority. He served with General Scott in the Mexican War as a lieutenant colonel, distinguishing himself at Cerro Gordo and leading a column at Chapultepec. He was wounded five times during the campaign. Having been promoted to lieutenant colonel of cavalry in 1855, he was in 1860 made Quartermaster General and promoted to brigadier general.

On the secession of Virginia, General Johnston was made a brigadier general in the Confederate army and, shortly after, the fourth ranking full general of the Confederacy. In April, 1861, Johnston took command in the Valley of Virginia, and in July, slipped away from his opponent, General Robert Patterson, joining Beauregard at Manassas to help oppose the Federal advance under Irvin MacDowell. He was in overall command during the battle of First Manassas, with Beauregard in executive command. The victory confirmed his reputation, and he remained in command of all of the forces in northern Virginia into the following year.

When in March, 1862, McClellan began his movement to the York–James Peninsula, Johnston shifted his army to Yorktown in order to oppose him. After retreating to Richmond, he attacked McClellan on May 31 at the inconclusive battle of Seven Pines, where he was twice wounded and, on this account, had to be superseded by General Lee. His plan was excellent, but execution was defective, aggravated by the inexperience and immature state of his command organization.

But, among Confederate generals, Johnston himself was a well-qualified military leader. He had commanded a major army longer than any of his colleagues, while his battle experience was exceeded only by that of his good friend, Lee. Johnston's field experience and recognized professional ability were amplified by an excellent theoretical background and extensive study and reading in the fields of military history and science. Johnston had exhibited "magnetic and winning qualities" which made "his friends and most of his subordinates devoted to him." Though he had displayed "unmistakable strategic sense," his military efficiency was clouded by deficiency in administrative capacity and lack of attention to detail. While lack of interest in administration and his characteristic method of excessive delegation of authority to subordinates kept his performance as an administrator from being first-rate, more serious was his "excessively reserved" attitude in dealing with the War Department and the President.[9] Though the caliber of his generalship was to be the subject of dispute during and after the war, of great importance for his supervisory command was his apparent disinclination for administration and his difficult and touchy character as a subordinate.

Johnston's insistence on his rights in dealing with the War Department, as well as his reticence, may have in part stemmed from past unpleasantness with his fellow West Pointer, Jefferson Davis. They had collided

[9] Notes on Johnston's library in the papers of R. M. Hughes, Norfolk, Va.; Johnston to Murray B. Dawson, May 26, 1873, Hughes Papers; Douglas Southall Freeman, *Lee's Lieutenants* (3 vols., New York, 1942–44), I, xxxviii.

in 1860 when Johnston had been made Quartermaster General. Davis, then chairman of the military affairs committee of the United States Senate, had endorsed his friend, Colonel Albert Sidney Johnston. Lieutenant Colonel Joseph E. Johnston was backed by his friend and connection, Secretary of War John B. Floyd, whom Johnston was later to describe as the "best friend my manhood has known." J. E. Johnston received the appointment, perhaps to the annoyance and chagrin of Senator Davis. That their relations lacked cordiality is borne out by Mrs. Johnston's warning to the general that, if he joined the Confederacy, Davis would "ruin" him.

Relations between President Davis and General Johnston underwent a severe strain when the full generals of the Confederacy were appointed in the summer of 1861. Johnston was outranked, not only by the elderly Adjutant and Inspector General, Samuel Cooper, but by A. S. Johnston and R. E. Lee as well—all colonels in the United States Army. Congress had provided that relative rank within grades should be maintained from the old army, so former Brigadier General Johnston should clearly have been senior to ex-Colonels A. S. Johnston and Lee. To an ambitious man who had seen in his promotion to Brigadier and Quartermaster General an opportunity to succeed the aged Winfield Scott as commander-in-chief, this demotion all but ended any similar ambitions in the Confederate Army. Johnston wrote an indignant and in some ways almost insubordinate letter to the President, protesting this unjust and illegal action. Though the dispute was limited to Davis' brief reply and their official relations remained correct and even cordial, a residue of animosity was retained. Also at this time their wives seemed to abandon a hitherto friendly relation.[10]

Johnston had already displayed a tendency to be secretive about his plans. This was probably due both to a natural disposition to keep his intentions to himself and to a fear of disclosure. He felt that Cabinet members were not discreet, for he once learned the same day of an important military decision taken by the Cabinet from two people who should not have known, one of whom was "too deaf to hear conversation not intended for his ear." Whatever the cause, failure to confide and report was bound to undermine confidence and to prevent the general and the President from fully understanding the other's point of view.

Another characteristic of Johnston which would effect his performance as western commander was his theory of command. He gave to his subordinates the same confidence and discretion which he seemed to require from his superiors. He strongly believed in delegation of authority and that a subordinate was an expert on matters with which he was familiar. At First Manassas he adopted Beauregard's plans, for Beauregard was familiar with the situation. Johnston's later campaign in defense of Atlanta was characterized by contsant consultation with his corps commanders and deference to their judgment on at least two occasions. His method was to seek

[10] Johnston to Mrs. R. W. Hughes, August 25, 1863, Hughes Papers; Gilbert E. Govan and James W. Livingood, *A Different Valor, The Story of General Joseph E. Johnston, C.S.A.* (New York, 1956), 23, 28, 65–71; Leslie J. Perry, "Davis and Johnston— Light Thrown on a Quarrel among Confederate Leaders—a Question of Rank," *Southern Historical Society Papers,* XX, (1892), 95–108.

his subordinate's views and advice. He did not tell them how to do their work but rather gave them his objectives and theory of operations, allowing them to work things out in their own way. Johnston did not believe in imposing his method on his junior commanders, believing that they could only work efficiently and whole-heartedly when carrying out operations as they saw fit. There is, of course, nothing wrong with this theory of command, but it presupposes a certain harmony and identity of views between the general and his commanders. A lack of this harmony in outlook and method and/or a failure by a subordinate to reciprocate or understand his confidence could radically mar the working of this system to which Johnston seemed irrevocably wedded. He appeared to believe that there was no practical alternative as effective as this system. Even if he had reservations about the ability of a lower commander and the soundness of his plans, Johnston apparently regarded it as preferable to let him proceed in his own way. The climate was favorable for this anomalous situation to arise, since Johnston had not selected his own subordinates.[11]

In common with many other Confederate generals, Johnston "was a devoted and stubborn advocate of the military strategy of concentration." The opinions presented to General Randolph illustrate an application of this viewpoint. Also significant for his western command was that, from his army command in Virginia and from his sick bed, Johnston had observed operations in the West during the year and concluded that large fortified points, such as Fort Donelson, were a serious mistake. He thought that, unless the Confederates were

[11] Johnston, *Narrative,* 36–42, 97, 305–47.

to be "weak at every point," it was necessary to have the minimum number of men in garrisons and the largest possible active army in the field.[12]

The general's reluctance to confide his plans to his superiors was aggravated by the paucity of his communications, his occasional acidity of tone, and by his habit of sometimes being so excessively concise that the import of what he said might well be missed. The principles of concentration and elastic defense which would guide his strategy were at variance with those of the President, though they were probably shared to some degree by the Secretary of War. While his manner of dealing with his superiors and the disagreement between their strategic views did not portend well for harmonious working of the new organization, his system of command was well-adapted to cordial relations with the President's appointees already in the West. Yet, if too rigorously applied, this method of extreme delegation and discretion could have largely nullified his own effectiveness as commander of such dispersed forces.

5

PROBLEMS FACING GENERAL JOHNSTON IN HIS new department were threefold: the nature of his command and his mission, the subordinates with whom he

[12] Alfred P. James, "General Joseph Eggleston Johnston, Storm Center of the Confederate Army," *Mississippi Valley Historical Review*, XIV (December, 1927), 354; Johnston, *Narrative*, 85–86.

had to work and on whom he must rely, and the Federal armies, now ready for new offensives.

Bragg's brilliantly conceived Kentucky campaign had succeeded in placing his army between Buell and Louisville. But, after inexplicable vacillation, Bragg had opened the way to Louisville, letting Buell re-establish his communications, while the Southern commander had gone to Frankfort to inaugurate Richard Hawes as Confederate governor of Kentucky. Governor Hawes's inaugural address had been interrupted by Federal shells, fired by the artillery of Buell's reinforced army sallying from Louisville. After some inept maneuvering, Bragg was checked at the battle of Perryville on October 8, 1862, and he soon withdrew from Kentucky. With the failure of the Confederate offensive in the West, the Federals were again preparing to advance. The Confederate problem was largely one of defense.

There were two major theaters of operations— Mississippi and Tennessee. In Mississippi the Confederates still held a section of the river between Vicksburg and Port Hudson, Louisiana, which were fortified to prevent the passage of Union gunboats and thus secure communication with the Trans-Mississippi Department. A powerful advance from the north was gradually getting underway, the Federal forces having the skillful and determined leadership of Ulysses S. Grant and William T. Sherman. Though their armies numbered about 100,000 men, only a little over one-half of these were available for an advance because of the necessity of guarding communications and of garrisoning west Tennessee and points on the river. A similar advance from the south was contemplated by a force of 30,000 men, directed by a former Speaker of the House of

Representatives, Nathaniel P. Banks, a man of only very modest military talent. The Federal Navy under Admirals David D. Porter and David G. Farragut provided formidable support.

Against these powerful and well-led forces the Confederates had about 45,000 men under Lieutenant General John C. Pemberton. This forty-eight-year-old Pennsylvanian had left the regular army to join the South primarily on the ground of principle, believing the South was right. His rise was rapid in the Confederate service. His duty had been almost solely at Charleston, "where the circumstances and conditions of his service . . . did not augur well for his future in Mississippi." Since Charleston was a static situation in which fortifications were the principal defense, his experience had not provided any background for leading a large field army. His promotion to lieutenant general had been almost fortuitous, arising from the necessity to give unity of command to the forces operating within his department.

His principal subordinate, forty-two-year-old Major General Earl Van Dorn had served in Virginia and Arkansas, as well as in his native Mississippi. He had twice held independent command, but his two major battles had been defeats. He had also had considerable experience with cavalry both in the Confederate and United States Armies. "Van Dorn was a brave and enterprising commander, touched with brilliance but dogged with fatal ill fortune."

Against the powerful Federal forces operating on the east bank of the Mississippi both Pemberton and Johnston hoped for aid from the forces in the quiescent Trans-Mississippi theater. However, little vigor could be expected from its bumbling commander, the "antiquated, domineering, and dangerously deaf" Lieutenant General Theophilus H. Holmes.[13]

The Tennessee armies of the Confederates were threatened by a Federal army of over 60,000 men at Nashville under the capable, if excessively deliberate, leadership of Major General William S. Rosecrans. Commitments in Kentucky and provision for the security of his communications prevented Rosecrans from taking the offensive with more than about 45,000 men, though additional forces in Kentucky were in position to advance on Confederate territory in east Tennessee.

Confederate forces holding central and eastern Tennessee along a roughly northeast to southwest line were divided into two departments. General Braxton Bragg commanded the major force, about 45,000 men at Murfreesborough, Tennessee, while Lieutenant General Edmund Kirby Smith, with headquarters at Knoxville, commanded the scattered garrisons of east Tennessee, totaling a little over 10,000 men. The odd situation of two separate departments in the same geographical area was made worse by the fact that Bragg's command extended to include the District of the Gulf which embraced Alabama and parts of western Florida and Georgia. This area was unrelated to General Bragg's army and received little attention from him, while it had an intimate relation to Pemberton's department to its west.

Kirby Smith, commander of the Confederate forces at Knoxville, was a friend of Johnston and an able

[13] Hay, "Confederate Leadership at Vicksburg," *Mississippi Valley Historical Review,* XI, 546–47; Henry, *First with the Most Forrest,* 128; Vandiver, *Rebel Brass,* 31.

soldier, but he was to leave in January to take charge of the Trans-Mississippi. He would be followed by several others, the department having seven commanders in five months. The already controversial Bragg was to remain however. The forty-five-year-old Bragg had displayed energy and capacity in organizing Confederate troops and had exhibited tactical skill at the Battle of Shiloh where he commanded a corps. Impressed with his ability, President Davis had elevated him to command in the West after the removal of Beauregard. His invasion of Kentucky had exhibited strategic insight, but his execution was faulty. He seemed unable to draw the correct conclusions from his intelligence information and, in spite of his undoubted capacity, degenerated to incompetence when actually facing an enemy.

Almost equally harmful to his efficiency was his suspicious and quarrelsome nature. While his inadequacies demoralized his subordinates, his fractiousness aggravated the situation. A story about him from his days in the United States Army, told by General Grant, illustrates his deserved reputation.

On one occasion, when stationed at a post of several companies, commanded by a field-officer, he was himself commanding one of the companies and at the same time acting as post quartermaster and commissary. He was first lieutenant at the time, but his captain was detached on other duty. As commander of the company he made a requisition upon the post quartermaster—himself—for something he wanted. As quartermaster he declined to fill the requisition and indorsed on the back of it his reasons for so doing. As company commander he responded to this, urging that this requisition called for nothing but what he was entitled to, and that it was the duty of the quartermaster to fill it. As quartermaster he still persisted he was right. In this condition of affairs Bragg referred the whole matter to the commanding officer of the post. The latter, when he saw the nature of the matter referred, exclaimed: 'My God, Mr. Bragg, you have quarreled with every officer in the army, and now you are quarreling with yourself!' [14]

Bragg's army was fortunate in having talented if not forbearing senior officers. The two corps of the army were commanded by two distinguished and capable lieutenant generals, William J. Hardee and the clergyman-soldier, Bishop Leonidas Polk. The cavalry had the benefit of the brilliant leadership of Nathan Bedford Forrest and Joseph Wheeler, and the Gulf District, after the middle of December, 1862, was under the able guidance of Major General Simon Bolivar Buckner.

Thus Johnston had as subordinates Pemberton and Bragg, one of whom was untried in the field and the other who had already revealed serious defects in character and capacity. Since Johnston was ignorant of Bragg's shortcomings and probably did not reflect on Pemberton's inexperience, he anticipated no difficulties in that direction. He did, however, have serious reservations about the organization of his department. He felt that Pemberton should co-operate with the forces of Holmes rather than those of Bragg. Not only were the Arkansas troops much closer but Bragg's army was

[14] U. S. Grant, *Personal Memoirs of U. S. Grant* (2 vols., New York, 1885–86), II, 88.

separated from Pemberton's by the Tennessee River, which was frequented by Federal gunboats. Grant's field army in northern Mississippi also lay between the two major armies of his department.[15] Holmes had been instructed to co-operate, but Johnston's authority was confined east of the Mississippi. His mission was to co-ordinate the forces within his department for its defense. Therefore, Johnston began with reservations as to the practicability of his task.

The western strategy of the Davis administration, evolved over two and a half months of reorganization in the West, was largely dependent for its success on the man selected to carry it out. The story of this significant effort to supply flexibility and central direction to Confederate operations in this critical area is best seen from the point of view of General Johnston.

[15] *O. R.,* Ser. I, XVII, Part 2: Johnston to Cooper, November 24, 1862, 758.

Chapter Seven

Johnston and Davis
Survey the Situation

1

WHEN GENERAL JOHNSTON TOOK UP HIS DUTIES as commander of the Department of the West, it was certainly without much enthusiasm. This was not the type of service for which he had a taste. He had charge of a large part of the area of the Confederate States, including two of its most vital fronts and embracing three departments. Although this area contained perhaps 100,000 men, none of them were under Johnston's direct command. He was unhappy with his geographical and administrative assignment, for to Johnston "command in the field was superior to any administrative post." It is probable that Pemberton or Kirby Smith, and certainly Bragg, were envied by Johnston for "though he held the higher rank," Bragg "held the more important assignment" to Johnston's way of thinking.

In addition to his dissatisfaction with this type of command, he expressed great concern for the condition of things in his department, feeling that "nobody ever assumed a command under more unfavorable circumstances." His concern was aroused by the fact that the two principal armies in his department were separated not only by the "formidable obstacle" of the Tennessee River but also by Grant's army. Receiving word that General Pemberton had retreated south before Grant's army as well as instructions to supply reinforcements for Pemberton from Bragg's army, he noted that Pemberton's "march is in a direction exactly away from Bragg, and the enemy's army is between, every day's march makes a junction . . . more difficult." He was thus led to feel that "if Rosecranz [*sic*] had disposed our troops himself, their disposition could not have been more unfavorable to us." [1]

This continuing realization of the problems inherent in his geographical command was sharpened when he actually began to grapple with them on the spot and was emphasized by the immediate crisis of General Grant's advance on Vicksburg. His pessimism must have been somewhat relieved, however, by the news that General Holmes had been "peremptorily ordered" to reinforce General Pemberton. While this did not seem to indicate the adoption of his and Randolph's plan to concentrate the forces of the two departments for an offensive to crush Grant's army, it must nevertheless have been comforting news to hear that at last the forces of these adjacent departments were at least going to cooperate.

In spite of his personnal reservations about his new post and his strong and well-founded position that his

[1] Govan and Livingood, *A Different Valor,* 181; Johnston to Louis T. Wigfall, December 4, 1863, Mrs. D. Giraud Wright, *A Southern Girl in '61* (New York, 1905), 99–100; *O. R.,* Ser. I: XX, Part 2—Cooper to Johnston, December 3, 1863, 435; XVII, Part 2—Johnston to Cooper, December 4, 1863 (letter and telegram), 780, 781.

department was not well adapted for the co-operation of the forces in it, General Johnston did not come west with an entirely negative attitude. He continued firmly convinced of the efficacy of his original solution of western problems: concentration of the Mississippi and Arkansas troops for an offensive against Grant. He was strongly resolved to try to have this remedy applied by constantly stressing to Richmond its value, both on its own merits and as a substitute for sending troops on the lengthy march from Bragg's army to Mississippi. He also attempted to have the plan adopted through the unofficial channel of asking his friend Senator Wigfall to speak to the Secretary of War. This plan, originally advocated in Richmond, might properly be described as General Johnston's strategy for the West. It was upon this that he pinned his hopes as he took up his new duties.

The problems of assuming command in a new theater with which he was comparatively unfamiliar were aggravated by the fact that there was an entirely new headquarters to be set up. There was no predecessor, no staff, no subordinates on hand to "brief" him. Equally important was that no established channels of communication for reports and intelligence of the friendly and enemy situation existed, nor had there been much of a "planning phase" in which to prepare. Johnston's headquarters had to begin functioning immediately upon his arrival in Chattanooga. The paucity of information in the possession of the commander of the new department is well illustrated by his reply to an inquiry from the Chief of Ordnance: "General Pemberton's suggestion should be adopted. I do not know the condition of things so well as the President."

So the first concern of the new commanding general was to acquaint himself with the situation in his department. Though there was presumably a Federal offensive in General Pemberton's department, he decided to go to General Bragg's headquarters at Murfreesborough, Tennessee, in order to learn the situation there at first hand. He determined to go to the nearer headquarters, not only because he had not "learned the enemy's attitude in Tennessee," but also because he presumed "that all information relative to conditions around Vicksburg and troop movements from Bragg's army there could be acquired at General Bragg's headquarters," which he planned to reach by railroad on December 5, 1862. However, to General Pemberton he dispatched this terse telegram: "Let me know by express which way you are moving and what your plans are. . . . I am without necessary information. Give it."

At Murfreesborough Johnston found the situation in General Bragg's department calm. Rosecrans had about 45,000 men available for offensive operations against Bragg, who had an almost equal number. Bragg thought that campaigning was over for the season and was going into winter quarters. Unknown to Bragg and Johnston, however, Rosecrans was under strong pressure from Washington to assume the offensive. Washington's urgings coincided with Rosecrans' own plans. He was delaying his advance only long enough to accumulate sufficient supplies to be independent of the interruptions of his supply lines by Confederate cavalry.

Grant, on the other hand, had already begun an offensive against Vicksburg on November 7, 1862. Though he had at least 55,000 men, he was able to use less than 40,000 for an overland advance from Corinth,

Mississippi. The remainder was required for garrisoning Memphis and protecting his railway communications which ran north all the way to Columbus, Kentucky. Pemberton, with about 35,000 men in his department, was in a like situation. Garrisons for various points, principally Port Hudson and Vicksburg on the Mississippi River, prevented him from opposing Grant's overland advance with more than 20,000 men. Pemberton's forces had just fallen back to hold the Yalabusha River at Grenada, Mississippi, on December 5, 1862. Grant was nearby at Oxford, Mississippi. This was the first strong attack against Vicksburg itself, and the situation seemed very critical to General Pemberton, especially as he overestimated Grant's army. Pemberton's reports and his recent withdrawal convinced President Davis and General Johnston that Vicksburg was seriously endangered and must be reinforced.[2]

2

JOHNSTON WAS APPARENTLY ABLE TO APPRISE himself rapidly of the condition of General Bragg's army and of the strength and intentions of the enemy on his

[2] *Ibid.*: XX, Part 2—Cooper to Johnston, December 3, 5, 1862, 435, 440; Johnston to Cooper, December 4, 6, 7, 1862, 436–38, 441, 444; Johnston to Pemberton, December 4, 1862, 437; XVII, Part 2—Johnston to Colonel Josiah Gorgas, December 4, 1862, 761; Johnston to Pemberton, December 4, 1862, 780; Pemberton to Johnston, December 5, 1862, 784–85; Johnston to Wigfall, December 4, 1862, Wright, *A Southern Girl*, 99–100.

front, for he projected a visit to Mississippi within a "few days." Undoubtedly he learned much of the state of affairs in Mississippi at Bragg's headquarters, but it is doubtful if Pemberton's rather full and analytical report had yet reached him. Therefore, while he must have felt the urgent necessity of going as soon as possible to Mississippi to see that department first hand, he still sent his estimate and recommendations to General Cooper, probably because he was being urged by the President to reinforce Pemberton from Bragg's army.

Johnston's estimate dwells at length upon the difficulty of moving troops to Mississippi, pointing out that they would have to be ferried over the Tennessee River or would have to utilize the circuitous route by railroad, which would take a month—equally as long as by going cross country. Having tried to establish that the President's plan to "use troops on both sides of the river" would not be feasible "until next summer," he stressed the disadvantages of the plan. The problem was the great difficulty of marching through Tennessee, northern Alabama and Mississippi in the winter, particularly the problem of crossing the Tennessee River without the aid of bridges. The alternative was the railway route followed by Bragg in the preceding summer, which involved going south to Mobile, Alabama, and then coming northwest to Jackson, Mississippi. Opinion at Bragg's headquarters supported this view and argued that "to send a strong force would be to give up Tennessee, and would, the principal officers think here, disorganize this army. Rosecrans could then move into Virginia, or join Grant before our troops could reach Pemberton's position." Two thousand of Bragg's cavalry would be used against Rosecrans' communications, he

reported, and four thousand more in west Tennessee
and north Mississippi on Grant's communications might
delay him. As far as General Johnston was concerned,
the solution for the problems of Mississippi remained
the reinforcements coming from the Trans-Mississippi.

General Johnston's visit with Bragg's army and his
plans for an immediate visit to Mississippi were cut
short by the news that President Davis himself was
coming west, both to settle military questions and to
improve civilian morale by his presence. Johnston
met Davis at Chattanooga on December 10, 1862, and
together they visited Bragg's headquarters the next day.
The President remained until the fourteenth, while
Johnston returned to Chattanooga a day or two earlier.
During their stay an important decision was made when,
after hearing all the arguments from both Bragg and
Johnston, Davis ordered Carter L. Stevenson's division,
about 9,000 men, to be sent to Mississippi. It was withdrawn from both the commands of Bragg and General
Kirby Smith. Bragg protested this decision and later
said that he had urged that "Grant's campaign would
be broken up by our cavalry expeditions in his rear
before Stevenson's command would meet him in front."
To Bragg's protest concerning the effect of this move
upon his own command, Davis replied, "Fight if you
can, and fall back beyond the Tennessee." Apparently
Davis did not take the same serious view of the loss
of east and middle Tennessee as Johnston had earlier
expressed to Cooper.

However, the necessity of Bragg's having to carry
out these gloomy instructions must have seemed quite
remote to the President in view of what was learned
during this visit. He saw Bragg's army and not only

found it "in good condition and fine spirits," but was informed that Rosecrans seemed to have only "defensive purposes." This intelligence certainly seemed to warrant his detachment of one-fifth of Bragg's force and, with the projected cavalry operations, seemed to indicate that everything possible was being done in Tennessee to give aid to Vicksburg. All this must have given the President cause for satisfaction. It was certainly otherwise for General Johnston. He was disappointed that the decision to send reinforcements to Mississippi, so strongly opposed by him, had been made. More important from his point of view was the fact that he had had "some tall castles in the air" just "blown away" by learning that Holmes had not had *"orders"* to reinforce Pemberton but "requests and suggestions instead— which he thinks himself unable to comply with and therefore will not comply with." Johnston's dreams of "crushing Grant with Holmes' and Pemberton's troops, sending the former into Missouri and with the latter, Bragg and Kirby Smith, marching to the Ohio" had thus ended in the rude awakening of finding that Holmes had not been "peremptorily ordered" after all.[3]

However, it is unlikely that he abandoned hope of his plan for the future. He was to be with the President some days longer as they journeyed together on a tour through Atlanta, Montgomery, Mobile, and Jackson to Vicksburg. This was an opportunity for "making an impression on the President," of which Johnston un-

[3] *Ibid.:* XX, Part 2—Pemberton to Johnston, December 5, 1862, 440–41; Johnston to Cooper, December 6, 7, 1862, 441, 444; Johnston to Bragg, December 4, 1862, 437; Bragg to Johnston, January 11, 1862, 493; Davis to Seddon, December 15, 1862, 449–50; Johnston to Wigfall, December 15, 1862, Wright, *A Southern Girl,* 104–105 (italics Johnston's).

doubtedly planned to avail himself to sell his scheme for the West. The opportunity for successful persuasion was probably not lessened by the adoption of Davis' plan of sending reinforcements from Tennessee. Having implemented his own plan, he might be more amenable to Johnston's suggestions. More helpful would be the continuing emergency at Vicksburg and the slow arrival of the troops from Tennessee.

As Johnston and Davis set out to see for themselves the military situation in Mississippi, problems other than those caused by the Yankees must have bothered them. Senator James Phelan of Mississippi had written a long letter to his friend, the President, which had just been received. After pointing out the strong criticisms of the enforcement of conscription, the system of buying substitutes, and the exemption of the owners of twenty slaves, the Senator had reported that the people of Mississippi had sunk "in listless despondency." The army was in a "deplorable state as to its *morale* and organization." The people had lost confidence in the military leaders. Pemberton had "not impressed himself either upon the people or the army," while Van Dorn was so covered with "universal opprobrium," the atmosphere being so "dense with horrid narratives of his negligence, whoring, and drunkenness," that "an acquittal by a court-martial of angels would not relieve him of the charge." The solution was for the President to "plant your own foot upon our soil, unfurl your banner at the head of the army." While the Senator's solution was not applicable, neither probably was the replacement at this critical juncture of the department commander or his senior major general. However, it must have been disquieting intelligence indeed to John-

ston, who had to rely so much on subordinates operating
at a great distance. An attack was made on the problem
of civilian morale when the President arrived, with an
address to the legislature and at least one other speech.

Johnston and Davis arrived in Mississippi about the
seventeenth of December, and the President remained
about ten days, visiting both Vicksburg and Grenada.
Apparently all that Pemberton's two superiors decided
about the conduct of operations against Grant was to
establish a reserve at Jackson, Mississippi. During the
President's stay the situation was quiet as Grant had
suspended his overland advance until Sherman should
make an attack by water, which began only as Davis left.
Much the more significant event of the visit from
Johnston's point of view was the qualified success of his
"selling" job which he had planned and presumably
carried out on the way from Tennessee with the President. The "impression" made on Davis is revealed in
a letter he sent to General Holmes, which is significant,
not only as evidence of Johnston's success, but also as a
reflection of Davis' views on Confederate strategy at
this time.

He felt that it was now "clearly developed that the
enemy has two principal objects in view, one to get
possession of the Mississippi River and the other the
capital of the Confederate States." Feeling that the capture of Richmond was only important for the loss of
its factories and the effect on public opinion abroad,
he stressed the importance of the Mississippi River.
Capture by the enemy of the river would have the
indirect advantage of depriving the Confederacy of its
use and the direct benefit of providing the "best possible
base for operations in the Valley." In addition, naviga-

tion and access to New Orleans would be given to the Union. In order "to prevent the enemy getting control of the Mississippi and dismembering the Confederacy," the principal reliance must be placed "upon maintaining the points already occupied by defensive works, to-wit: Vicksburg and Port Hudson."

Having expounded his strategic views, he then urged that it was "unquestionably best" to reinforce General Johnston in order to defeat the enemy, thus rendering Arkansas more secure. Stressing that the Trans-Mississippi was safe because it seemed "impossible that any large force can invade through the northwestern part of Arkansas," he contended that we "cannot hope at all points to meet the enemy with a force equal to his own, and must find our security in the concentration and rapid movement of troops." The matter discussed was important, as nothing would "so certainly conduce to peace as the conclusive exhibition of our power to hold the Mississippi River." Having thus presented his views to General Holmes, the President said that, since he trusted alike in his "patriotism and discretion," he was left "to make the application of them which circumstances" would permit.

The immediate importance of this letter was that Johnston's plan for the concentration of forces of the two departments was again to have the backing of Richmond, with the President himself writing to Holmes and enclosing a letter of Johnston's for which he asked consideration. This enclosure, presumably written for this purpose, outlined the situation at Vicksburg in some detail and reiterated his opinion that the "true system of warfare would be to concentrate the forces of the two departments on this side of the Mississippi, beat the enemy here, and then reconquer the country beyond it which" the enemy "might have gained in the meantime." [4] Johnston's success in impressing his views on Davis is measured by the fact that the President's words in favor of reinforcement and the principles of concentration were virtually the same as those customarily used by Johnston. Holmes was not, however, ordered to come to the aid of Pemberton. The question was still left to the discretion of the commander of the Trans-Mississippi Department.

On the departure of the President about the twenty-seventh of December relations between these two West Pointers must have been at a high point. They had come to a large measure of agreement over what was to be done. The President had had his way about sending troops from Bragg and that dispute was out of the way, while on the other hand, Johnston's pet scheme had been adopted. Johnston had probably been seeking to be agreeable in order to have his opinions accepted, while Davis must have been pleased to have the counsel of his distinguished appointee. Basic disagreements had either receded or were not yet realized. Harmony undoubtedly prevailed as they parted, for at that moment success greeted Southern arms. Though this success was not owing to the efforts of either of them, good news coming at the end of the President's visit could only have promoted good feelings.

[4] *O. R.,* Ser. I: XX, Part 2—Kirby Smith to Johnston, December 26, 1862, 463; LII, Part 2—Davis to Holmes, December 21 (?), 1862, 397–99; XVII, Part 2—Phelan to Davis, December 9, 1862, 788–92; Johnston to Holmes, December 22, 1862, 800–801.

3

GRANT'S FIRST EFFORT AGAINST VICKSBURG HAD developed into a two-pronged advance. One came overland under his personal direction, and the other advanced by the river under the guidance of Major General William T. Sherman. These separate advances were to co-operate as Sherman reached Vicksburg and secured a good position at the fortified bluffs north of the town. But on December 20 Pemberton's principal subordinate, Major General Earl Van Dorn, having passed Grant's left flank with the Confederate cavalry, destroyed the Federal base at Holly Springs, Mississippi. Deprived of his supplies, owing to Van Dorn and the Bragg-sponsored raids in west Tennessee of Forrest, Grant began to retreat on December 27, the same day that Sherman reached the vicinity of Vicksburg. Sherman was left to make the attempt on the Confederate fortifications unaided. Not only were these positions almost impregnable, both from the nature of the ground and the works that had been built, but Pemberton was now able to transfer troops from the army which had been facing Grant to strengthen the defense against Sherman. Sherman attacked on December 29 and was easily beaten off, losing nearly 2,000 men to a Confederate loss of a little over 200. Thus baffled at the battle of Chickasaw Bluffs, Sherman withdrew on January 2, 1863, and the immediate threat to Vicksburg was removed.

The safety of Vicksburg had been secured largely by the troops of its own department. Johnston's plan to have its defense assisted by reinforcement from Arkansas, much less his plan to concentrate the forces of the two departments for offensive operations, had not materialized in time to be of aid. Though General Holmes had been bombarded by Richmond with orders and requests, a successful resistance to any movement had been made by that officer. After Davis' and Randolph's original instructions, General Cooper had on November 19, 1862, asked Holmes, "Can you send troops from your command—say 10,000—to operate either opposite to Vicksburg or to cross the river?" To Holmes's reply, "I could not get to Vicksburg in less than 2 weeks," Cooper inquired, "Is not your force sufficient to make a detachment?" Three days later the Adjutant and Inspector General tartly insisted that Holmes "send without delay the infantry force you have been twice telegraphed for." Undismayed, Holmes explained that he "could not get there in twenty-five days, and all would be lost" in Arkansas before he could return, to which Cooper replied that "the President reiterates his orders." Standing his ground, Holmes argued that he regarded "the movement ordered as equivalent to abandoning Arkansas." On December 11 General Cooper capitulated, telling him, "you must exercise your judgment in the matter."

With the revival of the plan for reinforcement through the letters of Davis and Johnston, hope and expectation was aroused, and both Johnston and Pemberton constantly awaited news of reinforcement from the Trans-Mississippi. However, neither troops nor news had arrived before Sherman's withdrawal on January 2, 1863.

The falling back of Grant, the major crisis of the campaign, took place before any of the men ordered by President Davis had arrived from Tennessee. One half of Stevenson's division, two brigades, did arrive in time to be of assistance in repelling Sherman's attack. Reason for this slow movement was that they had to come an "appallingly circuitous route," as the more direct railway route over the Memphis and Charleston Railroad, the "vertebrae of the Confederacy," had been broken since April, 1862. In order to come by rail, the troops had to be routed from Murfreesborough, Tennessee, to Stevenson, Alabama, to Chattanooga, Atlanta, Montgomery, Mobile, Meridian, and thence across central Mississippi to Jackson and Vicksburg. In July, 1862, General Bragg had sent at least 25,000 men over almost the same route in about two weeks, but this move had been preceded by careful planning and elaborate preparations, including the sending of one division in advance which had served as a trial and a test of the arrangements.

While two brigades of Stevenson's division got away on December 18, about four days after they had been ordered, and arrived within ten days, the remaining two brigades "consumed more than *three weeks*, the division wagon trains, dispatched across country, being on the road only a little longer. Reasons for the delay are obscure but the Military blamed the carriers." Johnston, however, thought that the "management of the railroad was at least as good as usual in such cases." [5]

Efforts were being made by the Confederate government to improve this situation through shortening the route by building a line from Meridian to Montgomery, thus by-passing Mobile. This new route could promise little for improving the communications within the Department of the West, though completed with a steamboat link in December, 1862. It added very little to the speed of movement, as it required long advance notice of large troop movements and hardly provided an adequate substitute for the lost Memphis and Charleston.

Though Johnston's prediction as to the great travel time required between the two major portions of his command was borne out, this can hardly be called a conclusive argument against making the movement. President Davis, who ordered it, had been told that Bragg's army was not faced with an impending Federal offensive, while Vicksburg was clearly threatened. A part of Johnston's original argument against this reinforcement had been based on the expectation of reinforcements from Holmes, but when he ordered it, the President knew that Holmes was not coming.

However, this dispute points up an important difference over western strategy between the President and his principal western subordinate, which each revealed in his correspondence during December. Johnston had

[5] *Ibid.*: Correspondence of November 19, 22, 29, December 5, 6, 8, 11, 1862, 753–93 *passim;* Johnston to Pemberton, December 27, 1862, 806; Johnston to Davis, January 2, 5, 1863, 823, 827; Order, Headquarters, Department of Mississippi and Eastern Louisiana, January 1, 1863, 817; Robert C. Black, III, *The Railroads of the Confederacy* (Chapel Hill, 1952), 139, 158, 181–83, 192; Govan and Livingood, *A Different Valor,* 173.

stressed the importance of middle Tennessee, not so much for itself as for the consequences of its loss. The loss of this area would give the Federals new strategic capabilities. If Bragg were forced out of middle Tennessee, Johnston thought Rosecrans would then be able to move into either Virginia or Mississippi. Though neither of these possibilities which he feared turned out to be the actual outcome (Sherman's march to Atlanta and the sea), this still remains an important strategic insight on Johnston's part, not shared by Davis. It is clear that Davis did not have the former's concern for middle and east Tennessee, nor did he view the consequences of its loss in the same light as did Johnston. He was not only prepared for Bragg to fall back but did not even list this area as a major Union objective. This great difference in strategic concept between the President and the department commander undoubtedly played a part in their difference over the question of reinforcing Mississippi from Tennessee. It would have an important bearing on the management of the western theater of the war, producing conflicting policies and views on important strategic questions.

Other basic differences between the outlook of Johnston and Davis revealed themselves during the course of the month in which the new command had been in existence. While Johnston had seemingly convinced Davis of the value and importance of concentration, Davis' policy of territorial defense had actually remained unaltered. This policy is implicit in his argument that it was possible for Holmes to concentrate in defense of the strategically important Mississippi because Arkansas was safe from invasion. The President was still unwilling to give up territory in order to concentrate

at a vital point, its own territory always taking pre-
cedence for the army of any department. His policy
is further revealed in his point that the reinforcement
and safety of the Mississippi was necessary to show the
South's power of resistance in that vital area—to show
the North and the world the futility of trying to
conquer the South. While Johnston was thinking in
terms of concentration to defeat the enemy's army,
Davis' analysis was still that of defending territory and
of wearing down the North by a tenacious resistance
of all Southern territory. So the President's advocacy
and practice of concentration and elastic defense was
still strongly conditioned by and anchored to his basic
concept of the strategy of the war, and it reflected, too,
perhaps a basic optimism on his part that it would not
be necessary to give way anywhere.

Yet, as the concentration of the preceding winter had
shown, Davis was able ruthlessly to sacrifice small points
to save large ones. His reluctance to do this must have
been reinforced in the case of the Trans-Mississippi by
the knowledge that assistance for Pemberton was on the
way from Tennessee, an area within the jurisdiction
of the new Department of the West. The relations of
Davis and Holmes illustrate also the President's continuing reluctance to dictate to a department commander. Davis seemed to feel that if a department was
worth creating and its commander worthy of appointment, then the department commander's discretion
must be paramount.

Even on the very question of the methods to be
employed in the defense of the Mississippi Johnston
and Davis were in disagreement. The President stressed
holding the two important and extensively fortified

positions of Vicksburg and Port Hudson, while Johnston deplored the large garrisons required by their
fortifications. He stressed the importance of relying
primarily on the field army and wished to avoid tying
down too many troops in the defense of fortified places
in order to provide the largest possible force for the
field. Here was a fundamental difference in concept,
one stressing vital points and the other regarding the
army as the means to the objective of preventing the
severance of the Confederacy. In modern terms, it was
a difference between static and elastic or mobile defense.
Johnston felt that, if the army were defeated, the forts
would be lost, but if the army won, the forts, if lost,
could be regained. There was an analogous disagreement between Hitler and his generals in World War
II.

In his short time in his new theater Johnston seemed
to be beginning to see an important new role for cavalry.
The use of cavalry against the enemy's communications,
a project of both Bragg and Johnston, was a natural
idea in view of the long railway supply lines in the
western area and the excellence of Confederate cavalry
and its leadership. However, this concept of the use of
cavalry was just at this time being given extensive
application. Johnston, a cavalry enthusiast as well as a
veteran of that service, could appreciate the possibilities
which this arm of the service might have against communications in the West.

When he thought that 4,000 cavalry on his communications "may delay General Grant," he as yet
saw only limited possibilities in what this employment
of his old branch might accomplish. In his former
theater of operations, Virginia, the shorter lines of

communication did not give cavalry nearly the opportunity to play this role. Yet it is evident that Johnston was beginning to note the differences and the potentialities of the new area.[6]

When Davis left Mississippi about the twenty-seventh of December, Johnston had been in his new position only a little over a month, the major part of which he had spent either in Richmond, traveling or on tour with the President. What little time had been available to him he had spent either in getting his headquarters into operation or acquainting himself with the situation. He could, nevertheless, view events so far with some degree of satisfaction. Though he had lost the argument about detaching part of Bragg's army, his prediction about the time which would be consumed in travel was proving to be accurate. Also, if Holmes had not been ordered to send troops, at least the President himself had written him and hope was high that he would at last respond. His relations with the President were good. His maligned subordinates, Pemberton and Van Dorn, had done well, and Grant was in retreat. With Holmes on the way, perhaps, and the troops from Tennessee coming in, it might be possible to deal a real blow to Grant. While leaving Pemberton in command of the defenses of Vicksburg and the control of his army, Johnston established headquarters at Jackson, Mississippi, and began assisting Pemberton and imperceptibly taking control of the operations in the area.

[6] Johnston to Pemberton, December 31, 1862, Sarah A. Dorsey, *Recollections of Henry Watkins Allen* (New York, 1866), 173; *O. R.,* Ser. I: XVII, Part 2—Johnston to Bragg, December 17, 1862, 798; Johnston to Davis, January 2, 1863, 823; XX, Part 2—Johnston to Cooper, December 6, 8, 1862, 441, 444; R. M. Hughes to D. H. Hill, October 26, November 5, 1922, Hughes Papers.

Chapter Eight

The Inception
of Departmental Strategy

1

AFTER THE DESTRUCTION OF HIS BASE, GRANT withdrew on December 27, 1862, leaving only Sherman's doomed effort against the bluffs as a threat to Vicksburg. Yet the removal of the real threat to Vicksburg was not immediately clear to the Confederate leaders. Pemberton, naturally and correctly, was anxious to concentrate the maximum number of men against Sherman's effort, while Johnston wished to retain as many as possible as a reserve at Jackson to deal with the renewed effort by Grant which he feared.

Johnston, however, deferred to Pemberton's view and sent from Jackson as many men as Pemberton requested. This disagreement highlighted the anomaly of having two commanders in the same department. Though an effort may have been made to formalize their relations, they had still to be worked out in practice. A number of telegraphic disagreements and discussions reveal both the nature of the relationship and the difficulties encountered. It was certainly Johnston's desire to give Pemberton free rein for, disliking to interfere with his subordinates, he must surely have felt that Pemberton, "having studied and kept up with all the military circumstances, would be more competent to command at an important juncture than one just arrived."

That Johnston adhered to this principle of command is borne out by the fact that all operation orders were issued by Pemberton. While endeavoring to keep himself informed of Pemberton's movements and orders and to maintain a reserve at Jackson, Johnston yielded in every case to the local commander's wishes. However, with his headquarters now at Jackson on the scene of active operations and with Pemberton in Vicksburg, a "most important" position, but one which interfered "with the supervision of the other parts of the department," the inevitable happened. Johnston began not only to make suggestions and recommendations but to receive reports and intelligence from the other commanders scattered throughout Mississippi and eastern Louisiana.

Before the Federal forces withdrew, Jackson was fast becoming another headquarters. There are indications that the system did not work too well. After a telegraphic dispute over the number of men to be forwarded from Jackson to Vicksburg, Johnston reminded Pemberton that "it is necessary that we act together." Though Pemberton's reply fully explained his theory of operations and his need for men and concluded by expressing his "desire to work with" General Johnston, the latter again found it necessary to solicit greater co-operation from Pemberton. After "respectfully" requesting him to communicate "the substance of all orders" given "for movement of troops, and as much as practicable to confer . . . before giving them," he reminded General Pemberton: "I was brought here by the President to assist you. My great object is to do so."

Johnston's desire for information and to be consulted may well have been motivated by worry over the fact that he and Pemberton had, in Davis' presence, "differed widely as to the mode of warfare best adapted" to the defense of the Mississippi. Probably because of this and the disposition of Pemberton's troops, he felt it necessary again to elucidate his views on December 31, 1862. In what today would be known as a "policy directive" or "letter of instruction," Johnston contended that Vicksburg "should have just the force necessary to its defense: the remaining infantry, to constitute an active army," which, should Vicksburg be invested, "might attack the enemy in the rear." He thought to be inadequate the then active army of 11,000 men which, in the event of investment, "could not attack with decided hope of success." Evidently Johnston and Davis had agreed on a reserve or active army which was to be maintained at a specified strength considerably above 11,000, and his concern had been aroused by Pemberton's reducing it to this figure.

However, true to his principle that the man on the spot who had "studied and kept up with all the military circumstances" was "more competent to command at an important juncture," he did not take command but did provide Pemberton with guidance as to his views. However, the success of Pemberton's defense against Sherman and the failure of Grant to renew his advance gave no opportunity for the realization of Johnston's fears. All having turned out well, he felt that Pemberton deserved "high credit" for his conduct of the campaign.[1]

2

As EVENTS IN MISSISSIPPI WERE TAKING A favorable turn, Johnston's earlier fears were realized when General Bragg reported through Johnston's chief of staff at Chattanooga, Colonel Benjamin S. Ewell, that the enemy was "advancing in heavy force." Johnston directed that Kirby Smith send aid from east Tennessee to Bragg and that any of Stevenson's division still in the vicinity be stopped. Bragg was to receive little aid, as Kirby Smith had only 1,200 men available and Stevenson's troops had all departed. After doing what he could, the department commander waited in ignorance until December 31 when the good news arrived that General Bragg had attacked the enemy and driven "him from all his positions except his extreme left, taking thirty-one pieces of artillery and 4,000 prisoners."

Although absorbed with measures to defeat the still present Sherman, Johnston congratulated Bragg on his

[1] Johnston to Davis, March 2, 1863, Robert M. Hughes, *General Johnston* (New York, 1893), 167–68; Johnston to Pemberton, December 31, 1862, Dorsey, *Recollections of Henry Watkins Allen,* 173; Johnston, *Narrative,* 153; *O. R.,* Ser. I, XVII, Part 2 —Johnston-Pemberton correspondence, December 26, 1862, to January 3, 1863, 805–25 *passim;* Johnston to Davis, January 2, 1862, 823; Johnston to Cooper, January 4, 1863, 826.

"glorious termination of last year." On the following day he directed Bragg to press the Federals "vigorously" and again congratulated him. This good news from Tennessee acted as a spur to a plan which had been maturing since Van Dorn's great cavalry success on December 20. He had been interested in the possibilities of using cavalry on Federal communication lines since he had arrived in the department and had relied on this to delay Grant. Johnston was obviously impressed with the size, scope, and tremendously significant consequences of the cavalry raid which had destroyed the Union base at Holly Springs. This action, involving over 3,000 Confederate cavalrymen, destroyed more than a million dollars in property and captured a thousand prisoners. Most important, it helped to deprive Grant of the necessary supplies, compelling his withdrawal.

Van Dorn's was a far different type of operation from the raids of partisans, such as John Hunt Morgan. The advance of an army of nearly 40,000 men had been defeated by the combined action of this raid and that from Bragg's army against western Tennessee railways by that master railway-destroyer, Brigadier General Nathan Bedford Forrest. Fearful of a renewed advance by Grant, Johnston seized on a large cavalry force as the means to prevent another approach to Vicksburg.

Obviously a Federal base would not again be so easy a mark. Furthermore, if the result was to be commensurate with the means, a larger force was indicated. Here was an opportunity to secure the co-operation of the Tennessee and Mississippi departments through the mobility of the mounted branch of the service. Forrest's cavalry was at hand in western Tennessee and more could be concentrated near the scene of any projected

operations. So in the same message in which he announced Van Dorn's success to Bragg, Johnston communicated his intention to "unite Forrest and [Colonel
Philip H.] Roddey with Van Dorn for future operations"
and asked that they be told and that he be informed of
their whereabouts.

A large cavalry force was thus to be assembled, utilizing the resources of the two departments, and was to
be employed, not to delay, but, significantly, to "prevent
Grant's advance." This project, incidentally, was conceived apparently without any consultation with or
reference to Pemberton and was then announced to
him. Johnston reluctantly permitted Pemberton to use
some of the cavalry of his department. But by appropriat-
ing the major part of his cavalry force for a plan of his
own devising to accomplish an end which related purely
to the defense of Mississippi, Johnston, in reality, took
effective command of the Department of Mississippi and
Eastern Louisiana. Pemberton remained in charge of
the immediate defense of Vicksburg, and Johnston permitted his judgment to prevail in matters pertaining to
that. Thus, whereas the department commander had
heretofore limited his role to keeping himself informed
and consulted and to doling out the reserve, he had
now taken control of the cavalry and even gone so far
as to have "informally authorized Major-General Van
Dorn to visit his family" in Mobile without consulting
Pemberton. This act of granting Van Dorn a furlough
seems to indicate that Johnston clearly considered himself the general's commanding officer.

When congratulating Bragg on his success, Johnston
asked that Forrest and Roddey be directed to send to
him for their instructions. Bragg responded by reporting

that Forrest's expedition had "fully accomplished its object" and that Morgan too had been successful, the "enemy in Tennessee and Mississippi" being "without railroad and telegraphic communication with their Government." Upon receipt of this good news, Johnston embraced these successes in his renewed congratulations but repeated his requirements for putting Forrest and Roddey under his orders, as he wanted them "on this side of the Tennessee."

While his arrangements for concentrating half of Bragg's cavalry and most of Pemberton's under Van Dorn were in progress, Johnston received word from Pemberton that Sherman had apparently abandoned his effort before the Vicksburg bluffs, and was re-embarking his troops. Except for the fact that there was still no news of Holmes, the outlook in Mississippi seemed bright. The enemy attack by the river had just been repulsed, and a possible renewal of Grant's advance could be counteracted by the now-proven method of a cavalry attack on his communications. To accomplish this an enlarged force of cavalry, under the proven commanders, Van Dorn and Forrest, was in the process of formation.[2]

---

[2] *Ibid.:* LII, Part 2—B. S. Ewell to Johnston, December 27, 1863, 400–401; XX, Part 2—Johnston to Ewell, December 27, 1863, 463; Johnston to Cooper, December 8, 31, 1863, 445, 472; Johnston to Bragg, December 30, 1862, January 1, 2, 1863, 469, 475, 476; XVII, Part 2—Johnston to Bragg, December 17, 1862, 798; Johnston to Pemberton, December 30, 1862, January 1 (?), 1863, 813, 817; Bragg to Johnston, January 2, 1863, 476; Pemberton to Johnston, January 2, 1863, 820.

3

JOHNSTON MADE A RATHER FULL REPORT TO the President, giving his estimate of the situation. After making the same observations he had made earlier to Pemberton about keeping the field army near Vicksburg at the maximum size, Johnston pointed out that the latter was not adhering to his principle. Expressing his fears of a renewed advance on Grant's part and giving his opinion that the force of 11,000 effectives was too weak to do more than delay him, he then confided his plan to the President: "My hope of keeping him back is in Van Dorn, under whom I propose to unite all the available cavalry when Forrest and Roddey can be found."

In the light of his strategic principles Johnston voiced his fears for the future. He anticipated that, should Grant join Sherman by returning to Memphis and moving down the river, he could reach Vicksburg "as soon as we could learn whether he was embarking or moving along the railroad to Grenada." The city could thus "be invested by the combined armies." If this should happen, there would not be a "sufficient force to break the investment." Johnston felt that an added disadvantage of the elaborate defenses of Vicksburg and the heavy commitment of troops there was that the forces were "too widely distributed to be in condition for the offensive."

Turning to the need of "about 20,000 men . . . to make headway against both Grant and Sherman," he reported that there was "no news from Arkansas." Since this indicated that there would be no reinforcement from that quarter, would not "the great victory at Fredericksburg enable General Lee to spare a part of his force?" In conclusion, Johnston remarked that "should the enemy's forces be respectably handled the task you have set me will be above my ability. But the hand of Almighty God has delivered us in times of as great danger. . . . I will not lose hope."

In spite of his expressed fears, the tone of this letter was one of optimism. The President replied in the same vein, holding out hope of co-operation from General Holmes. This hope for aid from the Trans-Mississippi expressed by the President apparently spurred Johnston to obtain definite word. He directed Pemberton to have a messenger sent across the river "to ascertain whether there were any movements" there connected "with those on this side," a step which Pemberton on his own initiative had taken nearly a week before.

Meanwhile, it was becoming clear that there had been no great victory in Tennessee after all. A tone of urgency returned to General Johnston's communications, as well as criticism of the workability of his department containing two such widely separated armies. He must have not only felt keen disappointment over Bragg's retreat but annoyance that he should have been so misled as to the real situation. The latest turn of events in Tennessee deranged his plans. He was without adequate information as to the extent of Bragg's retreat, the condition of his army and, most important, whether he was still in peril. While he was awaiting information from Bragg, one element of uncertainty was removed from the picture. Word was received from the messenger sent earlier by Pemberton to Little Rock that "No troops will be sent."

Johnston's only immediate action in response to the situation as altered by Bragg's retreat was to return the cavalry of Forrest and Roddey to Bragg's control. However, preparing for any contingency which later intelligence from Bragg might bring, he sought official guidance from Richmond. Expressing the opinion that Grant was now unlikely to advance because the winter weather in Mississippi had made the country "impracticable," he asked whether Stevenson's division could not be sent back to Tennessee. He requested Stevenson only on condition that he was correct about Grant's enforced immobility and that there appeared to be "no danger in Mississippi except by the river." But he then posed a much more fundamental question when inquiring again about reinforcements for Bragg. He asked the President: "Which is the most valuable, Tennessee or the Mississippi?"

While the decision on the question of the return of Stevenson's men as posed was not dependent on the relative value of the Mississippi and Tennessee, an answer to this vital and inevitable policy question should have been given much earlier. But a decision by the government was certainly essential now that Johnston had begun to fill the primary role for which he had been sent west and for which the department had been established: the co-ordination of the defense of Tennessee and the Mississippi.

The answer he received, that the "whole or a part of Stevenson's division may be sent to re-enforce Bragg," and that "to hold the Mississippi is vital," was certainly not either sufficiently full nor clearly decisive to resolve such an important question. He did not, however, press for greater clarity. He had made his plans to deal with the changed situation.[3]

The plan evolved as reports from Tennessee began to indicate that Rosecrans was not immediately following up his success at Murfreesborough. An attempt was made to make up General Bragg's heavy losses from whatever source available, newly conscripted men or reinforcements from the east. But the main reliance was still to be on cavalry. The same interdepartmental cavalry force under Van Dorn was to be employed but this time to aid the forces in Tennessee as well as those on the Mississippi. The objective of the "cavalry expedition in the two departments" was reported to Pemberton as intended "to interrupt any movement into Mississippi or Middle Tennessee," to Bragg as covering his "left by preventing Federal troops from going from West to Middle Tennessee," and to the President that the 6,000 cavalry under Van Dorn were being sent "to Bragg's aid to operate on the enemy's communications."

The complete objective in organizing and dispatching this force is revealed in the three-fold mission given its commander. Its primary purpose was to aid Bragg by taking "part in a battle, in the event of the advance of the Federal army." Until the battle took place the

[3] *Ibid.:* Johnston to Davis, January 2, 6, 7, 1863, 823, 827–28; Johnston to Pemberton, January 6, 1863, 827; Order, Headquarters, Department of Mississippi and Eastern Louisiana, January 1, 1863, 817; LII, Part 2—Davis to Johnston, January 5, 8, 1863, 403–404; XX, Part 2—Johnston to Ewell, January 6, 1863, 487; Johnston to Davis, January 7, 1863, 487–88.

second part of its mission, attacking the enemy's communications, might be developed. This role was to be expanded, if there seemed to be no prospects of a battle, by moving "into Kentucky or farther." Yet the force would rarely be too far away to break the communications of any overland Federal advance against Vicksburg.

Thus the potentialities of the employment of cavalry against the communications of the Union armies were to be exploited on a grand scale, while at the same time co-ordination among the departments was to be obtained by using the greater mobility of cavalry. Infantry having failed to arrive in time by railroad, perhaps cavalry marching overland would have the necessary strategic mobility. It was to this large cavalry force, organized as a corps under Van Dorn, that Johnston attached "great importance" and relied on to aid Bragg and supply the only "pressure" which he regarded "possible by the troops in Mississippi."

Not only was it to remain an interdepartmental effort but its scope as such was enlarged. Colonel Roddey was to remain in the force after all, and additional cavalry was obtained from Major General Simon Boliver Buckner, now commanding the District of the Gulf at Mobile. Since the cavalry in Mississippi was "almost unorganized," General Van Dorn would require considerable time to concentrate and organize the various forces which were to make up his corps. Some of the troops from Alabama were even without arms. With the cavalry expedition thoroughly started in its preparation and organization, with appeals having been sent out for reinforcements, and with the situation momentarily quiet in both Mississippi and Tennessee, the department commander could turn his attention to other matters. Desiring to see the effects of the battle of Murfreesborough on Bragg's army, as well as to be present when Van Dorn arrived, Johnston set out for Tennessee. He was not rushed, however, and so stopped in Mobile for a visit of inspection.[4]

4

DURING THE MONTH OF JOHNSTON'S STAY IN Mississippi, especially the three critical weeks between the departure of the President and his own departure for Mobile, he had not only taken charge of the general conduct of operations in Mississippi but had begun to function as the commander of the Department of the West. Paucity of communications and adequate reports as well as, by modern standards, inadequate staffs limited the latter function. Nevertheless, action taken to secure reinforcements, harmonize a dispute between

[4] *Ibid.:* Johnston to Davis, January 8, 1863, 489; Bragg to Johnston, January 11, 1863, 492–93; Johnston to Cooper, January 16, 17, 1863, 498, 499; XVII, Part 2—Johnston to Pemberton, January 11, 1863 (two messages), 832; Johnston to Bragg, January 11, 1863, 832; Johnston to Simon Bolivar Buckner, January 11, 12, 1863, 832, 833; Johnston to Van Dorn, January 13, 1863, 833; Johnston to Davis, January 17, 1863, 838; XXIII, Part 2—*id.* to *id.*, February 3, 1863, 624; Johnston to Bragg, February 23, 1863, 646; Johnston to Van Dorn, February 24, 1863, 646; LII, Part 2 —Bragg to Johnston, January 7, 1863, 404; Campbell to Johnston, January 19, 1863, 410; Van Dorn to Johnston, February 22, 1863, 425. See also Johnston, *Narrative,* 160–62.

subordinates, reorganize departmental boundaries and, most important, to make strategic plans for the whole area, clearly indicates that the new headquarters was functioning as planned. It may not have seemed very significant to Johnston, for his direct activity and responsibility were not great compared to his command in Virginia, which had included an army directly under his command as well as departmental responsibilities.

This active period was also marked by the collapse of Johnston's dream of uniting the forces of the Trans-Mississippi with those of his own department. Not only did the special messenger bring this information but, at about the same time, Johnston received a long letter from General Holmes giving a full account of conditions in Arkansas and rhetorically asking "would it be justifiable to strip this country of its only means of defense, thereby allowing the enemy to overrun the State and win a wavering people from their loyalty?" There was little of which Johnston could complain in this communication, for the President's letter had not only left Holmes discretion but had assumed that the reinforcement could be accomplished without endangering Arkansas. So ended the last "tall castle in the air."

One reason so much reliance was placed in the forces of the Trans-Mississippi, not only by Johnston, but by Randolph and Davis, was the erroneous impression then existing in Richmond that General Holmes had a force of 50,000 to 55,000 men as well as being relatively unopposed by any sizeable or active Union forces. With a force of this size it was easy to conclude that Holmes was strong enough both to protect Arkansas and assist in the defense of Vicksburg. But, as Holmes said, the belief as to his "ability to render such assistance has grown out of a very erroneous impression" of his strength, which his "repeated reports to the War Department it seems have not been able to correct."

Though in part due to his constant demand for more weapons, the delusions about Holmes's strength apparently also originated in the office of General Cooper, the Adjutant and Inspector General. The Chief of the Bureau of War remarked: "As *Inspector General* one would suppose that the office highest in rank, the official keeper of the rolls whose specific duty it is to *know* the state of the army and *compel* proper returns, would in two and a half years have got some complete returns. Yet it is notorious that the returns are not complete even from the nearest and most stationary army, while of the Trans-Mississippi forces, they have almost no account whatever." Though, as Holmes said, they made a "very respectable show on paper," actually the army in Arkansas was about half the supposed 55,000 men, including Indians and unarmed men, two-thirds of them being far away in northwestern Arkansas. It was true, however, that the enemy, who was about half again as strong, was not on the offensive and, in fact, Holmes's forces took the offensive without success at the end of December, 1862.

Another factor was that the "Arkansas troops did not propose to give up their State" while the "Missouri troops which had crossed the Mississippi . . . were clamoring to return." It seems, nevertheless, that Holmes might have supplied perhaps as many as 10,000 men by the end of December, if he had acted in November to arrange affairs in his department in order to make it possible. However, in view of Holmes's poor performance while in Virginia and the fact that he was both "deaf and superannuated," it is unlikely that very much would have resulted even if positive orders had been sent him.[5]

When it became clear that there was to be no co-operation from the Trans-Mississippi, Johnston already had another plan for his department. If it were not so brilliant in its possibilities, it was probably sounder in actuality, for not only was it not based on any misconceptions about the strength of distant forces, but the troops which were to be employed were entirely under his control as department commander. This new plan was the one already discussed for the employment of the cavalry force being organized under Van Dorn. The idea of its potentialities displays a rapid development in Johnston's thinking. First it was to "delay" Grant, then it became his "hope of keeping him back." When the situation deteriorated in Tennessee, the mission, scope and potentialities of the force were expanded to include assisting both Bragg and Pemberton. The stationing of the cavalry with Bragg's army was to increase his strength in battle as well as to prevent reinforcements from being sent to Rosecrans, a contingency Johnston feared while Grant

[5] *O. R.*, Ser. I: XX, Part 2—Johnston to Bragg, January 9, 1863, 491; Johnston to Cooper, January 12, 1863, 495; XVII, Part 2— Davis to Cooper, November 29, 1862, 767; Holmes to Cooper, December 5, 1862, 783–84; Holmes to Johnston, December 29, 1862, 811; XIII—Holmes to Cooper, October 26, 1862, 883–85, 899; Johnston, *Narrative*, 148; Kean, *Inside the Confederate Government*, 87, entry of July 28, 1863; Livermore, *Story of the Civil War*, Part 2, 52; Daniel O'Flaherty, *General Jo Shelby, Undefeated Rebel* (Chapel Hill, 1954), 122, 123.

was inactive due to the bad weather conditions in Mississippi.[6]

Johnston had actually taken over most of the cavalry in his department. Not only was he taking most of Pemberton's and Buckner's from them, but he had assumed "full responsibility . . . for the use made of Bragg's." This large cavalry force, to be over 6,000 men, was specially organized by Johnston's direction under a commander of his own selection. Forces from the entire Department of the West were united to be employed on missions common to the interest of the whole department. In a sense this was to be the department commander's mass of maneuver or general reserve. For this reason the creation of this force can be called Johnston's strategic plan for his department at this time. It was his solution for the difficulty of transferring troops between the two major armies. Complaining that his command was a "nominal one," he was saying that he could not "direct both parts" of his department at once, at the very same time he is activating this plan. This disparity between words and deeds, however difficult to explain, is nevertheless quite clear. It is probable that, while he still felt his old objections and was in a sense committed to them, he was doing the best he could in the circumstances. He undoubtedly still desired the command of an army rather than this geographical or administrative post. His position in Mississippi in which Pemberton did most of the work and commanded the troops must have made him "repine" for his former position in Virginia.

[6] *O. R.*, Ser. I, XX, Part 2, Johnston to Cooper, January 12, 1863, 495.

In his first two months this dissatisfaction and lack of faith in the soundness of his mission does not seem to have affected his performance. The problem of communication between the two major armies received continued attention from both Johnston and Davis. The latter, in giving permission to return Stevenson's division to Tennessee, made the interesting and significant suggestion that a "double purpose" might be served if this force were placed at Meridian or Selma, points about halfway on the railway line between Bragg's army and that of Pemberton. There is no evidence that Johnston gave this possibility any active consideration.

He was absorbed in his cavalry movement for he had one of his staff officers, Major A. D. Banks, on the "valuable" employment of surveying the overland route between Columbus, Mississippi, and Decatur, Alabama, including the crossings at the latter place. In addition to reporting that there would be plenty of supplies for troops on that route, Banks sent his chief "a whole venison and a can of very fine oysters." This route was presumably intended solely for the use of the cavalry.

Familiarity with the conditions in his command made Johnston pessimistic about the prospects for the future. He felt that his department desperately needed reinforcements. Bragg had met Rosecrans at the battle of Murfreesborough on December 31, little inferior in force, having about 37,000 men to the Federal General's 43,000. The fact that he almost beat Rosecrans on the first day supports Bragg's argument that, had he had Stevenson's division, he could have won. As it was, Rosecrans entrenched and Bragg fell back about thirty miles to Tullahoma, Tennessee. While each side lost about thirty per cent of its army, Johnston's information was that the Union army had had its losses replaced while Bragg had had only one-third of his deficiency made good.

In addition to the 20,000 men Bragg estimated to be necessary "to enable him to hold Middle Tennessee," Mississippi badly needed troops. The situation appeared even more serious as it was correctly estimated that Grant now had nearly 70,000 men available for offensive operations, while a portion of Pemberton's 42,000 were necessary at Port Hudson to resist the northward advance of a Federal force of 30,000 under N. P. Banks. Should these forces move at the same time, "such a combination" could not be opposed with "present forces," Johnston told the War Department. He reiterated his previously expressed fear that "should a large portion of these forces act upon the river, they may invest our two positions, which would fall in the course of time, unless we have an active army to break the investment." The active army available—only about one-half of Pemberton's total strength due to the necessity for garrisoning the elaborate defenses of Vicksburg and Port Hudson—he obviously regarded as inadequate.

Nevertheless, Johnston's armies were no more outnumbered than were those of Lee, and the very reason he had been placed in his command was to utilize more efficiently the available men in that area. But Johnston may be pardoned for his requests for more men, as it is doubtful if there have been many commanders, however strong their forces, who did not feel the need of reinforcements. It was true that he was dangerously outnumbered, and he could truthfully say that he was making the best use of the men he had, carrying out his assignment of co-ordinating the resources of the area for its defense.

On his way to Bragg's headquarters, he had stopped at Mobile. While his inspection there was in progress, he received on January 22, 1862, a telegram from the President with directions to proceed "with the least delay" to the headquarters of Bragg's army. On the way he would find an "explanatory letter at Chattanooga." He promply cut short his visit of inspection and set out on what was to prove to be a very disagreeable task.[7]

[7] Kenneth P. Williams, *Lincoln Finds A General* (4 vols., New York, 1949–56), IV, 540; Johnston to Wigfall, January 8, 26, February 14, 1863, Wright, *A Southern Girl in '61*, 107, 121, 122–23, 125; O. R., Ser. I: XVII, Part 2—Johnston to Davis, January 6, 1863, 827; Banks to Johnston, January 13, 1863, 834; LII, Part 2—Davis to Johnston, January 8, 21, 1863, 404, 410; XX, Part 2—Johnston to Cooper, January 8, 12, 1863, 489, 495; Bragg to Johnston, January 11, 1863, 493.

Chapter Nine

Complications
with Personnel

1

JOHNSTON PROMPTLY LEFT MOBILE BY RAIL-
way and reached Chattanooga three days later on January 25,1863. While he found alarming reports from
Pemberton that Grant was before Vicksburg on the river
with 40,000 men, he discovered no letter from the
President explaining the purpose of his trip. Along
with his query for instructions, he telegraphed the
intelligence from Vicksburg to Richmond. After another inquiry, word was received on January 27 to go
on to Bragg's headquarters at Tullahoma. He arrived
there the following day, receiving the President's letter
there on the thirtieth.

Davis' letter informed him that "events connected
with the late battle at Murfreesborough and retreat
from that place, have led to criticisms of General
Bragg," which had caused the general to ask for the
opinion of his corps commanders, not only upon this subject, but "whether he had so far lost the confidence of
the army as to impair his usefulness." Though the
President could not understand why General Bragg
should have selected a "tribunal" of his corps commanders and "invited its judgment," he thought that

this condition of things required Johnston's presence. Since, if Bragg were distrusted by his officers and troops, a disaster might result, Johnston should investigate, deciding "what the best interests of the service require" and giving the President needed advice. The President added that his "confidence in General Bragg" remained "unshaken."

Bragg's retreat from Kentucky and his withdrawal after his announced victory at Murfreesborough had aroused the press and public against him to a degree which had begun to amount to a public outcry for his removal. In order to save his "fair name" and to "stop the deluge of abuse" which would destroy his usefulness and demoralize the army, he asked the lieutenant generals whether they had not supported the retreat from Murfreesborough and then asked them to be "candid" with him as to whether he had lost their "good opinion" and that of their subordinate generals. The opportunity offered by this invitation to candor, together perhaps with his offer to "retire without regret" if he had lost their good opinion, was embraced with alacrity by one corps commander, Lieutenant General William J. Hardee, and his able and popular division commanders, Patrick R. Cleburne and John C. Breckinridge. The other corps commander, Bishop Leonidas Polk, was absent, but he and his division commanders shared the view of Hardee and his colleagues. They had testified that, while there had been unanimity about the necessity of withdrawal after Murfreesborough, they felt that "a change of command" was "necessary." It was this discontent and virtual revolt of the generals which Johnston was charged to investigate and ascertain whether it warranted Bragg's removal.

Johnston directed his efforts in the investigation

toward ascertaining not only the views of the generals but the attitude of the men themselves, which necessitated visiting all of the units of the rather widely dispersed army. The required travel and interviews, delayed by constant rain, were not completed until February 12. He rendered two reports to the President in which he recommended that General Bragg not be relieved. Not only did he feel that it would be unwise to remove him when he had "just earned if not won the gratitude of the country," but he found the army "well clothed, healthy and in good spirits," its entire appearance giving "positive evidence of General Bragg's capacity to command." Recent operations of the army had, in Johnston's opinion, been "conducted admirably," the "effective fighting" in December exhibiting "great vigor and skill" on the part of General Bragg and "courage in the troops." He found dissatisfaction with General Bragg among the officers, especially of Hardee's corps, but felt that it was declining; the fact that they thought that the President "might give them a commander with fewer defects" did not, in Johnston's view, "greatly diminish his value." On the other hand, he thought that the confidence of the troops in their ability to beat the enemy was as great as when the President had been there in December. Regardless of what the President might do about removing General Bragg, Johnston was emphatic that "no one in this army or engaged in this investigation ought to be his successor." [1]

[1] *O. R.*, Ser. I: XXIV, Part 3—Pemberton to Johnston, January 24, 1863, 699–700; Johnston to Davis, January 25, 26, 1863, 602, 605; XXIII, Part 2—*id.* to *id.*, February 3, 12, 1863, 624, 632–33; Davis to Johnston, January 22, 1863, 613–14; LII, Part 2—*id.* to *id.*, January 27, 1863, 418; Horn, *Army of Tennessee*, 222–27.

Johnston obviously regarded the command of an army, especially a fine one like that of General Bragg, as a preferable post to his geographical command. Consequently, he felt it would be a promotion if he took Bragg's place and so thought it improper and "inconsistent" with his "personal honor" for him to receive Bragg's command as a result of his own investigative efforts. It would be even more improper, of course, for one of the lieutenant generals to receive it through agitation against their superior. Though it seems possible that Johnston supported Bragg to avoid this difficulty or to "protect his position as a department commander from the poaching of official Richmond and to rebuke the credence given to disloyal and insubordinate lesser commanders," it seems more likely that Bragg's operations and the state of the Army of Tennessee prompted his decision.

His inspection revealed to Johnston the fine state of the army, its high morale, efficient administration, and the recruitment of its strength through General Bragg's "vigorous system." It would be hard to believe that a commander who had so provided for his army that it lacked "no physical element of success" could be as inefficient as represented. Furthermore, as a distant spectator to Bragg's Kentucky campaign and the battle of Murfreesborough, Johnston was unable to see and evaluate his incapacity in active operations and on the battlefield, which was revealed there. If it were true, as Generals Henry Heth and Kirby Smith thought, that "there was no man in either of the contending armies who was General Bragg's superior as an organizer and a disciplinarian, but when he was in the presence of an enemy he lost his head," then Johnston saw only half

of the picture. The junior officers who had been campaigning with Bragg had naturally seen the other side
of him as well. Johnston, as did another observer,
Brigadier General William H. Bate, noted the effect
of Bragg's "force of character and discipline" and could
likewise come to no other conclusion than that Bragg
was misjudged by his officers and the public and was
perhaps a victim of discontented subordinates.

While his investigation was in progress, Johnston received an "unofficial" communication from Secretary
of War Seddon. After alluding to Johnston's feelings
that the parts of his department were too remote for
co-ordination, the Secretary expounded his views as to
the desirability of having "guiding direction and control" given to these distant departments by "a general
of the largest experience and greatest ability and reputation." Pointing out that another "great advantage"
was anticipated from his assuming command of any of
the armies in the department and giving them the
benefit of his "prestige and superior ability," he suggested that Johnston establish himself "permanently
with the central and leading army in Middle Tennessee," with or without General Bragg "as organizer and
administrator" under him. The Secretary concluded
his ingratiating letter by desiring to "learn candidly"
Johnston's own preferences. Since Johnston's official
communications as well as his private letters to Senator Wigfall had indicated his desire to command an
army and his dissatisfaction with his geographical command, Seddon was apparently making an effort to
accommodate him.

The points made in this communication were again
brought out officially by the President in a cordial

response to Johnston's recommendations with regard to Bragg. Davis said that he regarded lack of confidence in Bragg by his subordinate officers as a very serious matter, but it was anticipated that Johnston should "be present wherever most needed," and "command wherever present." He argued that, as the higher commander, his personal honor could not be involved as he "could have nothing to gain by the removal of General Bragg." Secretary Seddon in another letter reiterated this point and urged him to take command of Bragg's army. Confessing that he would prefer that Bragg "were recalled altogether," he undertook to overcome Johnston's "scruples," promising to try to obtain reinforcements and "thus measurably give the character of a combined army" to Bragg's command.[2]

The motives of the Secretary in this correspondence are a little obscure. Undoubtedly Johnston's efforts to find another post, that of an army command, through his friend Wigfall had succeeded in stirring Seddon to action. But Seddon's efforts to persuade him to replace Bragg may have been not so much an effort to accommodate Johnston's preferences as "unofficially" to induce him to supplant Bragg, a man in whom he had no confidence. It seems logical to assume that even the

[2] Govan and Livingood, *A Different Valor,* 179–81; Donald Bridgeman Sanger, "Some Problems Facing Joseph E. Johnston," *Essays in Honor of William E. Dodd,* ed. Avery Craven (Chicago, 1935), 265; *O. R.,* Ser. I: XXIII, Part 2—Johnston to Davis, February 12, 1863, 632–33; Davis to Johnston, February 19, 1863, 640–41; Seddon to Johnston, February 5, March 3, 1863, 626–27, 658–59; LII, Part 2—William H. Bate to Landon C. Haynes, March 24, 1863, 442–43; Memoirs of Major General Henry Heth (Alderman Library, University of Virginia), 140; Johnston to Wigfall, January 26, February 14, March 4, 1863, Wright, *A Southern Girl,* 121–22, 124–25; Wigfall Papers, Library of Congress.

influential Secretary had been unable to persuade the President to do more than to permit Johnston to exercise his discretion. Perhaps the Secretary was trying to induce Johnston to use his authority to remove the President's favorite, or at least to assume command of his army himself, thus nullifying Bragg's incompetence. In the case of Davis, it is more difficult to understand the motives. He had the power to remove Bragg or to order Johnston to adopt his interpretation of his orders. Was he unwilling himself to yield to public clamor and remove his favorite, or was he, as was probably Seddon, merely allowing what they regarded as the appropriate degree of discretion to the commander in the field?

Whatever may have been their motives, their efforts were abandoned when, on March 2, Johnston refused to yield, restating his position thus:

> I fear that it would be difficult to find a successor to General Bragg equal to him in all respects —especially now, when the season for active operations is so near that the successor might not be allowed time to learn well the theater of operations before the enemy's attack, and therefore regret very much that you think the impaired confidence of the superior officers in his fitness to command makes his removal necessary. I cannot think that troops who seem so full of spirit, and who their superior officers say, are full of confidence, can much doubt the capacity of their general. Besides a strong belief in his capacity, the injustice he endures from the country impels me to wish that you may find it expedient not to remove General Bragg. . . .

I thought that it was not intended that I should assume command at any time of either of the three departments; and having so expressed myself in writing to you early in January without being corrected, I was thus confirmed in my belief. It. seems to me that the exercise of such authority, except in rare cases would operate badly unless the officer exercising it be greatly superior to those commanding departments. . . . [The department commanders,] having studied and kept up with all the military circumstances, would be more competent to command at an important juncture than one just arrived. They could not be expected to serve with full zeal or interest if liable to be deprived, by my arrival at the last moment, of the fruits of long labor . . . The distance between these armies is so great, and each so near the enemy, that we cannot learn where the need is greatest until it is past. I could not have reached Murfreesborough in time for the battle if I had attempted to do so after the enemy advanced; if I had, it would have been a great hazard for me to have taken the command from General Bragg who had studied and learned the situation.[3]

If Johnston possessed "the power of keeping people at a distance" when he chose, he apparently exercised this talent on Secretary Seddon, for no more of the flattering and confidential communications came from that gentleman. Their correspondence was highly official, with strategic and policy questions giving way

---

[3] Johnston to Davis, March 2, 1863, Hughes, *General Johnston,* 168–69.

to subsistence problems as the topic of correspondence. Johnston's firm statement of his position to the President, however, caused no alteration in the pleasant and cordial tone which had characterized their communications since Johnston had taken up his new duties in December.

2

HAVING COMPLETED HIS INVESTIGATION AND made his report on February 12, Johnston again began to devote his full time to departmental duties. While this was probably more congenial than investigating Bragg, Johnston was still far from content with his position as a commander without an army. Not only was he indifferent and probably not an enthusiastic administrator, but he found very little to do, there being "very little office work." This was due to the fact that all departments were still corresponding directly with Richmond, and consequently the headquarters of the Department of the West received very little official paper. While Johnston was undoubtedly not sorry to be relieved of much of it, many channels tended to bypass him, thus depriving him of some information on which he might have based decisions and keeping from him problems on which he could have taken action.

In spite of the fact that he had been in his department for nearly ten weeks, Johnston had still to complete his inspection and familiarization of it. Therefore, he

returned to Chattanooga by way of Knoxville, the
headquarters of the Department of East Tennessee.
This long, narrow department, largely composed of
the extreme eastern portion of Tennessee and centering
on the railway running northeast to southwest from
Bristol, Virginia, to Chattanooga—"a mere line" as
Johnston described it to Davis—had just received a new
commander. Johnston's good friend, Kirby Smith, had
recently been sent to the Trans-Mississippi Department.
His successor, Brigadier General Henry Heth, had just
gone to Virginia, being replaced by an able Tennessean
of middle age, Brigadier General Daniel S. Donelson.
Donelson and Johnston discussed many of the problems
of the department. They were particularly concerned
with the inadequate numbers and scattered condition
of the 9,500 men available for its defense, lack of supplies, and a cavalry expedition into Kentucky with the
co-operation of Major General Samuel Jones, commanding the Department of Southwestern Virginia.

Johnston's major departmental strategy, that of Van
Dorn's cavalry force reinforcing Bragg and operating
on the enemy's communications, failed to develop according to plan. Despite the fact that the cavalry was "so
poorly equipped and the difficulties of supplying deficiencies so great" that the troops were unable to leave
northern Mississippi until February 7, they made the
overland march to Bragg's army in two weeks, and Van
Dorn was able to report his command for duty on
February 22. In response to Van Dorn's query as to
what his position would be, Johnston enlightened him
by explaining that he was intended to aid Bragg in
the event of a battle or to raid Rosecrans' communications if a battle was not imminent. He was instructed

further that "movements in General Bragg's theater of operations will be, necessarily, under his control; those from beyond it" Johnston would "at least inaugurate." [4]

Though he agreed with Van Dorn's desire "to cross the Cumberland and operate on the north bank of the Cumberland and on the banks of the Ohio," what seemed to be an impending advance by Rosencrans detained not only Van Dorn's cavalry corps but also that of Major General Joseph Wheeler. Guarding the flanks of the army and engaging in skirmishing and minor actions with the enemy was hardly the duty either Van Dorn or Johnston envisaged for the enormous cavalry force (nearly one-third of Bragg's 48,000 men) which had been assembled in Tennessee.

It was not entirely fear of a Federal advance which held the cavalry with the army. Van Dorn's corps accomplished another very important, if perhaps not anticipated, service. The stationing of his cavalry on the left flank of the army, near Columbia, enabled Bragg "to command all the resources of the Duck River Valley and the country southward," making it possible for him to feed his army and so remain in middle Ten-

[4] Arthur James Lyon Fremantle, *The Fremantle Diary*, ed. W. Lord (Boston, 1954), 93. Johnston's reply to Seddon's first letter is missing. It is not clear whether he replied to the second; Johnston to Wigfall, January 8, February 14, 1863, Wright, *A Southern Girl*, 106, 125; *O. R.*, Ser. I: XXIII, Part 2—Johnston to Cooper, February 17, 1863, 637; N. B. Forrest to Joseph Wheeler, February 18, 1863, 638; Johnston to Van Dorn, February 24, 1863, 646; Seddon to Humphrey Marshall, March 3, 1863, 660; Seddon to D. S. Donelson, March 3, 4, 1863, 661–62; Donelson to Ewell, March 4, 1863 (three letters), 661; Johnston to Davis, April 10, 1863, 745; LII, Part 2—Van Dorn to Johnston, February 22, 1863, 425; Johnston, *Narrative*, 161.

nessee. Johnston found that the question of food supplies—subsistence—was "the vital one," as the army
was "living from hand to mouth."

Bragg's army had been subsisting in the same area
for some months, and not only had the territory been
combed by the army's agents but by those of the Commissary General of Subsistence at Richmond as well.
After a long and sometimes severe correspondence in
which Johnston was unable to obtain any appreciable
quantity of subsistence from the Commissary General's
depot at Atlanta, he was obliged to establish what
was, in effect, his own commissary bureau for the
department. He sent out his own agents to obtain supplies throughout his department. While a similar dearth
of subsistence afflicted the Department of East Tennessee, which Johnston sought to remedy by foraging
raids into Kentucky, the situation was critical only in
Bragg's army. In Mississippi and the District of the Gulf
supplies were plentiful. The problem of subsistence
for Bragg's army absorbed more and more of Johnston's
efforts and attention as time wore on, and the situation
remained critical.[5] So, while the duty of Van Dorn's
cavalry was more prosaic and much less spectacular

[5] Livermore, *Story of the Civil War*, Part 2, 367; Johnston,
Narrative, 161; Sanger, "Some Problems Facing Joseph E. John-
ston," *loc. cit.*, 268–71; Archer Jones, "Tennessee and Mississippi,
Joe Johnston's Strategic Problem," *Tennessee Historical Quart-
erly*, XVIII (June, 1959), 138–39; *O. R.*, Ser. I: XXIV, Part 3—
Johnston to Davis, March 23, 1863, 686; XXIII, Part 2—W. P.
Johnston to Davis, March 24, April 15, 1863, 724, 757–73; David
Urquhart to Ewell, March 16, 1863, 700; Johnston to Seddon,
January 29, February 4, 25, March 4, 21, 1863, 618–19, 625–26,
647, 661, 724; Johnston to Ewell, February 8, 1863, 630; Seddon
to Johnston, March 3, April 17, 1863, 657–58, 775–76; W. W. Guy
to Johnston, March 9, 1863, 674–75; Banks to Johnston, March
11, 1863, 680; Banks to Ewell, March 13, 1863, 688–89; Johnston
to Bragg, Johnston to J. F. Gilmer, March 6, 1863, 663.

than that of raids on the enemy's communications, it was no less important in holding the Confederate position in middle Tennessee.

3

FEDERAL EFFORTS AGAINST VICKSBURG AT THIS time consisted of attempts to outflank the city by water. Four distinct routes were considered: either to get below Vicksburg by a canal or a bayou route west of the Mississippi or to approach from the north via two bayou and river routes east of the Mississippi. While Grant had little faith in them himself and they were all unsuccessful, this multiplicity of efforts was perplexing and often alarming to Pemberton and kept him constantly at work to thwart each of them. Pemberton's dispatches necessarily reflected the variety and confusing nature of Grant's operations, but his communications were neither numerous nor voluminous even to Richmond, much less to his distant superior in Chattanooga. After his first alarming message while Johnston was on his way to Bragg's headquarters in January, there is evidence of only three or four messages to Johnston until the beginning of March. As Johnston wrote Davis, Pemberton was certainly "not communicative." Perhaps the fact that the President was "sorry to learn" that Johnston did not have "as full communication from General Pemberton as is desirable" was relayed to Pemberton. Either because of the President's feeling or because of a query from Johnston which began: "The

Newspapers say . . . ," Pemberton became more communicative in March.

While available information from Mississippi did not indicate an immediate threat to Vicksburg, the possibility of a canal bypassing the city alarmed Johnston. This, together with a suggestion by the President that a visit by him to Mississippi might be helpful, undoubtedly persuaded him of the desirability of remedying his ignorance of the situation there by a personal inspection. A secondary reason for making the trip was undoubtedly the reported inefficient state of Pemberton's command. Though Pemberton's disputes with the railroads, mismanagement and waste of subsistence stores, and lack of discipline on the part of his troops were undoubtedly known to Johnston, he probably did not intend to take any drastic action himself against the President's appointee. Rather he hoped to have Davis do so. For this reason Johnston urged him to have an inspection made of Pemberton's department by one of the President's own aides so that Davis could have the facts from his own sources. Nothing came of this effort, however.

Equally important as his desire for an up-to-date estimate of the situation and his concern over Pemberton's management of his department was Johnston's wish to make a trip to Vicksburg to ascertain the possibility of co-operation between his department and that of the Trans-Mississippi. While he no longer anticipated combining the forces of Mississippi and Arkansas for an offensive, nor even obtaining reinforcements from across the river, he did look for combined operations on each side of the river or at least a diversion from the forces on the far side. His hopes in his old plan had been revived by the transfer to the command of the Trans-Mississippi of his friend and old subordinate, Kirby Smith, in whose military ability and judgment he had great confidence. While he did not expect much at this time due to the high state of the water in the river, he evidently wanted to make his views known to Kirby Smith and encourage him to take any measures he could.

General Kirby Smith had also been told by Seddon, before he left Richmond to take up his new duties, "that the most important operations" in his department would be "aiding in the defense of the lower Mississippi." Though Pemberton and Kirby Smith corresponded in an effort to co-operate, lack of men, crises in his own department, and other difficulties prevented Kirby Smith from ever doing more for the defense of Vicksburg than providing supplies. This hope, if not expectation, on Johnston's part contributed to his decision early in March to go to Mississippi. It was perhaps a propitious time to go for, in spite of the enemy's activity, Johnston and Bragg had come to the conclusion that he would not attack before the latter part of March, the state of the rivers and roads not permitting.[6]

[6] Sanger, "Some Problems Facing Joseph E. Johnston," *loc. cit.,* 267, 270–72; Johnston to Wigfall, March 4, 1863, Wigfall Papers; *O. R.,* Ser. I: XXIV, Part 3—Johnston to Pemberton, February 4, 8, March 2, 5, 6, 15, 1863, 615, 634, 649, 653–54, 670; XXIII, Part 2—Pemberton to Johnston, February 6, 9, 1863, 618, 643; Johnston to Davis, February 12, 1863, 633; Davis to Johnston, February 19, 1863, 641; Bragg to Ewell, February 27, 1863, 653; Wheeler to Kinloch Falconer, March 7, 1863, 668; Polk to Johnston, February 25, 1863, 649; LII, Part 2—Pemberton to Johnston, February 24, 1863, 421; Davis to Johnston, March 6, 1863, 430–31; XXIV, Part 2—Seddon to Johnston, February 14, 1863, 625; XXII, Part 2—Seddon to Kirby Smith, March 18, 1863, 802–803; XV— Kirby Smith to Pemberton, April 19, 20, 1863, 1046–47; XIV, Part 3—Taylor to Pemberton, February 20, 1863, 635; E. Surget to W. S. Lovell, March 21, 1863, 638.

4

JOHNSTON'S VISIT WITH BRAGG'S ARMY AND HIS trip to east Tennessee had undoubtedly given him a clearer picture of the problems and necessities of his department. His view of the importance of holding Tennessee was strongly reinforced, and his conviction grew that the value and importance of maintaining the present Confederate position in middle and east Tennessee was not properly appreciated by the authorities in Richmond. Johnston thought that the "government sees with Lee's eyes," and to those in Richmond the "near danger appears to be much greater than the distant one." Convinced of the importance of this area he labored to strengthen it. He succeeded in having the conscripts from Mississippi diverted to Bragg and sought to prevent sick leaves. A much more important source of manpower was a bureau established by Bragg to bring in volunteers and conscripts and return deserters and stragglers. Bragg was undoubtedly correct in describing Brigadier General Gideon J. Pillow, his appointee, to head the bureau, as in "a place fit for him, and a place he so exactly fits." For General Pillow's "energy and vigorous system" increased the army by 9,400 men—twenty-five per cent—in a little over a month.

In addition to these efforts, Johnston sought to secure reinforcements from beyond the department through appeals to Richmond, both official and unofficial, and by means of approaching the adjacent department commander, General Samuel Jones, in southwestern Virginia. Johnston's constant stressing of the importance of Tennessee, of Bragg's weakness relative to the heavily reinforced Rosecrans, and his appeals for men from the East produced no help for Bragg. More effective was his argument that, since Federal troops from southwestern Virginia had joined Rosecrans, Confederate troops from the same area should reinforce Bragg. The logic of this argument persuaded Seddon and Davis to direct Major General Samuel Jones and Brigadier General Humphrey Marshall in southwestern Virginia to assist by means of a diversion into eastern Kentucky. Orders from Richmond became involved with local arrangements, arrived at by means of direct negotiations among General Donelson and the two officers in southwestern Virginia. On one occasion Secretary Seddon, finding arrangements already made and Marshall himself at Donelson's headquarters, bowed out of the picture saying that he did not "intend to interfere with any movement" ordered by General Donelson.[7]

[7] *Ibid.:* XXIII, Part 2—Johnston to Polk, March 3, 1863, 659; Johnston to Seddon, January 28, February 25, March 2, 1863, 618, 646–47, 656; W. P. Johnston to Davis, April 15, 1863, 757–61; Seddon to Marshall, March 3, 1863, 660; Donelson to Johnston, March 1, 1863, 655; Donelson to Jones, March 1, 1863, 655–56; Donelson to Ewell, March 4, 1863, 661; Seddon to Donelson, March 4, 1863, 662; XX, Part 2—Johnston to Cooper, January 12, 16, 17, 1863, 495, 498, 449; XXIV, Part 3—*id.* to *id.*, March 3, 1863, 652; LII, Part 2—Campbell to Johnston, January 19, 1863, 410; Bragg to Davis, February 23, 1863, 426; Johnston to Beverly R. Johnston, May 7, 1863, R. M. Hughes, "Some War Letters of General Joseph E. Johnston," *Journal of the Military Service Institute of the United States,* L (May–June, 1912), 319–20.

Thus Johnston had to rely almost entirely upon the resources of his own area for its defense. In spite of his appeals to Richmond, he realized this and made his plans accordingly. While expressing the hope of taking the offensive and re-entering Kentucky in the spring, he was really fearful of an advance by Rosecrans' army, which he estimated at twice the strength of Bragg's. He anticipated that Bragg would prove strong enough to hold against a frontal attack, and in the much more likely event of an effort being made to flank him, an opportunity would be presented for attacking Rosecrans. He seemed to regard Bragg's position as not only more precarious but as more important than that of Pemberton and feared that the Federals, stymied temporarily in Mississippi, might reinforce Rosecrans. If Rosecrans, with or without reinforcements from Grant, succeeded in driving Bragg over the mountains, Johnston thought the Confederate situation would be critical.

Though he had made arrangements for the fortification of Chattanooga, he thought east Tennessee, because of its geography, indefensible even if the Confederate army could be subsisted there, which he doubted. But the loss of east Tennessee itself was of secondary importance. The capability for strategic movement which would thus be opened by the Union army was enormous. While Johnston did not now regard it as practical for Rosecrans to advance into Virginia, he could "move into Georgia, or cross the Tennessee and co-operate with Grant in Mississippi." The latter was more serious, as the Tennessee River would give the enemy a secure supply line, while in any advance into Georgia, Johnston thought that for supplies the Federal army "could not depend upon the long line of the railroad between Nashville and Atlanta." It was undoubtedly these possible consequences which caused Johnston to place such a high valuation upon the Confederate position in middle Tennessee.

The threat to Bragg and middle Tennessee, with its ominous consequences, was to be met by reinforcement from adjacent departments. The forces of the Department of East Tennessee and those in southwestern Virginia were either to aid Bragg or create a diversion in his favor, and troops from Pemberton's department were to be rushed by rail to Bragg's assistance. While Johnston retained his doubts about the feasibility of this distant army aiding Bragg, he had secured permission from the President for the return of Stevenson's division and had definitely incorporated this move into his plans. Seeking to reduce the time necessary for the transfer, he directed Pemberton to station some of his troops at Jackson and Meridian, Mississippi, so as to have a start on the long railway trip to Tullahoma.[8]

His concern for the protection of middle Tennessee did not mean that Johnston was ignoring the safety of Mississippi. Undoubtedly he felt easier about Vicksburg at this time than he did about Bragg's army. Evidently some of Pemberton's confidence that 100,000 men could not take Vicksburg had been communicated to John-

[8] *Ibid.:* XXIII, Part 2—Johnston to Polk, March 3, 1863, 659–60; Johnston to Seddon, February 25, March 2, 1863, 647, 656; Polk to Johnston, February 25, 1863, 649–50; Donelson to Johnston, March 1, 1863, 655; XX, Part 2—Johnston to Cooper, January 12, 1863, 495; Johnston to Kirby Smith, December 31, 1863, 473; LII, Part 2—James Nocquet to Johnston, January 26, 1863, 417; Davis to Johnston, January 8, 1863, 404; XVII, Part 2—Johnston to Davis, January 6, 1863, 827; Johnston to Wigfall, March 4, 1863, Wigfall Papers.

ston. Also the "skill and vigor" of Pemberton's operations against Sherman at the end of December contributed to his confidence. He did not fear another overland advance by Grant until the spring, and if it came, he thought that it could again be defeated by a cavalry attack on the Federal communications. For such an eventuality the cavalry force of Van Dorn was in an admirable position in the area around Columbia, Tennessee, to move rapidly into either northern Mississippi or western Tennessee. His primary concern seems to have been fear that Grant, via the canal in progress or by some other means, might get below Vicksburg and surround either it or Port Hudson. If this happened, Pemberton's forces were still too scattered to be concentrated rapidly enough, and one or the other of these essential strongholds would be invested without sufficient force being available to break the seige. He evidently hoped that, if co-operation from the Trans-Mississippi could be secured in time, Federal efforts to pass below Vicksburg could be obstructed.

So Johnston's plans for the defense of the Mississippi envisaged co-operation from Kirby Smith across the Mississippi and the utilization of Van Dorn's cavalry to block any overland advance or reinforce the area rapidly. He felt Bragg too weak and too far away to provide any assistance other than that of the interdepartmental cavalry force. The dispersed nature of Pemberton's forces, together with the danger of Grant's getting below Vicksburg, must have worried Johnston and were motives for his projected visit to Mississippi. He was not too optimistic, however, about changing things. His theory of command forbade him from ordering Pemberton's dispositions from a distance, and, in all probability, not only did he not fully realize the potentialities of the telegraph, but Pemberton's messages, usually unevaluated information rather than intelligence, would have made long-distance control quite difficult. He definitely felt that the man selected by the President for that particular post, who not only shared the views of the President as to its defense but also "had studied and learned the situation," could not and should not be told how to run his department. Apparently his experience in previous disagreements with General Pemberton indicated to him that Pemberton was not going to follow the guidance as to strategy and dispositions which he would give, particularly when Pemberton knew that Davis probably agreed with his concept of the defense. If, in person, he could persuade Pemberton of the efficacy of his ideas of keeping a field army concentrated, it would be valuable. But if he ordered Pemberton to change his arrangements and plan of operations to suit his "own ideas, the enemy might interrupt me," and "Pemberton, when again left in command, would naturally go back to his own system."

This desire to confer with Pemberton and "reach the state of things in the department" of Mississippi and eastern Louisiana and personally to "correspond with Lieutenant-General Kirby Smith, to ascertain if any of his troops" could "operate against the enemy's forces" which menaced Pemberton on the Mississippi, decided Johnston to make a trip which would enable him to complete his inspection of the defenses of Mobile and canvass the supply situation throughout his entire department. He must have left with some misgivings as the second "confidential" letter from Secretary Seddon had just arrived, and he naturally feared that the President entertained the idea of removing Bragg.

He had hardly departed when, on March 9, 1863, instructions were received in Chattanooga for Johnston to order General Bragg to report to the War Department "for conference." Johnston was himself to assume "direct charge of the army in middle Tennessee." Johnston did not allow this second interruption to cut short his visit in Mobile, for he did not reach Chattanooga until March 17 nor Bragg's headquarters until the nineteenth. He had prepared the way for his assumption of command by having the War Department send to Bragg a copy of the telegram sent to him.[9]

[9] *O. R.*, Ser. I: XXIV, Part 2—Memorandum, Van Dorn and Price, Grenada, Mississippi, January 23, 1863, 596–97; Johnston to Davis, January 2, 1863, 823; Part 3—Johnston to Pemberton, March 15, 1863, 670; XXIII, Part 2—*id.* to *id.*, March 12, 1863, 685; Johnston to Davis, February 12, 1863, 633; Seddon to Johnston, March 9, 1863, 674; Seddon to Bragg, March 16, 1863, 698; XVII, Part 2—Johnston to Pemberton, January 11, 26, 1863, 832, 605; LII, Part 2—*id.* to *id.*, May 5, 1863, 467; Ewell to Seddon, March 9, 1863, 432; Hughes, *General Johnston,* 167; Hay, "Confederate Leadership at Vicksburg," *loc. cit.,* 559; Johnston to Wigfall, March 4, 1863, Wigfall Papers.

Chapter Ten

Realization of Departmental Planning

1

Upon his arrival at Bragg's headquarters in Tullahoma, Tennessee, on March 19, General Johnston found that General Bragg was absent in Winchester, Tennessee, at the bedside of Mrs. Bragg who was ill with typhoid fever. Reporting this to Richmond, he said that he would not order Bragg to the War Department for this reason. Having already indicated his desire for Bragg to be retained, he pointed out that, since the country was "becoming practicable" for military operations, were the enemy to advance General Bragg would be "indispensable" in middle Tennessee. Johnston assumed command of Bragg's army unofficially without announcing it in any orders nor, out of consideration for Bragg, communicating to him his orders to go to Richmond.

Oddly enough, Johnston received no response from Richmond to this communication. He continued to exercise Bragg's command until his health, already poor, became so bad in April that he felt himself unable to command an army properly. He communicated this fact to the President in one of his regular letters, stating that Bragg's presence was therefore necessary in Tennessee to command the army. Apparently General Bragg was already available for duty again, but Johnston was awaiting additional instructions which never came. He suggested that if a conference with Bragg was still desired, then might not "a confidential officer" visit him for the purpose in Tennessee? To this suggestion, made again to Seddon on April 28, no response is recorded. Johnston apparently waited throughout the month of April and into May for some official response. Although Richmond seemed to have let the matter drop, Johnston thought that he was compelled to remain at Bragg's headquarters, though he wished to leave.[1]

Johnston's incapacity may have prevented Bragg being ordered to Richmond. On the other hand, it may have been the last unsuccessful effort of Secretary Seddon to put Johnston in Bragg's place by getting Bragg to Richmond and then diverting him elsewhere. While Johnston's relations with Seddon remained official and devoted almost entirely to the question of supplies, those with Davis consisted of a cordial exchange of letters in which each confided his views to the other. The President and his western commander enjoyed a harmonious correspondence, keeping each other informed and discussing strategy and reinforcements, while Johnston corresponded with Seddon and Cooper on the day-to-day questions of troop movements, sup-

[1] *O. R.*, Ser. I: XXIII, Part 2—Johnston to Seddon, March 12, 19, April 28, 1863, 684, 708, 799; Bragg to Ewell, March 18, 1863, 706; W. P. Johnston to Davis, April 15, 1863, 757; Johnston to Davis, April 10, 1863, 745; T. B. Lamar to Pemberton, April 7, 1863, 743; Hughes to T. R. Hay, July 29, 1924, Hughes Papers.

plies, and the latest intelligence of the enemy. It was to the Secretary of War and the Adjutant and Inspector General that Johnston's occasional sharp and critical comments were directed.

2

THOUGH HE SUFFERED FROM BAD HEALTH AND severe discomfort on horseback, resulting from his wounds of the previous year, and in spite of regarding himself as obliged to remain in Tullahoma, Johnston now entered on the period of true command in the West. He was able to give his whole attention to the problems of his department and for nearly two months was not interrupted by orders from Richmond.

His old problem of relations to Pemberton continued to plague him. The lack of intelligence from Mississippi, a condition which his abortive trip there was intended to remedy, continued to be a problem. He was probably unaware, however, of the degree to which Pemberton slighted him. The fact that Pemberton was seeking, as he wrote Cooper, "to keep General Johnston informed of any movement which may affect his army" indicates that he was doing what he thought necessary. He regarded the distant general at Tullahoma as command-ing the Army of Tennessee and kept him fully informed as to any movement threatening "his army" and any development in which that army could assist his in Mississippi. Almost all intelligence about operations in Mississippi which Johnston received was in either of these two connections. This misconception of Pemberton's was to a degree abetted by Richmond when the War Department would occasionally exercise Johnston's command for him and employ terminology indicating Bragg's army was Johnston's. Pemberton may have thought that, if Johnston was ordered to remain in Tullahoma, then his authority had been restricted to that area.

While Johnston had complained to Davis' aide, Colonel William Preston Johnston, that he was receiving "no intelligence from General Pemberton, who ignores his authority, is mortified at his command over him and received his suggestions with coldness or opposition," nothing was done by the President. After this and earlier complaints, Johnston did nothing more, saying nothing to the President or to Pemberton himself, though had he been fully aware of the latter's attitude, he might well have done more. His ignorance of Pemberton's attitude is indicated by the fact that Johnston was in the habit of forwarding to Richmond most of the intelligence received from Pemberton, obviously unaware that Pemberton was reporting more fully and more frequently to Richmond. Also he was unaware that Pemberton omitted to send him many reports about Federal activity on the Mississippi as they were not pertinent to the Army of Tennessee, thus giving Johnston a false picture of the situation in Mississippi. Hence, while he was not satisfied with Pemberton as a subordinate, he was unaware of the extent to which Pemberton's misapprehension about his position was keeping him in the dark.

One problem of the department about which Johnston thought he could take more positive action was that of the organization of the Department of East Tennessee. He had noted the badly scattered condition of the command and determined to remedy it. His proximity made him feel more at ease about giving orders for redisposition. More important, however, was the fact that, unlike Lieutenant General Pemberton, General Johnston was "greatly superior" in rank to Brigadier General Donelson. So in east Tennessee he had put into execution his concept of defense by directing Donelson to "form a strong reserve" from "his infantry not employed in guarding bridges or keeping the disloyal in subjection." Regarding the bridge defenses, like those of Vicksburg, as "too extensive," he had them reconstructed in order to require only the minimum garrisons. The troops thus concentrated were to be kept "at two or three points near the railroad" which were "selected with reference to movement into Middle Tennessee or toward the gaps in the Cumberland Mountains." Nor was there any difficulty in having his instructions carried out, for the department commander reported early in April that, with a few exceptions, "the entire infantry force of this department can be thrown to the railroad in three hours time."

Having had the infantry in the department concentrated and organized into brigades, he had the cavalry sent into Kentucky in order that they might supply themselves. The cavalry force beyond the mountains in Kentucky had the additional purpose of collecting "cattle for the army and be in position to learn the enemy's intentions and report them." [2] Thus, east Tennessee was reorganized and placed in position not only to defend itself but to take its place in the general scheme of interdepartmental reinforcement which was gradually evolving.

3

JOHNSTON'S PLANS FOR THE DEFENSE OF HIS theater, and the plans of the President as well, embraced emergency assistance from General Samuel Jones's department in southwestern Virginia. While he had made constant appeals for reinforcement from that quarter and both he and the Richmond authorities had organized diversionary raids into Kentucky with the assistance of General Jones, there had been no positive general instructions to provide assistance if need arose. However, despite frequent changes in leadership in east Tennessee, the commanders of the adjacent departments got together on a program of reinforcement. With the assistance of urgings from the Secretary of War, fellow

[2] *O. R.*, Ser. I: XV, Part 2—Johnston to Cooper, March 13, 1863, 1010; Pemberton to Johnston, March 11, 1863, 1009–10; XXIV, Part 3—*id.* to *id.*, April 17, 28, May 4, 1863, 751, 797, 827; Pemberton to Davis, March 12, 13, April 2, 1863, 663, 665–66, 709; Davis to Pemberton, April 7, May 1, 1863, 718, 807; Cooper to Pemberton, April 18, 20, 1863, 760, 767; Pemberton to Cooper, April 9, 17, 23, 1863, 739, 751, 778; XXIII, Part 2—W. P. Johnston to Davis, April 15, 1863, 761; Jones, "Joe Johnston's Strategic Problem," *loc. cit.*, 141–42.

Virginians—Samuel Jones in southwestern Virginia and Dabney H. Maury, currently commanding in east Tennessee—reached an agreement for assistance to Maury if he were threatened.

In spite of the difficulty of keeping the cavalry force in position in Kentucky, the capacity of east Tennessee to resist attack had been enhanced, both by providing for assistance from southwestern Virginia and the central cavalry force and by the new dispositions which were to give warning of an attack and permit the concentration of 5,000 infantry at the threatened point. Perhaps more important than increased defensive capabilities was the fact that the infantry was now in a position to come rapidly to the assistance of Bragg's army in middle Tennessee, while, in the absence of the infantry, warning of an enemy advance could be given by the cavalry and assistance would be at hand from General Jones.

Having thus arranged for assistance from Bragg's army from east Tennessee and perhaps indirectly from southwestern Virginia, Johnston continued his efforts to have a positive accretion of force for the army from the East. He asked his friend Senator Wigfall to tell the Secretary of War that "several divisions from Virginia ought to reinforce Bragg." He strengthened the argument by pointing out to the Secretary that the armies of Pemberton and Bragg were "more distant from each other in time than Eastern Virginia and Middle Tennessee." At the same time he reiterated the argument already made that, if Federal divisions had been moved from Virginia to Tennessee, "the troops which had been opposed to those divisions in Virginia should be sent to General Bragg without delay."

The President. who had previously expressed a desire to reinforce middle Tennessee when "practicable," must have raised Johnston's hopes when he announced that he would "endeavor to send a few troops" from the East. But an end was put to the hope, if not to Johnston's requests, when Davis said that, though "General Lee concurred . . . in an anxious desire to send" reinforcements and had "looked to and hoped for a condition of things . . . which might enable him to detach a corps for service in the West," no troops from Virginia would be sent due to "unexpected activity" by the enemy there. Though he hoped after Chancellorsville as after Fredericksburg that General Lee might supply something for the West, he heard nothing encouraging. The failure of the naval assault against Charleston, South Carolina, may have combined with Johnston's pleas to suggest to Seddon that General Beauregard might be able to spare some men. But, when finally underway, the project of sending them to middle Tennessee was interrupted by a more pressing necessity—a grave threat to Vicksburg in May, 1863.

While General Johnston obviously did not believe that Bragg's army could give up any infantry, he contemplated its aiding the adjacent departments with its large cavalry force. He thought that the difficulty of supplying an army invading east Tennessee would force it to bring its own supplies, thus making its supply trains an attractive and vulnerable target for cavalry. Even if the enemy occupied east Tennessee, cavalry, breaking communications, might well force withdrawal. Having Brigadier General John H. Morgan's large brigade particularly in mind, he intended that part of

Bragg's cavalry should be used to help east Tennessee in this way.

While the forces of the Gulf (now dignified by the title Department of the Gulf) were meager, its small force of cavalry assisted General Pemberton in northern Mississippi, even though the department was subject to the jurisdiction of General Bragg. It is not clear whether this co-operation was entirely due to arrangements between the respective commanders, Pemberton and Major General Simon Bolivar Buckner, or whether General Johnston instructed Buckner on the subject. Johnston did, however, have a role for Buckner's 3,000 infantry to play in his plan for reinforcing General Bragg.

In order to overcome the already demonstrated obstacle of the great amount of time consumed in transferring troops between Mississippi and Tennessee, Johnston intended that part of Pemberton's reinforcements should be at Jackson and Meridian in order to be partially along the way to Tennessee, yet within easy reach of the Vicksburg area. This was to be extended to include the infantry at Mobile. In the event that rapid reinforcement would be necessary, the troops at Mobile were to start to Tennessee to be replaced, if necessary, by the last troops to leave Mississippi. This was similar to the manner in which Bragg had moved his main body from northern Mississippi during the summer of 1862 and may have been suggested by Bragg. Thus Johnston hoped to expedite the transfer of forces from Mississippi to middle Tennessee by having the "pipeline" half full before the movement began. This would give him some of the advantages of President Davis' suggestion of stationing Stevenson's division in the center of the department at either Meridian or Selma, without having the disadvantage of any troops being removed from a possible scene of action.

Misgivings about Pemberton's dispositions which he could not correct, feeling as he did that he could not give orders when he was so far away, and the fact that the condition of Pemberton's command, especially quartermaster affairs and troop discipline, was "far less satisfactory than that of General Bragg's troops," undoubtedly made Johnston uneasy. However, when Pemberton described the batteries which he had established to block the exit from the Federal canal then in progress, Johnston expressed satisfaction at the "activity and vigor in the defense of the Mississippi" displayed by Pemberton. This degree of confidence that Pemberton could "maintain himself" on the river front was shared by the President. In addition, both Pemberton and Richmond authorities were in agreement with Johnston's hope that the capable new commander of the Department of the Trans-Mississippi would be able to co-operate in the defense of the river.[3] There must

[3] *Ibid.*, 142–43; Johnston to Wigfall, March 4, 1863, Wigfall Papers; *O. R.*, Ser. I: XXIII, Part 2—Johnston to Seddon, March 2, 12, 1863, 656, 684–85; Davis to Johnston, March 16, April 6, 1863, 713, 740; Johnston to Davis, March 16, April 6, 1863, 713, 740; Johnston to Dabney H. Maury, May 8, 1863, 824; Johnston to Pemberton, April 11, 1863, 734; W. P. Johnston to Davis, April 15, 1863, 761; LII, Part 2—Davis to Johnston, January 8, March 6, 1863, 404, 431; XVII, Part 2—Johnston to Davis, January 2, 1863, 823; XIV—Seddon to Beauregard, May 2, 1863, 923; XXIV, Part 3—Pemberton to Buckner, March 24, 1863, 687; R. W. Memminger to Ruggles, April 10, 1863, 733; Johnston to Pemberton, January 23, March 5, 15, 23, April 27, 1863, 597, 653, 670, 685–86, 791; Pemberton to Johnston, March 6, 14, April 18, 1863, 654, 688–89, 760; XXII, Part 2—Seddon to Kirby Smith, March 18,

have seemed to Johnston little more to be done about Mississippi, either in respect to increasing the force there or, from his headquarters at Tullahoma, of altering the system of the defense. Pemberton's success in repelling every Federal advance up to that point must have offset, to a degree, concern over his dispositions, the state of his army, and his lack of communicativeness.

Thus, in summary, Johnston's departmental plans for defense envisaged co-operation with the adjacent departments for his central and most menaced army in middle Tennessee. He had arranged for assistance to come to Bragg's aid from northeast and southwest and had so organized things that this aid could come more rapidly than heretofore. While no central reserve had been provided, the half-filled pipeline from Mississippi to Tennessee partially filled this role. In a sense, also, a pipeline was filled from southwestern Virginia in that, if troops from east Tennessee should aid Bragg, their places might be taken by contingents from southwestern Virginia. On the other hand, the defense of the peripheral departments was to be aided by the great concentration of cavalry at the center which could strike in either direction against an advancing enemy.

Johnston was naturally reticent about his plans, and after his experience of hearing his own most secret plans from an unauthorized person whose hearing was defective, he thought that the personnel of the Rich-

1863, 802–803; XV—Pemberton to Kirby Smith, April 18, 22, 1863, 1045, 1049–50; Kirby Smith to Pemberton, April 15, 19, 20, 1863, 1042, 1046, 1047; Returns, Department of the Gulf, February, May, 1863, 1001, 1068.

mond government was insufficiently security-conscious. He had stressed constantly to the President and the Secretary of War the difficulty, if not the impossibility, of co-ordinating the forces in Tennessee and Mississippi. These factors together would have prevented him from revealing to Richmond more than parts of these arrangements. Moreover, Johnston certainly never thought of these plans as a unified whole, but rather as a collection of specific measures contemplated to meet a number of particular contingencies. What he had done in the planning phase, nevertheless, was what he had been sent west to accomplish and had himself said could not be done.

4

THOUGH JOHNSTON'S PLANS FOR DEFENSE WERE fairly complete and, due to his weakness, he contemplated no offensive unless reinforced, he did make plans for the contingency of defeat. Again his attention centered on the critical area of middle Tennessee. He was fairly confident that Bragg's army could maintain its position if Rosecrans attacked without reinforcements. The Confederates were disposed more south than southeast of the Union position at Murfreesborough, in order to cover the area from which they drew their supplies. While this position made their left flank quite secure, it kept them off the direct line between the Union army and its objective—Chattanooga. For the same reason they were vulnerable to being outflanked on their right. Should the enemy pursue this most likely line of action, Johnston and Bragg thought that, if only a part of Rosecrans' army attempted it, either part of the divided forces might be successfully attacked, while the flank of the whole Union army would be vulnerable to attack on a flank march. Even if Rosecrans should succeed in a flanking movement with his whole army, Bragg could "exchange bases with him very advantageously," as his supplies were drawn from south of Murfreesborough already.

If Rosecrans' army were reinforced, however, Bragg's would be forced to yield to any advance, as the Federal army would be strong enough to threaten the Confederate communications while maintaining in front a force too strong to be attacked. Should the Confederates be thus compelled to abandon middle Tennessee, unpleasant alternatives were foreseen by Johnston. If the army should take up a position at Chattanooga, the lack of forage in east Tennessee and northern Georgia would not only make it necessary for the cavalry to be separated from the army, but it was even "doubtful if forage for a reasonable baggage train" would be available. It would be unlikely, therefore, that the army, weakened by the loss of its cavalry, would be able to hold an area as weak defensively as Johnston regarded east Tennessee. The indicated course would then be to withdraw south of the Tennessee River and defend east Tennessee and Georgia from there.

The alternative to this line would be to take the army into northern Mississippi, possibly occupying also part of western Tennessee. The movement there "would be attended with great risk," due to the lack of supplies en route through a country now held by the enemy as well as the difficulty of crossing the unbridged Tennessee River on the way. While supply difficulties were contemplated there also, and the presence of strong Federal forces at Corinth, Mississippi, complicated matters, there were compensating advantages. Not only would the Army of Tennessee be able to co-operate with Pemberton's army in Mississippi and draw reinforcements from it, but in that region of more plentiful forage the cavalry could be kept with the army. From this position Johnston thought that the army might be able to recross the Tennessee River in order to prevent any invasion of east Tennessee or to defend northern Georgia. Its position would, of course, be most advantageous if Rosecrans' army should, instead of marching toward Atlanta, come to Grant's assistance.

Johnston thought the retreat of the army into northern Mississippi was the preferable alternative, especially as he believed that the communications of any Federal advance on Atlanta would be very vulnerable and the Mississippi location of the army would best defend against the other major Union alternative, aiding Grant in Mississippi. He made his arrangements accordingly. He had earlier set on foot efforts to obtain pontoons, and now instructed General Pemberton to have his supply organization provide depots of supplies on or near the railway running north from Meridian to Corinth, Mississippi. While Pemberton said that these arrangements were under way, Johnston sent agents of his own departmental supply organization into the area to establish depots so, presumably, as not to have to rely in an emergency on Pemberton's supposedly deficient subsistence organization.

Johnston's departmental organization, which embraced plans for supply, reinforcements, and the contingencies of defeat, also included defense through deception by means of planted stories in the press. In order "to halt or delay any proposed attack on Bragg," misleading reports of Bragg's strength were placed not only in the press but into Federal intelligence channels through intercepted messages. One letter, intercepted by the Federals, exclaimed over Bragg's cavalry and described "a grand review of the army" at which the troops were reviewed by General Johnston, and 60,000 infantry—nearly double Bragg's actual strength in infantry—"marched in the grandest order before that old chieftain."

Insofar as his own efforts could affect the situation, General Johnston had probably prepared the Department of the West as well as possible for the test of the Union spring campaign and had certainly well represented its deficiencies and necessities to Richmond. While his plan to establish himself in the center of his department with headquarters at Montgomery, Alabama, was frustrated by the necessity of remaining in Tullahoma and his health made him unfit for field service, he was in most other respects as well prepared as he could expect to be.[4] He was resasonably satisfied

[4] *Ibid.*: XXIII, Part 2—Johnston to Cooper, April 6, 1863, 741; Johnston to Davis, April 10, 1863, 745–46; Johnston to Polk, March 3, 1863, 659–60; Johnston to Seddon, April 28, 1863, 799; Johnston to Ewell, February 8, 1863, 730; Banks to Johnston, April 23, 1863, 786–87; J. P. Baltzell to "Dearest Friend," April 11, 1863, 750–51; T. B. Lamar to Pemberton, April 7, 1863, 743; XXIV, Part 3—Johnston to Pemberton (letter and telegram), April 11, 1863, 734; Pemberton to Johnston, April 13, 20, 1863, 739, 768; Sanger, "Some Problems facing Joseph E. Johnston," *loc. cit.*, 282–83.

with the state of his command with the exception of
Mississippi, which condition he felt himself, rightly and
wrongly, powerless to alter.

5

SINCE THE BEGINNING OF MARCH THERE HAD
been Federal activity in northern Mississippi and on
the Tennessee River which had caused anxiety as to
whether it was intended as an overland advance against
Vicksburg, as a flanking movement against Bragg, or as
reinforcement for Rosecrans. Though Secretary Seddon
was quite alarmed in early March, Johnston was not
particularly concerned at that time, for he thought
that any movement was going to be directed against
Bragg and that it would not be begun until the country
in front of Rosecrans' army was suitable for a co-
operating advance by his army.

At the beginning of April, however, Johnston became
more and more concerned. A report came in which it
was indicated that Grant's troops might be in the
process of being withdrawn from before Vicksburg to
advance up the Tennessee River to get in the rear of
Bragg. Johnston instructed Pemberton that, if he
thought that Rosecrans was being reinforced, he was
immediately to dispatch Stevenson's division or an equal
number of men to Tullahoma. Indications of withdrawal from the Mississippi and movement east toward

Bragg became stronger as the month wore on. Finally, as "intelligence from Louisville, Nashville, and Memphis" indicated that "Grant's army may join that of Rosecrans," Johnston notified Buckner in Mobile of the plan, explaining that, if Pemberton should decide Grant was actually reinforcing Rosecrans, he would be notified by Pemberton who would be sending troops to Bragg. When he heard from Pemberton, Buckner was to send his infantry "as expeditiously as possible" to Tullahoma. Since they would start before Pemberton's reinforcements, they "could easily keep the lead." To Pemberton he sent co-ordinating instructions and suggested "placing a brigade at Jackson and another at Meridian."

Hardly had these arrangements been made when a message was received from Pemberton with a scout's report even more conclusive that Grant was going to Rosecrans' assistance. Pemberton announced that he was collecting troops at Jackson and could "send 4,000 at once, if absolutely necessary." Johnston responded, ordering the 4,000 men "immediately" and directing Pemberton to "prepare more troops for movement." Then a telegram arrived from Pemberton announcing that he was "satisfied Rosecrans will be reinforced from Grant's army" and was forwarding "about 8,000 men" as "fast as transportation can be furnished." But the troops which began the journey from Mississippi were not followed by more, as Pemberton began to have doubts four days later, on April 16, and thought that "no large part of Grant's army will be sent away." By the eighteenth the troops in transit, some of whom had got beyond Atlanta, were stopped by General John-

ston and were almost immediately on their way back
to Mississippi. The men from Buckner's department
did, however, reach Tullahoma.

While Johnston was uncertain for a day or two longer,
it soon became apparent that all the Federal activity
was intended to confuse the Confederates as to their real
objectives and to cover cavalry raids into Mississippi
and northern Alabama. The ensuing two and a half
weeks at the Tullahoma command post were confused
by conflicting reports and misleading intelligence, and
the situation was aggravated by the unrealized lack of
essential information from the critical area of operations, Mississippi, where Grant's major effort was at
last in progress. Grant was in the process, during the
last two weeks in April, of passing gunboats and transports past the Vicksburg batteries to meet his army
which had gone below the city on the west side of the
river. Then he was in a position to cross his army over
the river between Vicksburg and Port Hudson and
march to the rear of the Vicksburg defenses.

While Grant's operations were in progress, Johnston
was alarmed by repeated reports of an impending invasion of east Tennessee by the reinforced Union army
in Kentucky. In addition, the continued presence of
Union troops in northeastern Mississippi and northwestern Alabama absorbed his attention. Much more
important, however, was the fact that most of the communication and all of the co-operation with Pemberton
related to the cavalry raids in his department. They
exchanged intelligence, and Johnston sought to aid
him with 3,000 cavalry from Bragg's army, but they
were unable to reach Mississippi, being "employed"
by the Federal expedition from Corinth which was

still interposed between Bragg's and Pemberton's armies. While Pemberton reported to Richmond the movements of the Federal forces at Vicksburg, most of the intelligence he sent to Johnston related to the cavalry raids and his need for cavalry to meet them.

In the ten-day period, April 18 to 28, Pemberton neither provided Richmond nor Johnston with much information on Grant's activities other than lists of the Union vessels which had succeeded in passing the Vicksburg batteries and were in the river between Vicksburg and Port Hudson. Then the picture changed. Johnston learned on April 28 that the enemy was below Vicksburg on the west bank of the river opposite the Confederate position at Grand Gulf, and the next day Pemberton informed him that there was "very heavy firing," but it was not known whether the enemy had landed on the east side of the river. In response to the news on May 1 of the "furious battle" on the east bank and the opinion that Grant could cross over his whole army, Johnston suggested: "If Grant's army lands on this side of the river, the safety of Mississippi depends on beating it. For that object you should unite your whole force." The following day he instructed Pemberton that, "If Grant crosses, unite all your troops and beat him. Success will give you back what was abandoned to win it." [5]

[5] Jones, "Joe Johnston's Stategic Problem," *loc. cit.*, 145–46; *O. R.*, Ser. I: XXIII, Part 2—Johnston to Cooper, April 13, 28, 1863, 751, 799; Maury to Ewell, April 27, May 5, 1863, 798, 819; XXIV, Part 1—Johnston to Cooper, May 1, 1863, 214; Part 3—Ewell to Pemberton, April 20, 1863, 769; Johnston to Pemberton, April 23, 27, May 1, 2, 1863, 778, 791, 808, 815; Pemberton to Johnston, April 20, 27, 28, 29, May 1, 5, 1863, 769–70, 791, 797, 802, 808, 833; Pemberton to Cooper, April 20, 1863, 767–68; LII, Part 2—Johnston to Davis, April 30, 1863, 463.

With his cavalry still blocked, there was little that Johnston could do for Pemberton other than these general instructions which were, of course, by no means new to Pemberton. Johnston also inquired about Kirby Smith, saying: "Now is his time to co-operate." Johnston relayed Pemberton's reports to General Cooper and called for reinforcements from the East. To President Davis Johnston said that, though Pemberton asked for reinforcements, nothing beyond the cavalry could be sent from Bragg "without giving up Tennessee." Thus Johnston stood firm in his belief that Bragg could spare no infantry and was unaware that continued difficulties prevented the Tennessee cavalry from reaching Mississippi. Secretary Seddon, on the strength of these reports, obtained reinforcements from Beauregard in Charleston, which were promply dispatched to Vicksburg.

While Pemberton was describing to Richmond Grant's success in crossing over the bulk of his army and receiving instructions in turn, Johnston remained unaware that Grant's army had crossed the river and for nearly a week received no intelligence from Pemberton except that which related to operations in northern Mississippi. Finally, after twice asking the result of the "furious fight" reported on May 1 and the location of Grant's army, Johnston required Pemberton to inform him of the location of his troops, "number, and places, in cipher." The dispositions arrived the following day, May 7, along with the information that the "furious fight" had been lost. But this message still did not make it clear to Johnston that Grant's main army had crossed the river, for he replied, indicating that he regarded the dispositions as "judicious," since the forces "could be readily concentrated against Grant's Army."

Grant's alarming progress, of which Richmond was well-informed, had produced vigorous responses in the War Department, and so, on May 9, 1863, Johnston's career as the commander of the Department of the West in effect came to an abrupt end when the Secretary of War instructed him to "proceed at once to Mississippi and take chief command of the forces," adding that he should take with him from Bragg's army "3,000 good troops." On arrival he took command of operations, though he was "too late," for Federal troops were between him and Pemberton with the main army.[6] He remained in Mississippi, directing the unsuccessful efforts to relieve Vicksburg, into which Pemberton had withdrawn with more than 30,000 men, until the city finally fell to Grant's unrelenting seige on July 4, 1863.

6

AN ASSESSMENT OF JOHNSTON'S CAREER AS commander of the Department of the West is necessarily

[6] *Ibid.:* XXIV, Part 3—Johnston to Pemberton, May 1, 1863, 808; *id.* to *id.*, May 6 (two telegrams), 8, 1863, 838, 839, 844; Pemberton to Kirby Smith, May 1, 9, 1863, 808, 846; Pemberton to Davis, May 2, 3, 1863, 814, 831; Seddon to Pemberton, May 2, 1863, 1815; Beauregard to Pemberton, May 5, 1863, 833; Davis to Pemberton, May 7, 1863, 842; Pemberton to Johnston, May 7, 1863, 842; LII, Part 2—Johnston to Pemberton, May 5, 1863, 467; Ewell

difficult. He was severely handicapped, without positive policy guidance from the President as to the relative merits to the Confederacy of Tennessee and the Mississippi. Without this he could make no major redistribution of forces, had he wished to do so. His planning and preparation for defense and for the contingencies of defeat, as well as his organization and subsistence procurement within the department, entitle him to favorable consideration. It may be that in doing this he did all that was in his power. It is probable that a relatively slow reaction to a Federal offensive, made inevitable by troop transfers on circuitous routes over rickety railroads, was all that was possible for the Department of the West. The maximum potentiality of the department lay when on the offensive, with the initiative in Confederate hands, and the power to concentrate forces utilized.

While Johnston's plan to reinforce the middle Tennessee army proved its efficacy during the false emergency in April, the less extensive plans to aid the Mississippi from Tennessee broke down when the cavalry became involved with an intervening Federal force. In the absence of guidance from Richmond, Johnston decided that the importance of Tennessee and the precarious weakness of the army there precluded its being again weakened in its infantry strength. He could easily have provided for the same system of reinforcement for Mississippi from Tennessee as had been arranged for the movement of troops in the opposite

---

to Bragg, May 16, 1863, 472; Bragg to Ewell, May 16, 1863, 472; XXIV, Part 1—Johnston to Cooper, May 1, 1863, 214, Johnston to Seddon, May 13, 1863, 215; Johnston to Davis, May 1, 1863, 239; XIV—Seddon to Beauregard, May 2, 1863, 923; XXIII, Part 2—Seddon to Johnston, May 9, 1863, 825–26.

direction. Though stressing what to his mind seems to have been the paramount importance of holding Tennessee, Johnston was also holding to a relative certainty. He knew the situation in Tennessee, had confidence in the army and its commander, and thought that with the present balance of forces it could be held. On the other hand, he lacked that confidence and the same clear estimate with respect to the Mississippi. He undoubtedly preferred the bird in the hand.

One difficult problem which Johnston, as a department commander, failed to solve was his relations with Pemberton and his failure to have the forces in Mississippi arranged according to his views as they had been in east Tennessee. He had disagreed with Pemberton's policy in the presence of the President and had little faith in Pemberton's willingness to follow his concept of the operations. Pemberton himself not only had a peculiar idea of Johnston's position, but in his correspondence with Richmond was subject to instructions which conflicted with those from the department commander. Johnston's realization of his unsatisfactory relations with Pemberton seems to have made him fearful, if not resigned, to a disastrous outcome. Commenting on the "gloomy" aspect of affairs on May 7, he thought that Pemberton could not "comprehend that by attempting to defend at all valuable points at once," he exposed "his troops to being beaten everywhere." Johnston, having "urged him to concentrate to fight Grant," told his brother that he had "no hope that he will regard a suggestion of mine, and at this distance one can't give orders."

What faith Johnston placed in the assistance he was going to provide is not clear. He undoubtedly thought that he could defeat an overland advance again with his cavalry and presumably intended to return Pemberton's cavalry in the event he had to fight outside his fortifications. The reliance placed on the projected co-operation from General Kirby Smith in the Trans-Mississippi is not clear, though it may have been considerable. Pemberton had reported that he had had a conference with Kirby Smith and that they would "co-operate when practicable." Pemberton's continued success and usually optimistic reports must have kept the whole problem from ever appearing too pressing.

But should not Johnston have taken action to bring Pemberton into line? He three times complained to the President of Pemberton's lack of compliance and of the state of his army but seems to have taken pains to have had his relations with Pemberton pleasant and free of censure. What he might have done had he paid the contemplated visit in March is problematical. It is unknown how much time he intended to spend in Mississippi or what changes or new ideas he might have had. But he never made the trip, regarding himself as required to remain in Tullahoma. It is doubtful if he considered removing a man "selected" by and enjoying the "confidence" of the President and so decided to make the best of the situation, live with his subordinate, and let him apply his hitherto successful methods. To have sought Pemberton's removal probably would have been useless and would have destroyed his cordial and co-operative relations with the President, which Johnston may have valued more highly than a better man to replace Pemberton. He may have regarded the problem of his relations with

Pemberton as one for the President, "since he was in possession of the facts." [7]

Pemberton's reports supplemented Johnston's regular correspondence with Davis and the topical communications he exchanged with Seddon and Cooper. The President and the War Department were thus provided with a picture of what activity there was in the West, as well as a knowledge of Johnston's problems and many of his views on strategy. Intelligence from the West and Johnston's estimates made a deep impression in Richmond and gave rise to anxiety for the safety of the West.

[7] *Ibid.:* Part 3—Pemberton to Davis, May 3, 1863, 831; Davis to Pemberton, May 7, 1863, 842; Johnston to Pemberton, March 3, May 8, 1863, 652, 884; Pemberton to Johnston, March 6, 1863, 654; Johnston to Pemberton, March 25, May 8, 1863, 685, 844; XV—Pemberton to Franklin Gardner, May 8, 1863, 1080; XX, Part 2—Kirby Smith to Johnston, January 26, 1863, 462–63; XXIII, Part 2—Johnston to Davis, February 12, 1862, 633; W. P. Johnston to Davis, April 15, 1863, 761; LII, Part 2—Davis to Johnston, March 6, 1863, 430–31; Johnston to Beverly R. Johnston, May 7, 1863, Hughes, "Some War Letters of General Joseph E. Johnston," *loc cit.*, L, 319–20; Sanger, "Some Problems Facing Joseph E. Johnston," *loc. cit.*, 271–72. See also Johnston to Davis, January (?), 1863, Hughes, *General Johnston*, 167.

Chapter Eleven

The Gettysburg Decision

1

WHILE PEMBERTON REPORTED THE VARIOUS attempts of Grant's army to reach Vicksburg, his very success in repelling these Union attacks, together with Bragg's difficulties and Johnston's insistent emphasis on the dangers confronting Bragg, focused the attention of Davis and Seddon on middle Tennessee. Not only did the question of the relation of Bragg to his subordinates occupy them, but their concern was gradually more and more engaged by the larger question of the distribution of available Confederate troops. Johnston's expressed opinion that more men were required in both Tennessee and Mississippi broached a question which gradually became more pressing: Was the West strong enough? This was, of course, a relative matter, and the task of the President and the Secretary of War was to move troops from points more secure or stronger, in relation to the enemy, than the West. The areas and forces under examination from this point of view were usually Major General Samuel Jones's forces in south-western Virginia, Lee's army in eastern Virginia and

Beauregard's coastal command, the Department of South Carolina, Georgia and Florida. Active steps in this survey of resources seem to have been largely precipitated by real or apparent crises in the West.

Two measures for aiding Johnston had been tried in February, 1863. The project of providing reinforcements from General Humphrey Marshall's forces in southwestern Virginia did not prove feasible because of his small force of infantry. The effort to have a diversion by Marshall and other forces from southwestern Virginia to compel Rosecrans to divert a part of his force to protect Kentucky seemed also to have failed by early March, for there were reports that Major General Ambrose E. Burnside had left Virginia with a large force from Newport News to go into Kentucky. Just at the time that these measures had failed and it was feared that a part of Burnside's force might go to Rosecrans, the first reports came in of a Federal advance from Memphis and Corinth up the Tennessee River. Johnston did not think this a serious threat because no determined advance would take place until the roads and streams permitted simultaneous co-operating action by Rosecrans. Davis and Seddon took a more serious view.

On March 11 Davis called Lee to Richmond and discussed with him the possibility of sending reinforcements to Johnston. Davis was anxious to increase Bragg's army and reported to Johnston that General Lee had been equally anxious, hoping "for a condition of things, such as the enemy going into winter quarters or the like, which might enable him to detach a corps for service in the West." This March conference with Lee revealed, however, that nothing could be done due to "unexpected activity" by the enemy in Virginia. Yet, as the evidence multiplied that Burnside had gone west by railroad with as many as 20,000 men, the idea of a similar movement of Confederate troops from Virginia made a strong appeal to the President and the Secretary of War. While Johnston urged the logic of a "corresponding movement" by Virginia troops, the President already thought it "indicated." Since Davis had the move "under consideration," Secretary Seddon made arrangements accordingly. He warned General Samuel Jones to be prepared to add a portion of his command to any reinforcements going to Bragg. Though it was "impossible to say positively," if it looked as though Joseph Hooker's Federal army in Virginia would not advance, the President's idea of sending troops from Virginia might "ripen into action."

Exchange of intelligence over Burnside's movement brought General Lee into the picture again. He had remained unconvinced that Burnside had actually gone until his own scout reported that forty-seven trains had carried five divisions west on the Baltimore and Ohio. Lee reported that Hooker's army was undiminished and was "prepared to cross the Rappahannock as soon as the weather permits." He remained convinced of the efficacy of the measures the President had already applied. Though disappointed that Humphrey Marshall's expedition into Kentucky from southwestern Virginia had not caused a diversion of troops from Rosecrans, he hoped that it would yet prevent the reinforcement of Rosecrans by Burnside. For added strength for Bragg, General Lee relied on Johnston's concentrating men from the less menaced parts of the department. These ideas had already been given a trial, but it was found roops. Thus rather than reinforce Bragg from Pemberton's army when Grant sent men to Rosecrans, it was better, since Grant was weakened, for Pemberton "to take the aggressive and to call . . . back" the men sent to Rosecrans. Similarly, not only would "the readiest method of relieving pressure upon General Johnston" be for Lee's "army to cross into Maryland," but "greater relief would in this way be afforded to the armies in middle Tennessee." Furthermore, the Southern climate would soon provide relief and enable reinforcements to be brought from the lower South. The danger of a Federal attack on Charleston was now ended, for the enemy would be able to "accomplish nothing in the interior after May." Since the summer "season shall suspend operations," the "troops in the vicinity of Charleston, Savannah, Mobile, and Vicksburg will not be called in requisition at these places and no more will be necessary than to man the batteries." So not only would men be released from the defense of Charleston but from Vicksburg also, as Grant was withdrawing and would "hardly return to his former position there this summer." Therefore, General Johnston should concentrate these unmolested forces "and use them where they can be most effectively employed." He also advised that, if the Confederates in southwestern Virginia could "by judicious operations occupy General Burnside in Kentucky," it would "relieve General Johnston more than by sending their troops to him."

Of course, Lee had his own problems, too. Lack of forage and subsistence had plagued his army, and supplying this want was the objective of detaching Longstreet to southeastern Virginia. He was trying to get ready to advance by May 1, but the supplies to be

that the small force in east Tennessee was the only force General Johnston had available to reinforce General Bragg. General Lee, in making his second recommendation, did not know that Johnston had reported that the forces at Mobile were almost inconsequential and that Johnston was unwilling to weaken Pemberton, as the troops could not return in time to help were he attacked.[1]

While the President and the Secretary were meditating the possibility of detaching men from Lee's army if the enemy should seem quiescent in Virginia, a crisis forced them into action on April 5. General Johnston forwarded a collection of intelligence reports strongly indicating that a large part of Grant's army was being withdrawn to reinforce Rosecrans. This news impelled Seddon to write Lee telling him of the emergency and explaining that, "after anxiously surveying all the resources at command," the War Department was "unable to find troops at its disposal" unless they were available from his department. Asking for two or three brigades to be added to one from General Jones's department, he reasoned that, though he knew that Lee was "largely outnumbered," Burnside's transfer to the West "should be met by a withdrawal of at least a part" of the "defensive reserves" in Virginia. Seddon

[1] *O. R.*, Ser. I: LII, Part 2—Davis to Johnston, March 6, 1863, 430–31; XXIII, Part 2—*id.* to *id.*, March 16, 20, 1863, 713, 712; Johnston to Davis, March 18, 28, 1863, 713, 726–27; Johnston to Cooper, March 9, April 6, 1863, 674, 741; Seddon to Johnston, March 9, 1863, 674; Johnston to Davis, March 28, April 2, 1863, 726–27, 736; Johnston to Seddon, March 12, 1863, 684–85; LI, Part 2—Davis to Lee, March 10, April 1, 1863, 683, 690; XXV, Part 2—Seddon to Jones, April 1, 1863, 699; Lee to Davis, April 2, 4, 1863, 700–703; XXIV, Part 3—Pemberton to Davis, April 9, 1863, 729–30.

asked Lee's consideration of the project and requested his views.

The firmness of Seddon's and Davis' decision, once taken, is exhibited by the fact that they persisted in spite of an adverse reaction from General Lee. When Seddon originally solicited Lee for reinforcements, they had no knowledge of Johnston's plans to rush troops from Mississippi if Grant reinforced Rosecrans. The War Department was not immediately informed by either Johnston or Pemberton when they set in motion 8,000 men from Mississippi to go to Bragg's assistance, though Johnston and Pemberton had informed General Cooper of their intent to do so. Thus Davis' and Seddon's resolution was strengthened by a sense of crisis, deepened by reports from Johnston that Burnside might be moving against east Tennessee. In the face of what clearly appeared an enormous concentration of Union power against middle Tennessee, the President had Cooper write Lee, reiterating the necessity for help for Bragg and enlarging the request to John B. Hood's or George E. Pickett's division to help provide the 12,000 to 15,000 men needed to insure victory in Tennessee.

The pseudo-crisis was ended by the eighteenth of April when it was clear that Grant had not reinforced Rosecrans and Burnside's advance failed to materialize. Whether for this reason or because of General Lee's arguments and continued opposition, the matter of Virginia troops for Tennessee was dropped. No information concerning these efforts to obtain men was given to General Johnston, nor did he make any report on the reinforcements which had almost reached Bragg from Pemberton, though he had just sent two long

expositions of his strategic views, contingencies accompanying a re Bragg. Pemberton did report that he not until April 17. The President may well have been annoyed at bei fake crisis and thought that they h by Johnston on the significance of th Tennessee.

The request for men made of Ger "reflections" on the subject elicited general observations on Confederate In his letters to Seddon, Cooper, and 1863, Lee advanced two theses about coming year. While he had thought the enemy would stand on the defensiv transfer a part of its forces west for a there, the movement of Burnside wa support this view and, therefore, he t major offensive operations could be Hooker's very powerful army in Virg supported by his second hypothesis t would render active campaigning impos summer in the lower South. To these general principle: that it is "not so easy f troops from one department to another enemy, and if we rely upon that method, be too late."

As a companion to the concept that it to shift troops from one department to a idea that, when the Federal force before army was weakened by sending troops to the best plan was for the Confederate for offensive rather than to try to make a pa

collected by Longstreet were essential for this project, and Longstreet's men, too, were required if the Shenandoah Valley was to be cleared.

Lee's analysis sharply disagreed with one fundamental premise on which the President and the War Department were basing their operations. They had assumed that it was practical and desirable to shift men from one department to another to meet the paramount danger of the moment. In fact, it was on this hypothesis that the whole Department of the West had been founded. Except in the case where Lee thought the climate made operations impractical, he denied the validity of their operating assumption. That they would persist in the future in desiring to transfer troops indicates that they did not accept his view. That the theory about the Southern climate was Lee's own and not subscribed to by the President and the Secretary seems indicated by their failure to dwell on it in their correspondence.

General Lee's predictions that Hooker's large army would advance were realized at the end of April when the Federal army crossed the Rappahannock. With two divisions near Suffolk in southeastern Virginia, too far away to return in time for the battle, Lee was nevertheless able to inflict a severe defeat on Hooker at the battle of Chancellorsville during the first three days of May. Though Longstreet was returning to him, Lee's losses had been severe, and he repeated an earlier appeal for reinforcements. Men should be available from South Carolina as the enemy could do nothing against Charleston in the summer, so "no more can be needed there this summer than enough to man the water batteries. . . . If they are kept in their present positions . . .

they will perish of disease." [2] He was to be disappointed, for troops had already been sent from Beauregard's coastal department, having been first intended for Bragg and then rerouted to meet the emergency caused by Grant's having crossed the river below Vicksburg.

2

THE WAR DEPARTMENT SOON RECEIVED SOME unsolicited advice about what to do about the crisis caused by Grant's army having crossed the Mississippi south of Vicksburg. Lee's able and distinguished corps commander, Lieutenant General James Longstreet, had a plan of his own. His participation in the great defensive victory at Fredericksburg in December, 1862, had already suggested possibilities to Longstreet. In January, 1863, he had suggested to General Lee that half of Lee's army could be sent west to reinforce Bragg, while the other half, utilizing the power of the defense, just observed to be so strong at Fredericksburg, could hold Virginia. The plan was rejected by Lee, but Longstreet retained the desire to go west and either participate in an offensive campaign or have an independent com-

[2] *Ibid.:* XXIII, Part 2—Johnston to Cooper, April 5, 13, 14, 1863, 739, 751–52; XXV, Part 2—Seddon to Lee, April 6, 1863, 708–709; Cooper to Lee, April 14, 1863, 720; Lee to Seddon, April 9, 1863, 713–14; Lee to Davis, April 16, 27, May 7, 1863, 725, 752–53, 782–83; Lee to Cooper, April 16, 1863, 725–26; XXIV, Part 3—Pemberton to Cooper, April 17, 1863, 751.

mand. It must have been irritating to the senior lieutenant general to see his juniors—Holmes, Pemberton
and Kirby Smith—commanding departments while he
was still a subordinate. He had apparently desired the
Trans-Mississippi command which was given to Kirby
Smith.

But on his return from southeastern Virginia, Longstreet stopped in Richmond on May 6 and called on
Secretary Seddon. The Secretary, who, as historian
Douglas S. Freeman has observed, "had great art in
making his guests feel that their opinions were desired
on public questions," referred in their conversation
"to affairs in Mississippi, stating that the Department
was trying to collect an army . . . sufficient to push
Grant away from . . . Vicksburg." A discussion developed between the two in which the Secretary suggested that possibly Longstreet's corps of Lee's army
"might be needed to make the army strong enough to
handle Grant." On being asked his views, Longstreet
"replied that there was a better plan . . . for relieving
Vicksburg than by a direct assault upon Grant," proposing "that the army then concentrating at Jackson,
Mississippi, be moved swiftly to Tullahoma, where
General Bragg was then located with a fine army confronting an army of about equal strength under Rosecrans." These forces, in Longstreet's plan, were to be
met at Tullahoma by two divisions from his corps in
Virginia, making "a grand army at Tullahoma" with
which "General Johnston might speedily crush Rosecrans, and . . . then turn his force toward the north,
and with his splendid army march through Tennessee
and Kentucky and threaten the invasion of Ohio."

The Secretary and the general discussed this plan

"to equalize the contest by . . . skillful use of . . . interior lines," Seddon being impressed with the difficulty of withdrawing two divisions from Lee and having reservations about Longstreet's plan because "Grant was such an obstinate fellow that he could only be induced to quit Vicksburg by terribly hard knocks." While he was in Richmond Longstreet probably discussed his plan with his, Johnston's and Seddon's friend, Senator Wigfall, who was also an advocate of western reinforcement.

On his return to Lee's headquarters, Longstreet broached the plan to Lee. The latter was impressed by this new idea and gave it "unbiased consideration," but objected to it on the grounds that it would "force him to divide his army." Lee wished to make an advance beyond the Potomac. This changed Longstreet's view, for as he wrote Wigfall: "When I agreed with the Sect. & yourself about sending troops west, it was under the impression that we would be obliged to remain on the defensive here. But the prospect of an advance changes the aspect of affairs to us entirely." Since there was "a fair prospect of a forward movement . . . we can spare nothing from this army to re-enforce in the West." Longstreet thought that Pemberton would probably remain on the defensive, particularly since not enough men could be sent to make him much stronger than Grant. Therefore, it was better for no reinforcements to be sent him and that those available should either support Lee's contemplated advance or go to Bragg's army to enable it to take the offensive and thus make Grant "quit the Miss. River expedition." Furthermore, he did not feel that too much would be lost if Vicksburg fell. "We would be no worse cut off from the

West than we are now," with Federal gunboats between
Vicksburg and Port Hudson, while "as to the Yankees
using the river for trade, it cannot be done as long as
we have the banks." To what extent General Longstreet's chief, Lee, shared these views is unknown, but
they had discussed the whole field of Confederate
strategic policy together.

To General P. G. T. Beauregard, also, the events
suggested vigorous action. To this veteran of First
Manassas and Shiloh, now commanding in South Carolina, Georgia and Florida, a similar idea occurred,
reminiscent of his and A. S. Johnston's moves prior
to Shiloh. On May 15 he not only communicated his
new plan to Bragg and Johnston but, knowing his
"zeal, energy, and enlarged views on all military matters," to Senator Wigfall as well. Feeling that he was
out of favor in Richmond, he urged Wigfall to make a
"desperate effort" to have his plan adopted without
revealing its source. Beauregard felt that it was unwise
to take the offensive in Virginia because of lack of
supplies in northern Virginia and because "the threatened danger to Washington would arouse the whole
Yankee Nation to renewed efforts for the protection of
their Capital."

The best plan to save the Mississippi was to concentrate troops from Virginia and Mississippi with Bragg's
army where, "at the most favorable strategic point for
the offensive, Rosecrans could be suddenly attacked, and
would be either totally destroyed or the remnant of his
forces would be speedily driven beyond the Ohio." The
victorious army should then advance westward and
block the navigation of the Mississippi River above
Memphis, "and thus cut off Grant's communications

with the North. The latter officer (should he have delayed thus long his retreat north . . .) would then find himself in a very critical condition—that is, compelled to fight his way through a victorious army equal to his own in strength, on its own selected battlefield." The defeat of Grant's army would enable reinforcements to be sent to the Trans-Mississippi or "into Virginia, to reinforce the troops left there, should they be hard-pressed; but that is not to be dreaded, considering the terrible lesson the enemy has just had at Chancellorsville," and their reduced strength due to the expiration of terms of enlistment. Wigfall probably needed no encouragement to press for western reinforcement, unless perhaps his ardour had been cooled by Longstreet's defection to a Virginia campaign. Neither Johnston nor Bragg replied until much later, though they were in agreement with Beauregard.[3]

[3] Freeman, *Lee's Lieutenants*, III, 40, 42, 45; Longstreet to Wigfall, February 4, May 13, 1863, Wigfall Papers; James Longstreet, *Manassas to Appomattox* (Philadelphia, 1896), 326–28; James Longstreet, "Lee in Pennsylvania," *Annals of the War* (Philadelphia, 1879), 415–16; Beauregard to Johnston, May 15, 1863, Roman, *Military Operations of General Beauregard*, II, 84–85; *O. R.*, Ser. I: XXIII, Part 2—Beauregard to Wigfall, May 16, 1863, 839; Bragg to Beauregard, July 21, 1863, 920; XXVIII, Part 2—Beauregard to Johnston, July 1, 1863, 173–74. This account of Longstreet's views just given is an effort to harmonize his contemporary account to Wigfall, in which he displayed unreserved enthusiasm for an advance by Lee's army, with his postwar writings which voiced reservations about the advance.

3

MEANWHILE THE PRESIDENT WAS CONFINED
to his home by illness during the week of May seventh
to thirteenth, and Seddon was for the most part con-
ducting the military affairs of the Confederacy. The
situation seemed grave at this time. On May 7 Johnston
asked if men from Beauregard's department could not
be sent to help Pemberton, unaware that they had
been ordered five days before. But Pemberton had
reported these five thousand men which were on the
way to be "a very insufficient number. The stake is a
great one. I can see nothing so important." These,
however, were all the men which Beauregard could
spare.

Faced with this emergency and finding support from
Longstreet and presumably Wigfall, Secretary Seddon
revived the twice-considered idea of securing the needed
men from General Lee's army. On May 9, the same day
he had ordered Johnston to take command in person
in Mississippi, Seddon sent a coded telegram to General Lee, asking for Pickett's division for Pemberton.
Because of difficulties in deciphering the message, the
reply was not sent until the following day. General
Lee was firm in holding to his original opposition,
saying: "The adoption of your proposition is hazardous,

and it becomes a question between Virginia and the Mississippi. The distance and the uncertainty of the employment of the troops are unfavorable. But, if necessary, order Pickett at once." Shown to the President, he endorsed his agreement on Lee's response, saying that "the answer of General Lee was such as I should have anticipated and in which I concur."

Lee did not rely on his brief telegram but on the tenth and eleventh of May wrote both Seddon and President Davis letters after he had had an opportunity to consult with General Longstreet. In these two letters he again expounded his strategic views. Since he still thought Virginia was "to be the theater of action," his army ought to be strengthened "to oppose the large force which the enemy seems to be concentrating against it." If he were weakened, he might "be obligated to withdraw into the defenses around Richmond" by Hooker's already two-to-one superiority in numbers. Furthermore, it was useless to send troops to Mississippi, for not only would they "be greatly endangered by the climate" but, being unable to arrive until the end of May, the action in Mississippi would "be over by that time, as the climate in June will force the enemy to retire."

Having recalled his propositions that Virginia was to be the scene of the enemy's main effort and the limiting effect of the climate, he again indicated his doubts about the policy of troop transfers, reaffirming his belief that an advance by the army in Virginia would draw off enemy forces elsewhere, especially on the coast. Having explained the heavy odds against him in Virginia, Lee echoed his telegram when he concluded his letter to Seddon by asking the Secretary to "decide whether the line of Virginia is more in danger than the line of the Mississippi." [4]

Though Seddon telegraphed Lee that his letter was "conclusive against the suggestion made," he had another motive as well in abandoning the idea. He had developed misgivings about General Johnston. Johnston's complaints and apparent lack of any performance as commander of the Department of the West, his refusal of suggestions that he interpret his command so as to supersede the commander when he was present, and his failure to remove Bragg had undermined Seddon's confidence. Disappointed in Johnston, the Secretary "saw no reason to expect decisive results from him in May, 1863, even though reinforcements were sent him. This uneasiness about Johnston, in addition to Lee's convincing reasons, turned Seddon away from his original purpose."

Misgivings about the course to be pursued, together with the news that Grant had gotten between Pemberton and the newly arrived Johnston, decided the President to call a conference. His health was sufficiently recovered for him to come to his office, so he and Seddon met with General Lee and his subordinates, Major Generals S. G. French and J. E. B. Stuart. The conference decided on an invasion of Maryland and Pennsylvania by General Lee's army, and Lee recommended that Johnston promply attack Grant. Sed-

---

[4] *O. R.*, Ser. I: XXIV, Part 1—Johnston to Cooper, May 7, 1863, 214; Part 3—Pemberton to Seddon, May 6, 1863, 838; Davis to Pemberton, May 7, 1863, 842; XXV, Part 2—Lee to Seddon, May 10, 1863, 790 (Seddon's message not found in the *O. R.*, but its contents deduced from Lee's answer and Jones, *A Rebel War Clerk's Diary*, I, 325); Lee to Davis, May 11, 1863, 793. See also Freeman, *Lee*, II, 500–505, 562–63, III, 18–19.

don was fully convinced by Lee of the wisdom of the move, and completely abandoned his idea of sending reinforcements to Johnston. If Senator Wigfall approached him with Beauregard's plan, it did not sway him, for, when continued bad news from Mississippi induced the President to call a cabinet meeting to reconsider the whole question, Seddon supported Lee's plan. Postmaster General John H. Reagan was strongly in favor of aiding Vicksburg, as was public opinion. Though the President was still optimistic about the operations at Vicksburg, he must have been in doubt about what to do. Perhaps Seddon, at the height of his "powerful influence" with Davis, could have altered the decision, had he turned his "graceful and impressive manner as a speaker" and the "effective reasoning of his oratory" [5] against, rather than for, Lee's plan. But the cabinet decided overwhelmingly for the offensive by Lee.

4

THE ORDERING OF GENERAL JOHNSTON TO TAKE the chief command in Mississippi on May 9, 1863, effectively ended the life of the Department of the West, though it was not officially abolished until later. But

[5] *O. R.*, Ser. I: XXV, Part 2—Seddon to Lee, May 13, 1863, 797; LI, Part 2—Davis to Lee, May 26, 1863, 716–17; XXIV, Part 1—Johnston to Seddon, May 14, 1863, 215; Reagan, *Memoirs*, 121–22, 151–52; Patrick, *Jefferson Davis and His Cabinet*, 133–34, 137–39.

the decision to attack in Virginia symbolizes and high-
lights the collapse of hopes and plans for the West.
The Secretary was turned from an exponent of western
reinforcement into an advocate of an eastern offensive.
The role of Lee in the conversion of Seddon seems
strong. It is doubtful if he succeeded in persuading
Seddon of the fundamental error of trying to transfer
troops or communicated to him much of his optimism
based on the theory that the climate would force Grant's
withdrawal. Important, doubtless, was Lee's insistence
that it "becomes a question between Virginia and the
Mississippi." Lee asked, in effect: "As for the Army
of Northern Virginia . . . what better service could
it render the other Confederate armies and their common cause than to invade the North and threaten
Washington?" Therefore, more effective probably than
his arguments was the authority and prestige of General
Lee proposing an alternative program. Lee's capacity
to perform had been proven more than once, while
the performance of Johnston had been disappointing.
Better too, thought Seddon, to take assured safety of
Virginia than to risk it for Johnston's uncertain ability
to save Vicksburg.

The decision that led to Gettysburg has been subjected to much criticism. The making of it cast Lee
in the role of strategist for the whole Confederacy, a
task for which his absorption in his Virginia army un-
fitted him. Contemporary opinion was not all in agreement. When he learned of Lee's advance, Beauregard,
the inveterate westerner and disinterested observer,
wrote to Johnston asking "of what earthly use is this
'raid' of Lee's army into Maryland, in violation of all the
principles of war? Is it going to end the struggle,

take Washington, or save the Mississippi Valley?"
Beauregard retained a firm belief in his own plan. His
view is echoed by a modern critic who disparaged Lee's
"renewal of his luckless attempt to invade Pennsylvania." Though he might "scare the politicians at
Washington, and prevent reinforcements being sent
to Grant," his advance "could hardly have the immediate effect on Grant as one against Kentucky, nor even
as profound political reverberation." [6]

But the decision taken in May under the stress of
crisis had clearly been a reversal of the policy of the
preceding months. While no plan of campaign for the
Confederate armies for the year 1863 had been developed and presumably no conscious policy decisions
had been made, the underlying assumption of the
actions of Davis and Seddon during the late winter
and spring had been that the West was the weak point
in the Confederacy and that it needed strengthening.
The constant efforts to provide reinforcements indicate
that this was their working hypothesis. Furthermore,
there had been no decision to take the offensive that
year. The objective of their efforts was to make the
menaced positions in the West strong enough for a successful defense. Under the pressure of a crisis and the
urgings of General Lee they reversed themselves and
altered their plans from defensive to offensive, from
West to East, deciding to let the West get along without the reinforcements previously thought necessary.
Yet this decision was a half measure, for the troops that

[6] Freeman, *Lee's Lieutenants*, III, 45; *O. R.*, Ser I: XXVIII,
Part 2—Beauregard to Johnston, July 1, 1863, 173–74; B. H. Liddell Hart, *Sherman, the Genius of the Civil War* (London, 1933),
220.

were dispensable to Bragg and Beauregard were left with Johnston rather than used to augment Lee's offensive force. So what may be called the Confederate strategic reserve or mass of maneuver was divided, Lee retaining all of his men but receiving little other help.

The part played by the Department of the West in this policy reversal is difficult to assess. That the personal relations between Johnston and Seddon were cool after the cordiality of the latter's "confidential" communications seems clear. That Johnston would not use his power to remove Bragg and refused to interpret his orders in the manner suggested must have annoyed Seddon, as did Johnston's expressed lack of confidence in the practicality of co-ordinating the two main armies in the manner intended. It must have seemed strange to Johnston that, if it was desired that he automatically be in command wherever he was or that Bragg should be replaced by himself, he was not so ordered. On the other hand, if Seddon was not trying to use Johnston to get rid of or nullify Presidential appointees, Bragg and Pemberton, whom he regarded as incompetent, Johnston's refusal must have been exasperating. Not wishing to impose his views by orders, he offered Johnston what Senator Wigfall had led him to believe Johnston wanted, and it was refused. According to Wigfall, the President and the Secretary seemed genuinely confused by Johnston's refusal to take Bragg's army. Johnston, of course, wanted to return to his old command in Virginia and suggested that Lee should come west, but it is most improbable that he was being difficult about his command in an effort to exchange places with Lee.

Relations between President Davis and General Johnston were, on the other hand, quite cordial. They exchanged letters throughout February and March, and those of the President were extremely amiable, while in Johnston's there was none of the "jejune and ice tempered" [7] tone which he sometimes used with Cooper and Seddon. Their strategic correspondence ceased, however, after an April 10 letter in which Johnston explained in detail his views on the contingencies of Bragg's withdrawal, discussed the difficulty of the proposed transfer of troops from Mississippi to Tennessee, and the advantages of a diversion into Kentucky by General Samuel Jones. Perhaps Davis was satisfied and, having learned all he could from Johnston, had no important news for him. No note of asperity appears in their last letters.

While personalities loom large in both the history and the demise of the Department of the West, it has a story of its own, which, seen in perspective, not only casts much light on the actions and reactions of the personalities involved, but on Confederate western strategy during the period.

[7] Kean, *Inside the Confederate Government,* 50, entry of April 12, 1863.

Chapter Twelve

Shiloh to Vicksburg— An Evaluation

1

NEARLY ONE HALF OF THE STORY OF CONFED-
erate strategy from Shiloh to Vicksburg is concerned
with the Department of the West. The failure of this
significant attempt to implement better the fundamental
and continuing policy of decentralization with unity
of command was due largely to a lack of understanding
and of a common strategic evaluation between Joe
Johnston and his superiors. The role of personalities
is also important, but the history of the Department
of the West as distinguished from the relations of the
personalities provides a key to those relations. A significant mutual lack of communication is exhibited between the commanding general and the President and
Secretary of War. Also noticeable is a fading away of
the significance attached to the department by Richmond at the same time that it is beginning to function.
Changed circumstances largely account for the alteration in outlook.

The idea of a new unified command in the West
had had its inception in September, 1862, when President Davis and Secretary of War Randolph were dealing

with the problems of divided command in Mississippi. Though Randolph then thought that it should embody all of the West beyond the Appalachian Mountains, as modified, it excluded the region beyond the Mississippi River. This modified department marked a partial return to an arrangement which had existed six months earlier, when General Albert Sidney Johnston had commanded the whole western frontier. Circumstances were changed in that the Federal advance had pressed so far down the Mississippi that an enormous dent or bulge had been driven into the Confederate line. With the railroad from Memphis to Chattanooga cut, the Federal armies enjoyed, if not the advantages of interior lines, at least more rapid communication through their use of the rivers. Two separate fronts, middle and east Tennessee and the Mississippi, had in reality appeared and were so treated by both Northern and Southern commanders. Interchanges of troops between these two fronts were not frequent, but the North enjoyed the advantage in rapidity of movement.

Another fundamental difference existed in the fall of 1862 which had not been present when A. S. Johnston and Beauregard concentrated prior to Shiloh. Having been disastrously defeated by the fall of Forts Donelson and Henry and the evacuation of Kentucky and western Tennessee, they were ruthless in their concentration. They exposed Arkansas to invasion by calling all of its troops across the Mississippi, while New Orleans, Mobile and Pensacola were denuded of protection in creating a powerful army for offensive action. But the situation then had been desperate, and the defeated and dispersed Confederate armies were in serious danger from the powerful Union armies against whom they planned to concentrate and strike a blow.

The situation six months later was far different. Though offensive action had just been attempted, the Confederate state of mind was becoming defensive. The situation was stabilized. The complex series of offensives —actual and proposed, all requiring co-ordination— which were in progress when the department was conceived were no longer in progress or contemplated by the time the department had begun to function. The offensives of Bragg and Van Dorn had not regained much lost ground, and important positions in Mississippi and Tennessee had to be protected. With much to lose and little, apparently, to gain, safety first became the motto. That Johnston's mission in the West was purely a defensive one is borne out by the fact that he was the only one to mention the offensive in all of his communications with the government.

With the alternation from offensive to defensive, from desperation to relative security, the situation had changed. Concentration and strategic mobility of reserves became a different matter when on the defensive. The removal of the bumbling Halleck also changed the picture for the Confederates in that there were no longer any opportune diversions or pauses in Union activity. The problem for the Department of the West, as interpreted by Johnston, was to effect a shifting of troops from one of his major fronts to the other in the event one was attacked and the other not.

Thus the role to be played by the department was a passive one. Before anything could be done it was necessary for the enemy to do something. The inactivity of Rosecrans after December, 1862, and Grant's winter efforts, which were ineffective and in which he himself had no confidence, provided nothing for the department or its commander to do. It was natural, therefore, for Davis and Seddon to use Johnston as a trouble shooter to iron out the difficulties in Bragg's command. The declining significance attached to Johnston's role as co-ordinator is indicated by Seddon's willingness to give him the command of the Army of Tennessee, inevitably diminishing his ability to perform his functions as overall commander. The interpretation of his role as that of a roving expert who would take charge in emergencies also indicates a derogation of the departmental strategist functions. Johnston's exposition of the difficulties of carrying out his mission as strategic co-ordinator of so widely separated armies undoubtedly contributed to this change in point of view as also did the enforced inactivity of the departmental commander in his originally intended function.

Though Johnston felt that troop transfer in emergencies was not practical, he made an effective effort to solve the problem. The "pipeline" from Mississippi to Tennessee and the effort at a similar system with east Tennessee and southwestern Virginia was a concept that might have been profitably applied to all of the forces in the Confederacy. While Johnston's general plan of reinforcement, combining infantry forces flowing to Bragg and the centrally located cavalry striking northeast or southwest, seems about the best that could be made, it was dependent on higher questions of strategy and policy which were not squarely met by the Confederate government.

No real answer was given to Johnston's question: "Which is the most valuable, Tennessee or the Mississippi?" Without this essential policy guidance, Johnston was faced with a serious dilemma. He seems to have taken a logical step. While he regarded both Bragg's and Pemberton's forces as too weak, he thought Bragg could hold his own if Rosecrans were not too strongly reinforced. His familiarity with the commander and the army and his agreement with Bragg on fundamentals put him in the position of dealing with relatively ponderable quantities. He was strongly impressed with the importance of Tennessee and the serious consequences of its loss. His preparations for Bragg's enforced withdrawal introduced another calculable item into his thinking. Though the impression that he would have made a clear-cut decision in favor of Tennessee is strong, he must in addition have been strongly inclined to choose this relative certainty.

Compared with the clearly measured probabilities and contingent security in Tennessee, the situation on the Mississippi was obscure and gloomy. Not only were 20,000 more men necessary for its successful defense, but the principles on which that defense was being conducted were radically wrong. The intricacies of steam gunboat warfare were new and not thoroughly understood by Johnston. By comparison, Tennessee was sure; Mississippi, doubtful.

Another consideration made Johnston put the security of Tennessee ahead of that of the Mississippi. The worst that could happen, he thought, would be that the forts and communication with the Trans-Mississippi would be lost. But since the government persisted in making the serious mistake of not unifying the efforts and resources of the two departments, he must have felt that the stake was not as great a one as it might at first appear, for one of the most important advantages of the transit of the river was being wasted.

So, in the absence of guidance from Richmond, Johnston made his plans on the basis of securing Tennessee and letting the Mississippi make do. This decision was an implicit one and never conveyed to Richmond as such, just as he never viewed his reinforcement plans as a comprehensive whole. He probably could not have told Richmond these plans, for they were not clear as such to him.

Johnston remained in Tullahoma from the middle of March, 1863, on, under the apprehension that he should not leave until the matter concerning the projected conference with Bragg was settled. It was during this time that Pemberton labored under the apparent misconception that Johnston was commanding Bragg's army, with that as the new limit of his authority. This idea had some currency elsewhere, for both Lee and Longstreet appear to have regarded Bragg's army as Johnston's. The President and the War Department aided Pemberton's misconception by referring to the army in middle Tennessee as if it were Johnston's; not only this, but they began to exercise Johnston's functions for him. During the apparent emergency in April caused by the Federal advance up the Tennessee River from Corinth, the President asked Pemberton for any reinforcements he could spare for the army at Tullahoma. When Pemberton later reported that he needed the men he had sent, he was instructed to take them back. Though the troops had, of course, been sent and recalled by arrangement between Johnston and Pemberton, neither of them mentioned this. Perhaps Richmond's authority was necessary to make Pemberton adhere to Johnston's wishes, but as far as was known in Richmond, Davis and Cooper had both begun and ended the troop movement from Pemberton, also without their having themselves ever mentioned it to Johnston. Therefore, Richmond seemed to have viewed Johnston's functions as a department commander as having lapsed even before the department itself was abolished, though his nominal authority was maintained.

What did Richmond regard as his mission? Perhaps General Bragg put his finger on it with his disgruntled comment after Johnston had left for Mississippi in May; "he was kept here to watch me too long." Whatever was the thinking in Richmond, Johnston's last month before going to take charge in Mississippi was one of being ignored by the President and the War Department.

When the real crisis came in May, 1863, with Grant finally passing below and behind Vicksburg, the disparity in point of view and the failure of communication clearly revealed themselves. What reality still remained in the department was nullified by this failure. Johnston had not told Davis and Seddon his plans beyond what he might do if Bragg were forced to withdraw and his plans for reinforcing him. This, together with the enforced inactivity and complications with Bragg, had caused Richmond to discount the Department of the West and now led them to nullify its commander's discretion. When Pemberton was threatened, Johnston did nothing but move his cavalry and direct Pemberton to obtain aid from the Trans-Mississippi. This action was not enough for Richmond. That Johnston was not sending greater reinforcement to Pemberton from Bragg was due to Johnston's own plan, made in the absence of guidance from Richmond. He would not seriously jeopardize Tennessee on the chance of affecting the outcome in Mississippi. On the other hand, if the Confederate government did not value the Mississippi above Tennessee, they were at least willing to risk Tennessee to improve the chances of saving the Mississippi.

Charged with co-ordinating the defense of Tennessee and Mississippi, Johnston obviously felt that the Federal forces were so strong that, should they be "respectably handled" and "some great blunder" avoided, he would be defeated. This recognition of the possibility of defeat and of the necessity of being prepared to sacrifice one vital area to save the other had led him to ask Davis: "Which is the most valuable, Tennessee or the Mississippi?"

Though Davis had shown that he did not attach to holding Tennessee the same importance as did Johnston, his answer, "To hold the Mississippi is vital," does not seem intended so much to choose between the two as to impress on Johnston the importance of the Mississippi. Davis did not discount the possibility that both might be attacked simultaneously,[1] nor was he unable to make this kind of hard decision, having the previous year ordered the abandonment of Pensa-

---

[1] Johnston's views on the strategy of the war, probably written in 1864, Wigfall Papers; Longstreet to Wigfall, May 13, 1863, Wigfall Papers; Govan and Livingood, *A Different Valor,* 197; *O. R.,* Ser. I: XXV, Part 2—Lee to Davis, April 2, 1862, 700–701; XVII, Part 2—Johnston to Davis, January 2, 1863, 823; XXIV, Part I—Johnston to Seddon, June 15, 1863, 227; XXIII, Part 2— Davis to Johnston, March 16, 20, 1863, 713, 712.

cola and Mobile in order to strengthen Sidney Johnston's army in Tennessee. Rather, this failure to choose
seems to indicate Davis' belief that the decision was
unnecessary, that both could be saved; a manifestation
of that faith in success, that refusal to contemplate
defeat, which was brought so sharply into focus at
the end of the war.

It is this disparity in point of view that, in large
measure, accounts for the differing reactions to the
crisis on the Mississippi on the part of the Richmond
government and the commander of the Department
of the West. If the government had provided Johnston
with more positive official guidance as to the relative
merits of the Mississippi and Tennessee, his plans could
have been accommodated to their views. This absence
of agreement, long present, had not revealed itself
in the absence of a crisis.

While this basic difference in outlook between the
President and the general handicapped operations during the Vicksburg crisis, it contributed also to another
serious consequence of the fall of Vicksburg. Since
Davis implicitly assumed that, with good Confederate
generalship, victory was possible, defeat made necessary
a search for who was responsible. This search for a
scapegoat was impelled, too, by the bitter disappointment at defeat, a prospect Davis had not realistically
contemplated. The President usually found what he
sought. After the Fort Donelson disaster, the luckless
John B. Floyd was put out of the army; after Shiloh,
Beauregard was removed; and after Vicksburg, the
deepest of the President's enmities was directed toward
Johnston. It was only natural that Davis should find

the defective leadership in the general about whom he already had misgivings or toward whom he felt some latent or suppressed animosity.

The record of this new effort at unity of command in the West through a supreme commander is one of failure. But it surely did not have a fair trial. It is an interesting speculation as to what the record would be if Rosecrans, as he was urged to, had advanced before Grant was ready. Bragg, with his army heavily reinforced from departmental resources and the advice of Johnston available, might well have won Chickamauga north of the Tennessee River.

Yet this important episode in the strategy of the West, though marked by failure and misunderstanding, is not entirely discreditable to the participants. Johnston's strategic insight, Seddon's active concern, and Davis' sympathetic understanding and reluctance to intervene are characteristic of the history of Confederate strategy from Shiloh to Vicksburg, as are also the strategic dilemmas which faced Johnston and Davis. The methods and difficulties of Confederate strategy are illustrated well by the story of the Department of the West, not only in its relations with the President and the War Department, but because Johnston's problems and methods in his department reproduced in microcosm those faced in Richmond in the direction of Confederate strategy as a whole.

2

WHILE SOUTHERN STRATEGY AS A WHOLE WAS concerned with defending the territory of the Confederacy through forces assigned for the defense of specific areas, central strategic direction in the West was supplied by the very arrangement of the departments and districts charged with this defense. The organization of the departments and districts, with the periodic reorganization, redelineation of their boundaries, and redefinition of their missions, provided strategic mobility of reserves. A district or department commander was given the mission of defending a geographical area and given the command of the troops within it in order to carry out this mission. Delegation of authority and responsibility for this was complete, and the commander had discretion to practice the principles of concentration and elastic defense within his department and to take the offensive, if he were able and thought it proper. He could, if he chose, abandon one district to save another. While he was on his own, the very construction of his department was based on the President's and the War Department's view of the strategic necessities of the situation. When a departmental commander's territory was enlarged, not only were his responsibilities increased, but his resources for the task were correspondingly augmented, and the scope of his activity as well as his opportunity for maneuver extended. Thus the changing departmental picture constituted, in a real sense, the strategic direction supplied by the Richmond government to the Confederate defense.

But this very system militated against any larger control of strategy. The reliance on the policy of departmental arrangement and organization tended to exclude other methods of strategic direction. The very laudable and proper delegation of authority and discretion to the local commanders hampered inter-departmental movement of troops. In a sense the President and the Secretary of War had given away all of their men and had no mass for maneuver left to themselves. The very tailoring of the departments to the necessities of the situation and the fact that the department commanders were charged with territorial defense made President Davis extremely reluctant to go against the wishes of his appointees. Having given the authority to a man personally selected by him to carry out a particular mission, which had usually been rather recently defined, it was naturally difficult for the President to go against the judgment of a local commander.

Before pointing out the defects of the system in actual practice, its significant and valuable theoretical and practical advantages should be noted. The system was flexible, not only because departments and districts could be and were changed as frequently as the situation demanded, but because of the absolute delegation of authority and responsibility to the local commander who knew the situation. The strategic shifts from Richmond were of the most general sort under this system. Troops were rarely moved, but rather the authority to move troops was altered, as in the case of the extension of General Bragg's authority over Department No. 1 in June, 1862. This efficiently harmonized the overall grasp of the strategic picture, possessed by the President and the Secretary of War, with the familiarity with local conditions which the field commanders had.

While tremendous reliance was thus placed on the capacity of the department commanders, it was undoubtedly the best system, in the absence of modern communications and apparatus of command which would have provided better intelligence and increased facilities for centralized direction. This is why Confederate military history is so largely biographical and why the defects of Bragg and Pemberton loom so large in any history of western operations. The problem of finding officers qualified for high command is an important part of the story of Confederate and Union war efforts.

One major deficiency in the strategic management was the difficulty the President and his advisers had in treating the Confederacy as one big department. This was particularly true in the case of the eastern and western theaters. While at one time most of the West was united in one large department and much of it was at one time united to the Southeast, and the Southeast for a period was joined in effect to the East, the two principal theaters always remained linked only through the President. President Davis was very slow in behaving as he expected his department commanders to behave—concentrating the resources of his department for its defense or for offense.

The concept of local defense and the departmental system undoubtedly blinded the President to the necessity for more direction from above. That he could write that General Bragg had "bravely and patriotically" endangered his department by sending troops to aid in the relief of Vicksburg, indicated that the departments had a real identity for him and that he sometimes tended to see the war through the eyes of his department commanders.

Perhaps Davis saw too clearly the limitations of trying to direct operations from Richmond. When he behaved as a co-ordinator rather than a commander in asking, instead of ordering, Holmes to send troops, he was obviously aware of the difficulties of trying to command without the necessary information or freedom to move around and see the local situations for himself.

A partial answer to these problems was, of course, a commander-in-chief. This, however, was a temperamental impossibility for Davis. He would not delegate the post of commander-in-chief, not only because he thought himself well-qualified to fill it, but also because he felt the responsibility constitutionally belonged on his shoulders. He had "neither the power nor the will to delegate" the command.[2]

Secretary of War Seddon obviously wanted the President and the War Department to play a more active role in the strategic direction of the war. The view of Johnston and of Seddon that the West was weak became the working hypothesis of the President by the spring of 1863, and in spite of their having recently made departmental arrangements to remedy the weakness of that theater, they were ready to play the role of department commanders for the whole Confederacy. Their efforts foundered, in part, on the rock of the

[2] *Ibid.:* LI, Part 2—Davis to Lee, May 26, 1863, 716–17.

authority which they had delegated to the local commanders and which they were unwilling to override.

When the crisis at Vicksburg in May, 1863, made decisive and immediate action imperative, their views collided with those of General Lee. To a President who had been recently ill and who was unsure in his own mind of the best course of action, the prestige of General Lee, thrown unequivocably and forcefully behind a proposal to continue to rely solely on the departmental organization, must have been overwhelming. The general not only supported reliance on departmentalization, but had attacked the very premises underlying Seddon's proposal, arguing that interdepartmental troop movements would "always be too late." If Longstreet couldn't reach the Rappahannock from Suffolk in time for Chancellorsville, then what chance would Pickett have of reaching Vicksburg in time? That the idea, held during the winter and spring, that the West needed reinforcement died hard is indicated by the cabinet meeting called to review the decision to advance into Pennsylvania.

Seddon was isolated, his chief persuaded by General Lee. If he had been inclined to stand his ground, Lee's emphasis on the "distance and the uncertainty of the employment of the troops" might have touched a sensitive spot with Seddon. General Johnston had disclaimed any ability to affect the situation favorably, had not done what Seddon wished about Bragg, and may well have icily rebuffed the Secretary's confidential approaches. It is not surprising that Seddon too was persuaded of the lack of wisdom of a withdrawal of men from Virginia. Perhaps, also, Seddon wanted to

ficult to make a case. It is hard to conclude that an army twice the size of that actually available could have broken the ring around Vicksburg.

On the other hand there is the personal equation. What success could an army assembled *ad hoc* from all over the Confederacy and hastily concentrated in Tennessee expect to have in accomplishing the great things Beauregard envisioned? Was Joseph E. Johnston capable of executing this dashing offensive? No answer to this question could command agreement. Could a general—temperamentally committed to the defensive, burdened with General Bragg, and facing the capable and astute Rosecrans, fortified in Nashville—have much chance of success? But if the achievements of the Army of Tennessee, accomplished in spite of its generals, are remembered, then success might well have been possible for this army, with its excellently led corps and divisions and its fine cavalry. With a general in whom it had full confidence—one who would have, at last, been given the opportunity to fight against a weaker enemy —the Army of Tennessee might well have lived up to Beauregard's hopes.

3

AFTER ALMOST A CENTURY OF WRITING, IT IS clear that much work remains to be done on the history of the Civil War. An approach to Confederate military history from the strategic point of view will yield rich rewards to both the professional scholar and the amateur enthusiast. For it is clear from the limited period and area surveyed that traditional estimates of men and events must be carefully reviewed. Randolph, a consumptive Richmond lawyer and armchair strategist— Secretary of War for eight months—clearly used a limited, almost sporadic, influence with President Davis very beneficially for the Confederacy, shaping manpower policy and contributing substantially to a much-needed reorganization of the West, an area to which more attention was henceforth given.

The strategic reorganization, initiated under Randolph and carried out under Seddon, took the form of a new western department. While there are serious objections to the Department of the West as constituted, it is difficult to conceive a better organization. To have added the Trans-Mississippi would have tended to create for the department commander the very problem which beset the War Department—an area too large to be managed effectively. To have united east and middle Tennessee with Virginia is appealing, however, because of the direct railway connections between these two areas.

Resentful of the bad luck of a wound which had given the command of "his" army to General Lee and transferred him to an administrative command outside his home state, Joe Johnston, nevertheless, ingeniously exploited the opportunities for strategic co-ordination in his department. While impressing the War Department with the needs of the West, he also impressed it with his dissatisfaction of his command and disappointed and alienated the influential Secretary of War, James A. Seddon.

When a dangerous crisis arose in Mississippi, aggravated by the serious difficulties and lack of rapport between Johnston and Pemberton, Seddon acted quickly to implement his matured plans for strengthening the West with reinforcements from Virginia and South Carolina. In respect to the troops from Virginia, Seddon met the immovable opposition of General Lee. It is not surprising that Davis preferred the advice of Lee or even that Lee's firm stand converted Seddon himself to relying on Lee rather than Johnston to save the situation.

But the decision itself was a compromise in that Lee received no significant reinforcements for his important mission, while available troops from South Carolina and Tennessee were sent to Vicksburg. In a sense this compromise attempted two things at once and failed in both. Also, in essence, a plan of concentration in the West was abandoned on General Lee's advice, and the old system of departmental self-sufficiency was retained.

On only abstract and theoretical grounds can Davis and Seddon be blamed for thus reversing themselves. General Lee's prestige and personality would have been overwhelming, even to bigger and less worried and harrassed men than they.

When asked whether he could spare any men, General Lee, subconsciously perhaps, cast himself in the role of strategic oracle for the Confederate government, yet he seems to have viewed the situation through the glasses of a local commander. While he knew that his general views would be welcomed, he assumed a great responsibility. It is difficult to reach any other conclusion than that Lee failed to measure up to the task he set for himself. With his judgment clouded by concern for the Virginia front and his army, he presented a plan based on erroneous hypotheses and which, by its very rejection of principles later accepted by him, indicated that it had not received careful study or had been produced to support his own predilections. In this case the grandiose plan of the disinterested Beauregard seems better than that of Lee.

What may be said of the Davis methods during this year of war in the West? Sometimes tardy and uneven in application, the departmental system seems to have been a good one. It was well-adapted to strategic necessities as well as to the task of supply and manpower administration. War Department direction seems quite adequate also. The crisis of the fall of Fort Donelson was vigorously met, though the hard decision to concentrate was too long postponed. East Tennessee was supported by a similar decisive display of energy, and successive reorganizations were responsive to changing strategic necessities. The problems of the West received sympathetic and imaginative consideration during the fall and winter of 1862–1863.

It is clear that Davis' strategic sense was inferior to that of Beauregard, Bragg, and Joe Johnston. But while Davis did not realize the great strategic importance of Tennessee as the road to Atlanta nor fully appreciate the fatal defects of fortified points as a means of defending the Mississippi, his management had many strong points. His method was sound; his application competent. If he was too sensitive to the wishes of local commanders and had difficulty rising above his system and providing the needed measure of central control, too much centralization would have been a far worse error. With the exception of Pemberton, his choice of the commanders on whom he relied so heavily was, if not uniformly fortunate, soundly based on good principles of selection and knowledge of the candidates.

Confederate strategy, territorially and logistically oriented, seems realistic and adapted to conditions. Its implementation through a decentralized departmental command system was wise, and the measure of central control was adequate. Davis and his War Secretaries bear scrutiny well. While genius was absent, ability and insight were demonstrated.

Bibliography

I. MANUSCRIPTS

Edgehill-Randolph Papers. Alderman Library, University of
Virginia, Charlottesville, Va. About one hundred letters,
mostly from Randolph to his niece, Mary B. Randolph,
during the 1851 to 1861 period.
Daniel Harvey Hill Papers. Virginia State Library, Richmond, Va. Three letters from Randolph to Hill in 1862.
Memoirs of Major General Henry Heth, C. S. A. Typescript
in the Heth-Selden Manuscripts, Alderman Library,
University of Virginia, Charlottesville, Va. Interesting
primarily for his and Edmund Kirby Smith's view of
Bragg.
Robert Morton Hughes Papers. Norfolk, Va. This interesting collection, still in the hands of the family of Joseph
E. Johnston's first biographer, was courteously made available to me by Mrs. R. M. Hughes, Jr., and Mr. R. M.
Hughes, III. In addition to containing some interesting
unpublished wartime letters, it includes much correspondence of R. M. Hughes connected with the writing
of his biography of Johnston, including his unpublished
reminiscences of the general and material accumulated by
him after the publication of his biography.
Kean Collection. Property of Dr. Robert H. Kean of Richmond, Va. A few letters from Randolph and Mrs. Randolph to Randolph's nephew by marriage, Captain
R. G. H. Kean of Lynchburg, Va., mostly in the post-war
period; a manuscript sketch of about 3,000 words con-

cerning Randolph's career as brigadier general and stopping just after he became Secretary of War, which was presumably written by R. G. H. Kean; a few notes on Randolph's early life, presumably by Mrs. Randolph; and a draft amnesty petition for Randolph, probably by Kean.

James L. Kemper Papers. Alderman Library, University of Virginia, Charlottesville, Va. Correspondence of Major General James Lawson Kemper, C. S. A., a Virginia politician as well as soldier, with John B. Floyd, Henry A. Wise, R. M. T. Hunter and others, including one letter from Randolph. The letters contain some material concerning Randolph's early career in military legislation and his journalistic activities.

George Wythe Randolph Papers. Confederate Museum, Richmond, Va. Several letters from Randolph to J. Thompson Brown in 1862 and early 1863.

Virginia War Records. Virginia State Library, Richmond, Va. Photostats of the original appointments of officers and organization of units.

Louis T. Wigfall Papers. Library of Congress. This Confederate brigadier general and senator from Texas was a friend and advocate of many prominent general officers. His papers contain many wartime letters from such men as J. E. Johnston, James Longstreet and Wade Hampton.

II. PUBLIC DOCUMENTS

Candler, Allen D. (ed.). *The Confederate Records of the State of Georgia.* 8 vols. Atlanta, 1910.

Flourney, H. W. (ed.). *Calendar of Virginia State Papers and Other Manuscripts.* 10 vols. Richmond, 1861.

Journal of the Congress of the Confederate States of America. 8 vols. Washington, 1905.

Journal of the Convention of 1861. Richmond, 1861.

Ordinances Adopted by the Convention of Virginia at the Adjourned Session in November and December, 1861. Richmond, 1861.

Richardson, James D. (ed.). *Messages and Papers of the Confederacy.* 2 vols. Nashville, 1906.

The War of the Rebellion: A Compilation of the Official Records of the Union and Confederate Armies. 128 vols. Washington, 1880–1901.

III. NEWSPAPERS

South Carolina. Charleston *Mercury.* March, 1862, through May, 1862.
Virginia. Richmond *Enquirer.* February, 1862, through November, 1862.

IV. BOOKS

This is not, of course, an attempt to give a complete Civil War bibliography, but merely those books which were particularly helpful in this work.

Letters, Memoirs, and Diaries

Chamberlayne, J. H. *Ham Chamberlayne—Virginian,* ed. C. G. Chamberlayne. Richmond, 1932.
Chesnut, Mary Boykin. *A Diary from Dixie,* ed. Ben Ames Williams. New York, 1950.
Daniel, Frederick S. *Richmond Howitzers in the War.* Richmond, 1891.
Davis, Jefferson. *The Rise and Fall of the Confederate Government.* 2 vols. New York, 1881.
———. *Jefferson Davis, Constitutionalist, His Letters, Papers and Speeches,* ed. Dunbar Rowland. 10 vols. Jackson, Miss., 1923.
De Leon, T. C. *Belles, Beaux and Brains of the '60s.* New York, 1909.
———. *Four Years in Rebel Capitals.* Mobile, 1890.
Dorsey, Sarah A. *Recollections of Henry Watkins Allen.* New York, 1866. A defense of Pemberton's conduct in the Vicksburg campaign is contained in this work, including a significant letter from Johnston to Pemberton, not found in the *Official Records.*
Fremantle, Arthur James Lyon. *The Fremantle Diary,* ed. W. Lord. Boston, 1954.

Gordon, John B. *Reminiscences of the Civil War*. New York, 1903.

Grant, U. S. *Personal Memoirs of U. S. Grant*. 2 vols. New York, 1885–86.

Harrison, Mrs. Burton. *Recollections Grave and Gay*. New York, 1912.

Johnson, Robert U., and Buell, C. C. (eds.). *Battles and Leaders of the Civil War*. 4 vols. New York, 1887–88. An account of the war written by the participants then living, very well edited.

Johnston, Joseph E. *Narrative of Military Operations*. New York, 1874. This is J. E. Johnston's memoirs and defense of his wartime career.

Jones, J. B. *A Rebel War Clerk's Diary*, ed. Howard Swiggett. 2 vols. New York, 1935.

Kean, Robert Garlick Hill. *Inside the Confederate Government, the Diary of Robert Garlick Hill Kean, Head of the Bureau of War*, ed. Edward Younger. New York, 1957.

Lee, Robert E. *Lee's Dispatches*, ed. Douglas Southall Freeman. New York, 1915.

Longstreet, James. *From Manassas to Appomattox*. Philadelphia, 1896. Longstreet's war memoirs and his defense of himself.

Macon, T. J. *Reminiscences of the First Company of Richmond Howitzers*. Richmond, 1909.

Reagan, John H. *Memoirs*. New York, 1906. Memoirs of the Confederate Postmaster General.

Roman, Alfred. *The Military Operations of General Beauregard*. 2 vols. New York, 1883. General Beauregard so closely supervised this work that it is usually deemed autobiographical.

Smith, Gustavus W. *Confederate War Papers*. New York, 1884. A defense of his war record by this Confederate major general.

Stephens, Alexander H. *A Constitutional View of the Late War between the States*. 2 vols. Philadelphia, 1868.

Stiles, Robert. *Four Years under Marse Robert*. New York, 1903.

Taylor, Richard. *Destruction and Reconstruction.* New York, 1879.

Wise, John S. *The End of an Era.* New York, 1909. Reminiscences of Richmond and the war by the son of Governor Henry A. Wise of Virginia.

Wright, Mrs. D. Giraud, *A Southern Girl in '61.* New York, 1905. This memoir contains some wartime letters of General J. E. Johnston to Senator L. T. Wigfall.

Biographical, General and Other Works

Black, Robert C., III. *The Railroads of the Confederacy.* Chapel Hill, 1952.

Catton, Bruce. *U. S. Grant and the American Military Tradition.* Boston, 1954.

Christian, W. Asbury. *Richmond, Her Past and Present.* Richmond, 1912.

Coulter, E. Merton. *The Confederate States of America.* Baton Rouge, 1950.

Davis, Varina Howell. *Jefferson Davis, ex-President of the Confederate States of America, a Memoir by His Wife.* 2 vols. New York, 1890. Mrs. Davis' defense of her husband, carrying on his feuds with other Confederate personalities.

Donald, David. *Lincoln Reconsidered.* New York, 1956.

Drill Book of the Howitzer Company of the First Regiment of Virginia Volunteers. Richmond,1860.

Earle, Edward Meade (ed.). *The Makers of Modern Strategy.* Princeton, 1952.

Eaton, Clement. *A History of the Southern Confederacy.* New York, 1954.

Eckenrode, H. J. *Jefferson Davis, President of the South.* New York, 1923. A provocative survey of Davis.

Eliot, Ellsworth, Jr. *West Point in the Confederacy.* New York, 1941.

Evans, Clement Anselm (ed.). *Confederate Military History.* 10 vols. Atlanta, 1899.

Freeman, Douglas Southall. *R. E. Lee.* 4 vols. New York,

1935. This is the standard work, a biography of profound scholarship and attractive style, especially outstanding for its fine battle descriptions.

———. *Lee's Lieutenants.* 3 vols. New York, 1942–44. A history of the Confederate armies in Virginia, brilliantly developing and analyzing the leaders. It is scholarly and well written.

Fuller, J. F. C. *The Generalship of Ulysses S. Grant.* London, 1929.

———. *Grant and Lee, A Study in Personality and Generalship.* New York, 1933.

———. *The Second World War, 1939–45.* New York, 1949.

———. *A Military History of the Western World.* 3 vols. New York, 1954–56.

Govan, Gilbert E., and Livingood, James W. *A Different Valor, the Story of General Joseph E. Johnston, C. S. A.* New York, 1956. This is an excellent biography, friendly to the subject, which very effectively uses much new material.

Henry, Robert Selph. *First with the Most Forrest.* New York, 1944.

Hittle, J. D. *Jomini and His Summary of the Art of War.* Harrisburg, 1947.

Horn, Stanley F. *The Army of Tennessee.* New York, 1941.

Hughes, Robert M. *General Johnston.* New York, 1893. A defense of Joseph E. Johnston by a relative whom he had designated as his biographer. While admittedly partial and designed by the editors of the Great Commanders series to be friendly, it is based on thorough research and Mr. Hughes's own manuscripts, not frequently used.

Johnson, Bradley T. *A Memoir of the Life and Public Service of Joseph E. Johnston.* Baltimore, 1891. A discursive work by a distinguished soldier and lawyer, a close friend of General Johnston, containing some interesting observations as well as much unrelated material.

Johnston, Richard Malcolm, and Browne, William Hand. *Life of A. H. Stephens.* Philadelphia, 1884.

Liddell Hart, B. H. *Sherman, the Genius of the Civil War.* London, 1933.

————. *Strategy, the Indirect Approach.* New York, 1954.

————. *The Ghost of Napoleon.* New Haven, 1935.

Livermore, Thomas L. *Numbers and Losses in the Civil War in America, 1861–65.* New York, 1901.

Livermore, William Roscoe. *The Story of the Civil War.* 2 vols. New York, 1913.

Maurice, Major General Sir Frederick. *Statesmen and Soldiers of the Civil War.* Boston, 1926.

Meade, Robert Douthat. *Judah P. Benjamin, Confederate Statesman.* New York, 1943.

Moore, Albert Burton. *Conscription and Conflict in the Confederacy.* New York, 1924.

O'Flaherty, Daniel. *General Jo Shelby, Undefeated Rebel.* Chapel Hill, 1954.

Parks, Joseph H. *General Edmund Kirby Smith, C. S. A.* Baton Rouge, 1954.

Patrick, Rembert W. *Jefferson Davis and His Cabinet.* Baton Rouge, 1944.

Pemberton, John C. *Pemberton, Defender of Vicksburg.* Chapel Hill, 1942.

Polk, William M. *Leonidas Polk, Bishop and General.* New York, 1893.

Pollard, Edward A. *Life of Jefferson Davis with a Secret History of the Southern Confederacy.* Philadelphia, Chicago, St. Louis, Atlanta, 1869.

Ropes, John Codman. *The Story of the Civil War.* 2 vols. New York, 1898.

Shanks, Henry T. *The Secession Movement in Virginia, 1847–61.* Richmond, 1934.

Vandiver, Frank E. *Rebel Brass, the Confederate Command System.* Baton Rouge, 1956.

Williams, Kenneth P. *Lincoln Finds a General.* 4 vols. New York, 1949–56.

Williams, T. Harry. *Lincoln and His Generals.* New York, 1952.

————. *P. G. T. Beauregard, Napoleon in Gray.* Baton Rouge, 1954.

Wise, Jennings Cropper. *The Long Arm of Lee.* 2 vols. Lynchburg, Va., 1915.

V. ARTICLES

Atkinson, Charles Francis. "Infantry," *Encyclopedia Britannica* (11th ed.), XIV, 527–28.

Bach, Christian A. "Ulysses Simpson Grant," *The Dictionary of American Biography,* eds. Dumas Malone and Allen Johnson, VII (New York, 1928–36), 492–97.

Bruce, Brevet Lieutenant-Colonel George A., U. S. V. "The Strategy of the Civil War," *The Papers of the Military Historical Society of Massachusetts,* XIII (Boston, 1913), 393–412.

Curry, Roy Watson. "James A. Seddon, A Southern Prototype," *Virginia Magazine of History and Biography,* LXIII (April, 1955), 123–50.

"Extracts from an old 'Order Book' of First Company, Richmond Howitzers," *Contributions to a History of the Richmond Howitzers* (Richmond, 1878), pamphlet No. 4, 33–64.

Freeman, Douglas Southall. "James Longstreet," *D. A. B.,* XI, 391–93.

Ganoe, William A. "Henry Wager Halleck," *D. A. B.,* VII, 150–52.

Gordon, E. C. "The Battle of Big Bethel," *Contributions to a History of the Richmond Howitzers,* pamphlet No. 1, 14–84.

Hay, Thomas Robson. "Confederate Leadership at Vicksburg," *Mississippi Valley Historical Review,* XI (March, 1925), 543–60.

Hudnall, Captain Henry. "The Origin of the First Company," *Contributions to a History of the Richmond Howitzers,* pamphlet No. 1, 3–10.

Hughes, R. M. "Some War Letters of General Joseph E. Johnston," *Journal of the Military Service Institution of the United States,* L (May-June, 1912) 319–28.

James, Alfred P. "General Joseph Eggleston Johnston, Storm Center of the Confederate Army," *Mississippi Valley Historical Review,* XIV (December, 1927), 342–59.

———. "The Strategy of Concentration, as used by the

Confederate Forces in the Mississippi Valley in the Spring of 1862," *Proceedings of the Mississippi Valley Historical Association,* X (November, 1921), 363–72.

Jones, Archer. "Tennessee and Mississippi, Joe Johnston's Strategic Problem," *Tennessee Historical Quarterly,* XVIII (June, 1959), 138–39.

Lanza, Conrad H. "Joseph Eggleston Johnston," *D. A. B.,* X, 144–46.

Longstreet, James. "Lee in Pennsylvania," *Annals of the War* (Philadelphia, 1879), 414–46.

Maude, Colonel Frederic N. "Strategy," *Encyclopedia Britannica* (13th ed.), XXV, 986–97.

Owsley, Frank Lawrence. "Local Defense and the Overthrow of the Confederacy: a Study of States Rights," *Mississippi Valley Historical Review,* XI (March, 1925), 490–525.

Pearson, C. C. "Theophilus Hunter Holmes," *D. A. B.,* IX, 176.

Sanger, Donald Bridgman. "Some Problems Facing Joseph E. Johnston in the Spring of 1863," *Essays in Honor of William E. Dodd,* ed. Avery Craven (Chicago, 1935), 257–90.

Vandiver, Frank E. "Jefferson Davis and Confederate Strategy," *The American Tragedy* (Hampden-Sydney College, Va., 1959), 19–32.

White, W. S. "A Diary of the War," *Contributions to a History of the Richmond Howitzers,* pamphlet No. 2, 89–286.

Williams, T. Harry. "The Military Leadership of North and South." Lecture delivered at Gettysburg College, Gettysburg, Penn., November 17, 1958.

Wood, W. Birkbeck. "American Civil War," *Encyclopedia Britannica* (14th ed.), I, 754–67.

Index

Allies, 31
Apalachicola River, 64
Appomattox, Va., 7
Army of Northern Virginia,
  198, 204, 207, 211, 234,
  235
Army of Tennessee, *vii*, 154,
  175, 176, 186, 217, 222,
  224, 236
Army of the West, 64, 65, 74
Atlanta, Ga., 7, 12, 27, 55, 64,
  68, 71, 102, 118, 125, 127,
  162, 169, 186, 239

Balkans, 31
Balitmore and Ohio Railroad,
  200
Banks, Maj. Gen. Nathaniel
  P., 8, 105, 106, 148, 149
Bate, Brig. Gen. William H.,
  155
Baton Rouge, La., 74, 76
Beauregard, Gen. P. G. T.,
  22, 34, 53-57 *passim*, 61,
  62, 63, 66, 67, 71, 86, 99,
  102, 108, 180, 192, 199,
  206, 209, 210, 211, 215,
  216, 217, 221, 227, 235,
  236, 239
Benedek, Ludwig von, 44
Benjamin, Judah P., 36, 55
Bowling Green, Ky., 52, 53
Bragg, Gen. Braxton, *xviii*,
  6, 13, 51, 53, 55, 56, 62-
  87 *passim*, 94, 105, 107-
  228 *passim*, 231, 233, 236,
  239
Bragg, Mrs. Braxton, 173
Breckinridge, Maj. Gen. John
  C., 36, 152
Bristol, Va., 160
Buckner, Maj. Gen. Simon
  Bolivar, 109, 142, 147,
  181, 189, 190
Buell, Maj. Gen. Don Carlos,
  6, 13, 52, 54, 57, 63, 67,
  68, 69, 71, 75, 76, 105
Buena Vista, battle of, *ix*, 16
Burnside, Maj. Gen. Ambrose
  E., 13, 199-205 *passim*

Cavalry, Confederate, *vii*, 114,
  117, 118, 129, 130, 135-

142 *passim,* 146, 148, 162, 163, 171, 177, 222, 236
Cerro Gordo, battle of, 99
Chancellorsville, battle of, 180, 205, 210, 233
Chapultepec, battle of, 99
Charleston, S. C., 17, 62, 80, 180, 192, 204
Chattahoochee River, 64
Chattanooga, Tenn., 6, 55, 57, 63-76 *passim,* 97, 113, 117, 125, 134, 150, 151, 160, 164, 169, 172, 184, 185
Chickamauga, battle of, 6, 228
Chickasaw Bluffs, battle of, 123
Churchill, Sir Winston, 31
Cincinnati, Ohio, 75
Cleburne, Maj. Gen. Patrick R., 152
Climate, effect of, *viii,* 57, 140, 147, 203, 204, 212, 215, 234, 235
Columbia, Tenn., 162, 170
Columbus, Ky., 52, 54, 115
Columbus, Miss., 27, 148
Conscription, Confederate, *vii, xix,* 33, 35, 42, 43, 45-48, 49, 119, 167, 237
Cooper, Gen. Samuel, 53, 55, 61, 66, 67, 70, 71, 93, 101, 116, 117, 124, 145, 174, 175, 191, 197, 202, 203, 218, 225
Corinth, Miss., 6, 54, 56, 57, 62, 64, 67, 80, 81, 114, 186, 199, 224
Cumberland Gap, Tenn., 65, 66, 67, 75
Cumberland Mountains, 177
Cumberland River, 13, 52, 54, 78, 161

Dardanelles, campaign of, 31, 32
Davis, Jefferson, *v, viii, ix, xix, xxi,* 15-29 *passim,* 36, 45, 46, 47, 49, 53, 55-97 *passim,* 100, 101, 110, 115, 117-203 *passim,* 205, 211-213, 214, 216-19, 222, 224, 225, 227, 230, 231-35, 237-240; relations with J. E. Johnston, *v, vii, viii,* 95, 97, 100-102, 122, 174-75, 217-18, 226-28
Decatur, Ala., 148
Department, Western. *See* Department No. 2
Department of Alabama and West Florida, 51, 55, 56, 62, 63
Department of East Tennessee, 56, 64, 65, 160, 162, 169, 177, 178, 179, 183, 201
Department of the Gulf, 181
Department of Mississippi and Eastern Louisiana, 82, 136, 172
Department No. 1, 51, 63, 64, 71, 80, 231
Department No. 2, 51, 56, 61, 62, 63, 64, 65, 71, 220, 231
Department of South Carolina, Georgia and Florida, 199, 206, 209, 211
Department of the Trans-Mississippi, 71, 105, 106, 108, 117, 122, 125, 128, 139, 144, 145, 146, 160, 165, 171, 182, 195, 207, 223, 225, 237

Department of the West, *vii,*
xvii, xix xx, 97, 111, 113,
126, 128, 143, 160, 175,
187, 192, 193, 194, 205,
213, 214, 217, 218, 219-22,
225, 228, 237
Department of Western Virginia, 167, 169, 178, 179,
183, 198
District of the Gulf, 64, 107,
142, 162. *See also* De-
partment of the Gulf
District of Mississippi, 64
District of Western Louisiana,
78
Donelson, Fort, 6, 34, 52, 54,
103, 220, 227, 239
Donelson, Maj. Gen. Daniel
S., 160, 167, 168, 177

Europe, eastern, 14
Ewell, Col. Benjamin S., 134

Falkenhayn, Erich von, 32
Farragut, Rear Adm. David
G., 106
Fiske, John, *vii*
Floyd, Brig. Gen. John B.,
101, 227
Forney, Maj. Gen. John H.,
64
Forrest, Brig. Gen. Nathan
Bedford, 27, 28, 109, 123,
135-40 *passim*
France, 32
Frankfort, Ky., 105
Frederick II, "the Great" of
Prussia, 15
Fredericksburg, battle of, 139,
180, 206
Freeman, Douglas S., 207, 234

French, Maj. Gen. Samuel G.,
213

Gettysburg, battle of, *vii*
Gorgas, Col. Josiah, 113
Grand Gulf, Miss., 191
Grant, Maj. Gen. Ulysses S.,
5, 6, 12, 13, 14, 15, 52,
53, 54, 57, 82, 84, 105,
108-140 *passim*, 146, 151,
163, 164, 168, 169-71, 186,
188, 189-93, 198, 201, 202,
204, 206-10, 213, 215, 216,
222, 225, 228
Great Britain, 32
Grenada, Miss., 115, 120, 138
Gunboats, 13, 105, 110, 223

Halleck, Maj. Gen. Henry
W., 4, 53, 54, 57, 69, 221
Hardee, Lt. Gen. William J.,
109, 152, 153
Harpers Ferry, W. Va., 40, 75
Hawes, Gov. Richard, 105
Henry, Fort, 6, 34, 52, 53, 220
Heth, Maj. Gen. Henry, 154,
160
Hill, Maj. Gen. Daniel Har-
vey, 42
Hilliard, Henry W., 68
Hitler, Adolf, 129
Holly Springs, Miss., 6, 123,
135
Holmes, Lt. Gen. Theophilus
H., 13, 72, 84, 85, 87-89,
94, 106, 107, 110, 112,
118, 120-30 *passim*, 137,
139, 144, 145, 207, 232
Hood, Maj. Gen. John B., 13,
202
Hooker, Maj. Gen. Joseph,
13, 200, 205, 212

Island No. 10, Tenn., 57
Italian War of 1859, 39, 44, 93
Italy, 31

Jackson, Miss., 116, 118, 120, 125, 130, 131, 132, 169, 181, 189, 207
Jackson, Lt. Gen. Thomas J., 13
James River, 9
Johnston, Gen. Albert Sidney, 34, 51-57 *passim*, 61, 64, 86, 101, 209, 220
Johnston, Beverly R., 195
Johnston, Gen. Joseph E., *v, vi, vii, ix, xvii, xviii, xix, xx*, 12, 22, 27, 58, 59, 60, 84, 86-88, 92, 94-105, 109-111, 117-204 *passim*, 207-209, 211, 213-28 *passim*, 232, 233, 236-39. For relations with Jefferson Davis, *see* Davis, Jefferson, relations with J. E. Johnston
Johnston, Mrs. Joseph E., 101
Johnston, Col. William Preston, 176
Jomini, Baron Henri, 14, 15, 21, 22
Jones, J. B., 69
Jones, Maj. Gen. Samuel, 167, 178, 198, 201, 218

Kean, Capt. R. G. H., 26, 27, 90, 91
Kirby Smith, Lt. Gen. Edmund, 55, 64-71 *passim*, 73, 75, 104, 107, 111, 117, 118, 134, 154, 160, 165, 171, 172, 182, 191, 195, 207

Knoxville, Tenn., 52, 54, 55, 69, 160

Lee, Gen. Robert E., *v, vii, ix*, 7, 12, 13, 22, 29, 48, 58, 59, 60, 61, 69, 75, 82, 86, 96, 99-101, 139, 149, 166, 180, 198-217 *passim*, 224, 233, 234, 235, 237, 238, 239
Lexington, Ky., 75
Liddell Hart, B. H., *vii*; quoted, 216
Lincoln, Abraham, 4, 5, 7, 40, 41, 60, 65
Little Rock, Ark., 140
Longstreet, Lt. Gen. James, 13, 59, 204, 208-12 *passim*, 224, 235
Louisville, Ky., 75, 105, 189
Lovell, Maj. Gen. Mansfield, 51, 54, 63, 80-82
Ludendorff, Erich, 31, 32

McClellan, Maj. Gen. George B., 4, 19, 58, 59, 60, 61, 99
MacDowell, Maj. Gen. Irvin, 99
Manassas, First Battle of, 7, 33, 53, 58, 99, 102, 209
Manassas, Second Battle of, 75
Marshall, Brig. Gen. Humphrey, 167, 168, 199, 200
Marshall, Texas, 72
Maury, Maj. Gen. Dabney H., 179
Memphis, Tenn., 27, 57, 74, 138, 189, 199
Memphis and Charleston Railroad, 57, 66, 74, 125, 126
Meridian, Miss., 125, 126, 148, 169, 181, 182, 186, 189

Mexican War, 16
Mill Springs, battle of, 5, 33, 53
Missionary Ridge, battle of, 7
Mississippi River, 5, 6, 13, 14, 23, 28, 52, 54, 57, 61, 62, 63, 74, 79, 87, 105, 120, 121, 127, 128, 137, 140, 141, 163, 165, 171, 172, 176, 182, 191, 192, 208, 220, 223, 226, 227, 235
Mobile, Ala., 17, 51, 55, 71, 72, 116, 118, 125, 136, 142, 143, 150, 151, 172, 181, 189, 201, 204, 227
Montgomery, Ala., 71, 118, 125, 126, 187
Morgan, Brig. Gen. John Hunt, 135, 137, 180
Murfreesborough, battle of, 148, 151, 152, 154
Murfreesborough, Tenn., 6, 114, 125, 141, 143, 184, 185

Napoleon III, 44
Nashville, Tenn., *vii*, 6, 34, 66, 75-78, 169, 189, 236
New Bern, N. C., 34
New Orleans, La., 5, 51, 54, 57, 63, 73, 74, 80, 81, 121
Newport News, Va., 199
Norfolk, Va., 59, 60

Ohio River, 76, 87, 118, 161
Oxford, Miss., 115

Patrick, Rembert W., *vi, vii, xvii*
Patterson, Maj. Gen. Robert, 99
Pea Ridge, battle of, 34

Pearl River, 64
Pemberton, Lt. Gen. John C., 13, 80-84, 87, 97, 106, 109, 111-16, 118-51 *passim*, 163, 164, 165, 168, 169-172, 175-204 *passim*, 207, 208, 211, 213, 217, 223, 224, 225, 226, 231, 232, 238, 239
Peninsula campaign, 7, 58, 59, 99
Pensacola, Fla., 51, 55, 226
Perryville, battle of, 105
Phelan, James, 119
Pickett, Maj. Gen. George E., 202, 211, 212
Pierce, Franklin, *ix*, 16
Pillow, Fort, Tenn., 57, 62
Pillow, Brig. Gen. Gideon J., 167
Pittsburg Landing, Tenn., 54, 57
Polk, Lt. Gen. Leonidas, 52, 94, 109, 152
Pollard, E. A., 97
Pope, Maj. Gen. John, 13, 61, 69, 75
Port Hudson, La., 5, 74, 105, 115, 121, 129, 149, 170, 191, 209
Porter, Rear Adm. David D., 106
Potomac River, 208
Price, Maj. Gen. Sterling, 74-79

Randolph, George W., *v-ix passim, xviii, xix, xx*, 36, 37, 38-49, 58, 59, 60, 61, 67-69, 73, 77-80, 83, 84, 87-96, 103, 112, 124, 144, 219, 237, 240

Rappahannock River, 9, 205, 233

Reagan, John H., 214

Red River, 74

Red River expedition, 8

Revolution, American, 9

Richmond, Ky., 75

Richmond, Va., 8, 9, 12, 17, 18, 28, 29, 34, 38, 39, 40, 41, 45, 46, 48, 57, 58, 59, 60, 61, 69, 86, 96, 98, 120, 130, 151, 162, 165, 174, 232

Roanoke Island, N. C., 34, 36

Roddey, Col. Philip H., 136, 137, 138, 140, 142

Rosecrans, Maj. Gen. William S., *vii*, 6, 13, 57, 78, 87, 107, 112, 114, 116, 118, 127, 141, 146, 148, 161, 167, 168, 184-89 *passim*, 199, 200, 201, 202, 204, 207, 209, 221, 223, 236

Ruggles, Brig. Gen., Daniel, 72, 73

Russia, 14

Sadowa, 3

Savannah, Ga., 17, 204

Schofield, Maj. Gen. John M., 13

Scott, Lt. Gen. Winfield, 4, 99

Seddon, James A., *vi, viii, xvii, xix, xx*, 26, 90, 95, 96, 113, 155, 156, 157, 159, 165, 167, 168, 172, 174, 175, 180, 184, 188, 192, 193, 197-203, 205, 207, 208, 211-40 *passim*

Selma, Ala. 148, 182

Seven Days, battle of, 60

Seven Pines, battle of, 60, 99

Shenandoah Valley, 205

Sherman, Maj. Gen. William T., 7, 8, 13, 14, 15, 27, 105, 120, 123, 125, 127, 131, 133, 134, 137, 138, 139, 170

Shiloh, battle of, *ix, xix*, 6, 57, 61, 62, 66, 209, 220, 227

Sibley, Brig. Gen. Henry H., 72

Smith, Maj. Gen. Gustavus W., 59

Solferino, 3

Sparrow, Edward, 47

Stevenson, Ala., 125

Stevenson, Maj. Gen. Carter L., 117, 125, 134, 140, 148, 169, 182

Strategy, *viii-ix, xix, xx-xxi*, 240

"Anaconda," 8

concentration, 103, 104, 121, 122, 229

Confederate, 15-32, 229, 235-36, 237, 240

defensive, 17-21, 22, 229

departmental, *viii*, 25-28, 51, 52, 55-56, 62-63, 69, 71-73, 79-82, 84, 85-86, 97-98, 128, 155, 165, 219-22, 223, 226-227, 229-33, 238-39

East *vs.* West, 8-9, 12, 28-32, 180, 216-17

elastic defense, 23, 104, 129, 229

exhaustion, 14, 15, 20-22

Jominian, 14-15, 21, 22

local defense, 18-25, 229

Napoleonic, 14, 235

offensive, 18

offensive-defensive, 21-22, 235-36
technology, effect on, 9-12
U. S., 3-15, 19, 21, 23, 29
views of
  Beauregard, P. G. T., 22, 54, 61, 66-67, 209-10, 215-16, 235, 239
  Benjamin, J. P., 55
  Bragg, B., 55, 70-71, 73-76, 84
  Davis, J., 17-22, 25-27, 53-54, 55, 56, 58-60, 61, 66-68, 69, 71-73, 77-82, 83, 93-94, 104, 115, 116-19, 120-122, 126, 129, 140-41, 180, 181-182, 199-202, 205, 212, 213-14, 216-17, 226-27, 233, 239-40
  Johnston, A. S., 53, 54
  Johnston, J. E., 22, 59-60, 87, 103-104, 109-13, 115-122 *passim,* 126-130, 135-42, 146-149, 160-61, 167-171, 177-89, 191, 193-95, 201, 222-226, 237
  Kirby Smith, E., 66-67, 70
  Lee, R. E., 22, 59-60, 61, 180, 199-201, 203-206, 208-209, 211-14, 215, 233, 238-39

Liddell Hart, B. H., quoted, 216
Lincoln, A., 60-61, 65
Longstreet, J., 206-209, 235
McClellan, G. B., 4, 19, 58
Pemberton, J. C., 84
Price, S., 76-77
Randolph, G. W., 59-60, 67-68, 71-73, 77-82, 83, 87, 93-94, 112
Reagan, J. H., 214
Seddon, J. A., 96, 104, 155, 165, 180, 199-202, 205, 207-208, 211, 213-217, 233-34, 238
Van Dorn, E., 76-78, 84-85
Wigfall, L. T., 210
Stuart, Maj. Gen. J. E. B., 213
Suffolk, Va., 43, 205, 233
Sumter, Fort, 53

Tactics, 9-12, 29
Taylor, Maj. Gen. Richard, 72, 73, 80
Technology, influence of, 10-11, 13
Tennessee River, 13, 52, 53, 54, 78, 112, 116, 117, 169, 185, 186, 188, 199, 225, 228
Thomas, Maj. Gen. George H., 7, 13
Tullahoma, Tenn., 148, 151, 170, 175, 176, 183, 187-190 *passim,* 196, 207, 224
Tupelo, Miss., 57, 67, 71
Turkey, 31

United Nations, 31

Van Dorn, Maj. Gen. Earl, *vii*, 52, 54, 62, 63, 64, 65, 72, 74-82, 84, 93, 106, 119, 123, 130, 135-46 *passim*, 161, 162, 163, 170, 171, 221
Vandiver, Frank E., *xviii*
Vicksburg, Miss., *ix*, *xix*, 3, 6, 24, 25, 57, 72, 74, 105, 112, 114, 115, 118-38 *passim*, 142, 143, 144, 149, 151, 163, 164, 165, 170, 171, 180, 181, 188, 190, 191, 192, 193, 204, 206, 207, 208, 209, 214, 215, 225, 232, 233, 235, 236, 238

War Department, Confederate, *xx*, 17, 36, 50, 53, 56, 58, 61-69 *passim*, 78, 79, 82-95 *passim*, 98, 100, 113, 121, 124, 140, 145, 154, 159, 164, 166, 167, 168, 173, 174, 176, 191, 192, 194, 202, 205-207, 219,

224, 225, 226, 229, 230, 232, 234, 237, 239
War Department, U. S., 114
Washington, D. C., 7, 28, 34, 57, 58, 75, 209, 215, 216
West Point, Ga., 64
West Point, U. S. Military Academy at, 4, 14, 16, 90, 100
Wheeler, Maj. Gen. Joseph, 109, 161
Wigfall, Louis T., 47, 113, 155, 156, 179, 208-11 *passim*, 214, 217
Williams, T. Harry, 97
Wilmington, N. C., 17
Winchester, Tenn., 173
Wise, Brig. Gen. Henry Alexander, 90
World War I, 10, 12, 30-32
World War II, 3, 31, 129

Yalabusha River, 115
Yorktown, Va., 60

Zollicoffer, Brig. Gen. Felix K., 52, 53

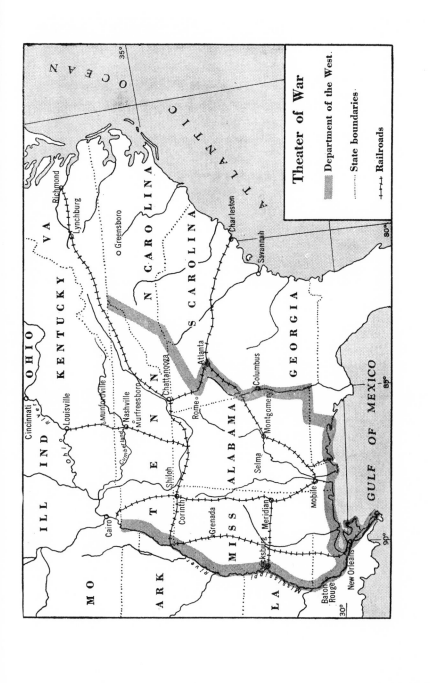

Theater of War

■ Department of the West.

········ State boundaries

+↔+ Railroads

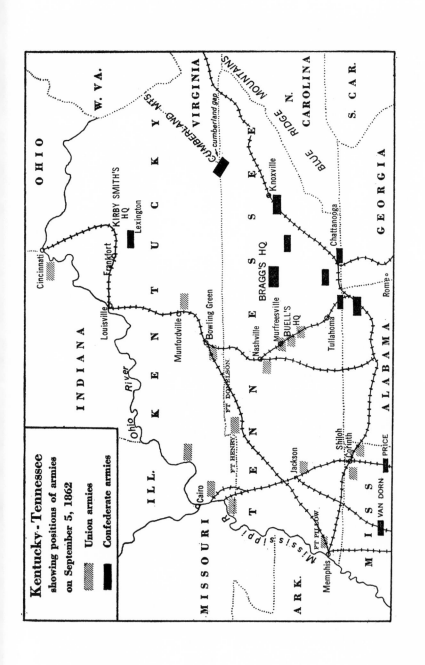

Kentucky-Tennessee

showing positions of armies
on September 5, 1862

Union armies

Confederate armies

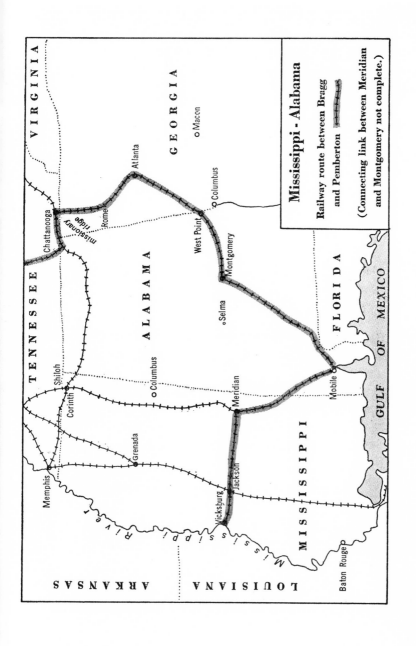

Mississippi - Alabama

Railway route between Bragg and Pemberton

(Connecting link between Meridian and Montgomery not complete.)